LADY REF

LADY REF

Making Calls in a Man's World

SHANNON EASTIN
WITH KATE ST. VINCENT VOGL

ROWMAN & LITTLEFIELD
Lanham • Boulder • New York • London

Published by Rowman & Littlefield
An imprint of The Rowman & Littlefield Publishing Group, Inc.
4501 Forbes Boulevard, Suite 200, Lanham, Maryland 20706
www.rowman.com

86-90 Paul Street, London EC2A 4NE, United Kingdom

British Library Cataloguing in Publication Information Available

Library of Congress Cataloging-in-Publication Data

Names: Eastin, Shannon, author. | Vogl, Kathryn St. Vincent, author.
Title: Lady ref : making calls in a man's world / Shannon Eastin, with Kate
   St. Vincent Vogl.
Description: Lanham, Maryland : Rowman & Littlefield, [2023] | Includes
   bibliographical references. | Summary: "Lady Ref is the eye-opening and
   inspiring memoir of Shannon Eastin, the first female official for the
   NFL, who continues to encourage and motivate others through her mentoring
   and training of young officials"—Provided by publisher.
Identifiers: LCCN 2023004701 (print) | LCCN 2023004702 (ebook) | ISBN
   9781538181591 (cloth) | ISBN 9781538181607 (epub) Subjects: LCSH:
Eastin, Shannon. | Football referees—United
   States—Biography. | National Football League—Officials and
   Employees—Biography. | Football—Rules—History.
Classification: LCC GV939.E26 A3 2023 (print) | LCC GV939.E26 (ebook) |
   DDC 796.332092 [B]—dc23/eng/20230228
LC record available at https://lccn.loc.gov/2023004701
LC ebook record available at https://lccn.loc.gov/2023004702

In memory of Tom Scarduzio and Dan Evans.
Thanks for opening doors and letting me in.

CONTENTS

AUTHOR'S NOTE

It was the honor of a lifetime to officiate for the NFL and be the first woman to do so. Through sharing my story, I've wanted to give proper thanks to those who lifted me up as I climbed toward my dream. I hope I did justice in making these men and women know how much I love and appreciate them. Life can be all too short for some.

To be the first, you inevitably will meet up against obstacles. I share my challenges so that those striving to achieve their dream know something of what it is you may have to face over time, to offer a little added strength and insight to help find your way. For me, I am stronger as I put my faith in God, when I strive to value people, and when I live intentionally with a positive attitude.

Putting my words to paper, I wanted to provide readers with the best and most honest account of what happened along the journey I traveled. Though I've checked this story against my albums and news articles and the memories of others, a memoir is by definition the author's memory of what happened. When I couldn't place the date of an event or otherwise confirm what happened, I included it in the story in a way to reflect that memory. And some names I have shielded to protect privacy.

What I share about Aiden was the most difficult to write. I've wanted his part of the story to be perfect, to honor a great friend and Aiden's memory. I've talked about Aiden so many times, starting with handing out wristbands to the last time I stopped by the hospital with more bears. I still can't tell his story without getting tears in my eyes. I know his memory will forever be carried in the hearts of his family and friends. With his story getting out into the world, it's nice to imagine how you'll now carry him in your heart too.

My wish for you is that, in coming along on this journey with me, you will be inspired when facing challenges to fight and rise above them, that you will focus on what you can control and surround yourself with those who support you. Beyond that, God knows what you need and will be there to love, comfort, guide, and forgive—and to send light along your path when it seems a bit dark. I pray you remember that, as I have found, there are far more people who will be there to support your hard work than to throw bricks to make you stumble. I pray you are encouraged that nothing is impossible when you believe.

Shannon Eastin
December 2022

1

OFFSIDE?

SEPTEMBER 16, 2012

You're not supposed to see me, though I'm standing right on the gridiron during an NFL game. Time's running down in the half. Players rush by me on one side, mill about on the other. You'll want to focus on them, on the game. Not on an official like me.

Unless I've done something wrong.

Late afternoon sun casts long shadows on CenturyLink Field, perfect weather for Seattle's home opener. Honestly the sky could have been pouring buckets, and I'd still consider it a beautiful day.

Now it's third and short, with the Seahawks in possession, vying for a few last yards to get within field goal range. Every point counts. The Cowboys have closed in on Seattle's early lead. The energy inside the stadium escalates as the twelfth man shows up. The roar of a crowd sounds different when you're on the turf. Louder.

But I tune out the crowd noise. That's what I do. It's what I've always done. Working as an official, I can't let myself be distracted or get caught up in emotion. I straddle the line of scrimmage and focus on the job.

My dream job, actually—as line judge for the NFL. This is my sixth game, the second in the regular season, though this season so far has been anything but regular for officials. The NFL locked them out back in July, and I'd been one of the few from a Division I conference willing to step in. The media keeps me pinned under the microscope—they keep all of us replacement officials there. Everything I do, though, is magnified even more, given that I'm the first female official in the NFL. It doesn't escape me that a description of every interaction I've had with a player since that first NFL preseason game has made it into print—from receiving handshakes

1

before the game to breaking up a skirmish on a punt. Online, ESPN makes note of the boos the fans give me and judges whether I deserve the jeers.[1]

In the middle of a game, though, I can't waste time wondering what commentators are second-guessing and whether the cameras near me are taking any pictures. I'm concentrating on the play at hand. At the D1 level, I'll see only a few players moving at a pro's speed. With twenty-two pros on a field, the tempo of a game picks up a bit.

I'm one of the officials in charge of deciding what movement is legal before the snap, so I'm watching as quarterback Russell Wilson lines up under center and barks a hard count. A linebacker jumps toward the neutral zone, but I do not throw the flag for him being offside.

And then Seattle fails to convert on third down and punts the ball over to Dallas. Dallas runs a play, and time expires.

Seahawks coach Pete Carroll yells as I run past. "Come on, Shannon," he says. "No flag?" He's riding me about the no-call.

This question I want to answer. Pete Carroll isn't just any NFL coach; he's one of only three coaches to win both a Super Bowl and a college football national championship. He's a legend. And why he's not happy is clear: The five-yard penalty would have given them a first down, keeping their drive alive, and they might have kicked a field goal before time ran out— reestablishing their comfortable lead, making sure they don't fall to 0–2.

I know what Pete Carroll saw. I also know I made the right decision not to throw the flag. What I don't know is how much time I have remaining on an NFL field. And neither of us knows just how soon the referee lockout will be over because of a questionable call on this field as the clock runs out.

What matters now is this moment, what I have to say—this chance I get to explain myself. So many times in my life I've been the youngest, the first, the only. I'm ready for this. I draw a breath as the fanfare of a professional halftime is about to start. I know where to begin.

2

EARLY PROMISE

Before an NFL coach ever questioned my on-field decision; before I officiated my first football game; before I took on a lot of training and hard, hard work; and before I accepted God into my life and then strayed for too long—before all of this came a powerful drive. A feeling I was born with something extra—that I not only *could* be the best but that I *should* be the best. So I had to do something about it.

Even as a kid, watching the Olympics, this feeling kicked in. Whenever the games were on, I'd be glued to the TV, no matter the sport—track and field, diving, figure skating, gymnastics. I remember watching the swimmers and imagining how I'd slice through that water. Be an Olympian.

Growing up, I'd heard my mother build the family lore of how she discovered I'd been born strong. On my first night home from the hospital, our German shepherd woke her, pawing her bed, barking, until Mom followed Ginger back to the nursery. There she found my body dangling out of the crib, my head stuck between crib bars. Mom twisted my shoulders to slide my limp form back up between the bars, lifting me free. She clutched me to her chest, and my little lungs filled once more with air, furiously pinking me up again. From my first days, she witnessed the relentlessness of my desire to get *somewhere*. She knew from the beginning I'd be strong.

Often, I surprised her with what I'd try to do. A lot of times, I was just trying to keep up with my big brother. When I was just nine months old and already walking, Mom brought us to Coes Pond, over in Worcester; she looked away for only a second before finding me floating facedown. She was a single mom shouldering worlds of responsibility, and she feared what she'd lift from the water when she reached me. But I wasn't drowning, I was only blowing bubbles. I was fine.

As improbable as it may seem, a number of different physical activities came to me as naturally as swimming first did. While growing up, I found that competitions somehow seemed tailored to showcase what I could get my body to do. In an elementary school challenge to complete as many sit-ups as possible during gym, I'd started out doing more than a sit-up a second. Then someone accidentally kicked me in the face. That slowed me down. Still, I managed to squeeze in 525 sit-ups before the bell rang, setting a record that stood for years.

Yet I didn't get the presidential award for fitness. I couldn't run the fifty-yard dash under the time required. I can remember how many times I tried, how my fantastic PE teacher Mr. T cheered me on. All to no avail. I wasn't as fast as I needed to be. The fifty-yard dash was a requirement, and I couldn't deliver.

Though a lot of sports felt intuitive to me, I still had my limits. Every tournament required a lot of hard work and intensive training to prepare. I tell you this so you know that, as willing as I was to face many physical challenges, I learned at a young age that in trying anything, I had to be willing to sit up and do the work. I was willing to get the breath knocked right out of me.

I just didn't know what I could do about it then.

∾

In 1976, I turned six, and Mom married Paul. Life got easier for her and much more interesting for me. Everything in my brother's room disappeared into boxes, then everything from my room squared inside one box or another, too, including my favorite stuffed animal, Cubby Comfortable Jr. We were moving out of our apartment and into our new chapter of happily ever after.

I loved Paul's modest house in Oxford, Massachusetts. I loved having him as a dad. I loved climbing up on our tan sofa to sit with him. My brother would be off with his friends. Dad and I didn't talk much, but we loved watching television together. He was the quiet type, a former navy guy, but when football was on, he'd get all excited, especially while watching the Patriots. They were our home team, and that was their Cinderella season.

We had a routine for those Sundays, which included eating bowls of double-scooped ice cream while on the couch watching New England play. Dad predicted their plays, explaining what to anticipate. When a player intercepted the ball and ruined the prediction, Dad would say something to make me laugh. Too soon, we'd reach the bottom of our bowls, but then he'd bring me close, arm around me, and point to the screen.

"See that?" he'd ask, eyes transfixed on the players and refs. "That was a personal foul."

A shrill whistle drew my gaze back to the screen. Play had halted. Athletes gathered themselves as a man in knickers and a striped shirt strode to the middle of the field. The official signaled to the crowd: Arms up, fists clenched, he gave a single, strong strike to his arm. *Yep*. Dad agreed with a nod and gave me a squeeze. I felt his approval and his happiness, though I didn't yet understand football. Dad knew it well; he'd played in high school. I paid attention to how Dad paid attention. On big plays, Dad stroked his brown mustache, dark eyes as wide as hubcaps. Every time we watched Steve Grogan drop back into the pocket to make a pass, Dad and I scooted to the edge of our seats. The seat cushions got some wear that year, as the quarterback closed in on—and then set—a record of twelve rushing touchdowns that season.

Clips of Walter Payton dominated SportsCenter the year I learned to play football. With my fingers on the laces, my neighborhood would disappear as I imagined the roar of Soldier Field. Here I was in the end zone, the ref signaling a touchdown. Nothing ever felt so right.

As much as I loved pretending I was Payton, we were Patriots fans in my house, and I remember the year the Patriots made it to the playoffs for the first time ever. But that fall turned into winter, and that winter outside of Boston was terrible. So much snow fell that we opened the front door to a wall of the white stuff, and it wasn't because of a drift. We kids made snow tunnels leading from our house through the carport and out to the other side. Trash bags worked as makeshift sleds down a hill out behind our place. I loved how fast we could go.

Mom did not love being snowed in. Snow had covered up her car. "Where can you get transferred?" she kept asking Dad. "And how soon?"

He had a good job as an X-ray repair technician; he had options. Arizona popped up as a possibility, which seemed the perfect opposite of Massachusetts. And it was. When we landed in Phoenix, the first thing I noticed was a line of majestic palm trees. They are still my favorite tree.

Mom loved everything she found grounded in Arizona. She liked that my brother and I could be outside all year, and she loved the nearby desert landscapes, the distant mountains. Mom kept an eye out for a couple of cacti for our front yard. One day, she came home to our three-bedroom ranch with a Saguaro and an Arizona barrel cactus stuffed in the back of her Subaru wagon. We didn't know at the time that you couldn't just pull them from the desert. And we still don't know how she managed to get them home without getting poked. Dad figured out how to plant them while Mom looked on, beaming with pride. Every time she caught sight of the cacti while pulling in the driveway, she smiled.

With us settled in our new home, Mom could fully focus on me and my brother again. She brought us to the Maryvale parks and recreation facility to play and found a co-ed soccer league for us. First match, I scored two goals, though I hadn't played before. That year, I also played some softball. Eventually, I did some dance, too, performing a tap recital in a nearby mall. Mom had done a lot of dance—she'd even been a go-go dancer, and she looked the part, with her dancer's body and her long and shining light brown hair. But she didn't push me to do more tap lessons. She could see it wasn't me. She signed me up for other sports instead. She kept my hair cut short and permed it into tight little curls, which she thought looked cute and which I thought was ridiculous. All that time stuck in a chair getting a perm wasn't my idea of fun, either. As we all figured out what worked best those first couple of years in Arizona, my brother did a bit of soccer with me and some swimming, too, but it turned out he liked to just have fun while playing. I liked more to compete. Mom let us follow our own paths.

Mine first led me to competitive swimming and diving, like I'd seen in the Olympics. By eight, I was doing complicated dives off a springboard. It was hard. I needed complete silence to do it, and I got crap for that. *Shannon's up, silence please.* Once, in competition, I didn't jump far enough away from the board while doing an inward dive, and I scraped the length of my back, creating a spine of a wound before hitting the water. That stung.

Mom could tell I itched to do more, so she had me look through the flyers at the parks and rec center to decide what sport to join next. I knew what I wanted to do; I'd been messing around playing it already for a few years in PE and at recess. I even collected cards of my favorite pros and exchanged them with friends. I burned to play the game more. "What about football?" I asked.

She paled. "Football?"

"I've been thinking about it a while," I said. "Please? I think I'd be really great at it."

"Absolutely not. It's too dangerous. No way is my little girl going to play football."

I figured Mom worried about the tackling. But contact never bothered me—except for maybe how my brother and I sometimes fought. "Okay, Mom," I said.

I was like that as a kid, understanding while other kids might protest and practicing while other kids might procrastinate. I tended to act a lot older than my years. My friends ended up teasing me about it. *How old is Shannon today?* they'd ask.

No matter my age, football was what I wanted. Maryvale parks and rec did offer something else that caught my eye, though. I'd seen it at the Olympics. "Hey, if I can't play football," I said, "how about I try some martial arts?"

Mom didn't love that option, either.

I tilted my head. Gave an innocent smile. "I could learn to protect myself."

She gave me a look. Mom knew what happened whenever I dove into something new. She also had faith in what came next. She sighed, then tousled my curls.

"Okay," she said. "We'll try it."

∿

First came karate. The first class, I went in so excited. I was not as excited coming out. I don't think I lasted a month. The form wasn't for me. Those beginners' classes didn't have near enough action. Fortunately, the rec center offered another martial art that did—judo.

I took to judo like I took to swimming. Even so, in the beginning, at the Nishi Tani Judo Club at Maryvale, there was never any talk about tournaments or competitions. That wasn't the focus of my first instructors, who were advanced black belts. Though I was a kid, only eight, and though competitions weren't the focus, the training offered wasn't kid's play.

Their instruction focused on the art of judo, which means "the gentle way" in Japanese.[1] From the first time I stepped into the dojo as a judoka (a person who practices judo), I was taught not only the physical moves but also the intellectual and moral choices involved. Turns out the sport's teaching philosophy is deeply rooted in its origins. And given that judo arose from the practice of self-defense found in certain forms in jujutsu, it's no wonder that the key to judo is harnessing an opponent's strength and using that same force against him. Or her.

To do that, first you need to learn how to fall. The better you can dissipate energy by, say, giving your hand a hard *smack* on the mat, the less likely you are to get hurt when thrown. The key to not getting thrown in the first place is to establish a solid footing and lower your center of gravity. For this, we were taught to keep our knees soft and our feet flat. On your toes, you're a half step closer to getting thrown since you're already lifting off the ground. On your toes, you're doing half of your opponents' work for them. In judo, you're supposed to make it harder, not easier, for an opponent to knock you off your feet.

Besides practicing how to fall in that first class, we also learned the rituals to follow for each match. Whether at practice or in competition, you begin a match by facing your opponent and taking a bow in your *gi*—that traditional white-robed garment. Once the referee signals the start, you grab your opponent by the lapel on one side and by the sleeve on the other. Where you grab the gi factors into how you can throw or, rather, flip your opponent to the ground. There were girls in my classes, but from my first sparring days, I most often practiced against guys. I never saw that as a big deal. I liked playing with the boys in my neighborhood.

Later I learned how competitions are scored. You can win by scoring the most points before time runs out or by scoring an *ippon* (a full point), which ends the match immediately. There are a couple of ways to score an *ippon*—either by throwing your opponent on his or her back with "considerable force and speed"[2] or by pinning your opponent for thirty seconds. Over the years, that length of time has been cut down a bit. Older judoka can score an *ippon* using two other methods: Choke an opponent until he or she passes out or taps out (by tapping either the mat or your competitor to show surrender). Or use an arm bar on an opponent until the arm breaks or he or she taps out. People usually tap out.

Judo instructors drilled us on the basics over and over and over again: how to land, how to throw, how to pin. It wore on me to have all this repetition without the promise of more. If you've ever seen *The Karate Kid*, you might remember Daniel facing a similar problem. (Though I hadn't fallen in love with karate, I did love that movie when it came out a few years later. I even hung an eight-by-ten of Ralph Macchio from *Teen Magazine* inside my closet door—near one I had of Shaun Cassidy.) The karate kid learns the value of waxing on, waxing off, painting the fence, and sanding the floor, but that approach didn't add up for this kid who turned from karate after a few weeks. I was used to competing in swimming and diving, doing everything from freestyle to individual medleys, from springboard to high dive. Finding out what I could do and learning how improve myself through competitions already meant too much.

Though we had top-notch Japanese instructors, I'd grown bored of practice without any outlet for competition. To be honest, as much as I appreciated the old-school approach, if my instructors didn't let me compete, I planned to quit.

It didn't come to that. In 1979, as I started third grade, I entered my first tournament, the Desert Judo Championship in Scottsdale, Arizona. Though I was still wearing a white belt, I took second place in my age and weight class. Second overall for my first competition was something to celebrate. No one expected me to win it all that first time much less get as far as I did. Up on that winners' podium, I was hooked. I wanted more.

A couple of months later, I competed in the Fiesta Bowl Champion-ship at Arizona State University. I was little but didn't think twice about the size of the facility or the number of attendees. Didn't matter to me that most people there wore a higher-level belt than I did—yellow and orange and blue and purple. I was just excited to compete again. For each match, we were randomly paired with others in our age and weight groups. Mom cheered like wild for me, but I didn't hear her while I was on the mat. My focus was on what I had to do. Between matches, I held that focus, all the way through until I'd completed the championship match. This time, I won. I climbed to the winners' podium wearing my white belt. I remember bringing that first-place trophy home. My first.

Of all the trophies I've ever won, that Fiesta Bowl award was the most stunning. Most trophies have that standard wood stand topped with a gold figure striking a pose representative of the sport. Most of my awards over the years looked like that. The only difference was the overall size and height of the stand. That first big Fiesta Bowl award, though, was made of crafted marble excavated from an Arizona quarry. As much as Mom loved those cacti dug out of the desert, I loved that stone-cold beauty dug from the ground. A trophy isn't what I usually get sentimental about, but that's one I wish I hadn't given away.

The next year, starting as a yellow belt, I took part in nine tourna-ments across three western states. Trophies started taking up space in my room. People like to focus on how I won the Junior Olympics as well as state and regional competitions as a low-level belt, but what belt I wore didn't much matter to me. Or maybe it did given how much I enjoyed beating someone wearing a higher-degree belt when we faced off in those big competitions.

In all honesty, I think the whole belt thing has changed over the years. Walk into any dojo now, and you'll see a room full of little kids with black belts. Rooms with that view seemed designed to appeal to parents seeking proof they're not wasting their money and their kids really are progressing. To me, the color of my belt wasn't what mattered. What I loved was the chance to compete, which might explain why I racked up so many sit-ups in Mr. T's gym class. Once I started a challenge, any challenge, I didn't want to stop.

Mom brought me where I needed to go for competitions—the next school facility, the next sports complex, the next convention center, whether older or brand new, whether its wall paint had peeled in spots or smelled fresh. By that June, I'd earned an orange belt. Even by then, the middle of my second year competing, all the places I went to for tournaments blurred together.

Except for the championships held in Vegas every November. These I remember because Mom always treated me to Circus Circus afterward as a way to celebrate that year's accomplishments. In my first full year of competing, I'd managed to win first place in seven tournaments and placed second in the other two. Not a bad start. And I loved ending the year at a place like Circus Circus. I was ten in 1980 and couldn't gamble, but I could play a whole slew of midway games lining the floor just above the main level.

Since my first carnival back in Massachusetts, I've had a knack for winning. To get the prize I wanted when I was five—a Smokey the Bear bigger than me—I had to toss a dime inside a nickel-sized circle without touching any of its edges. First try and I won. Seriously. Let's be real, though. You know how those games go. I could probably throw a thousand more dimes and not ever have that happen again. Now, most of what I've achieved over the years meant working hard to perfect skills and strength. But when luck counts too, the game often breaks my way, starting with the time I won that Smokey the Bear. (For the record, I loved that big bear. I carried him proudly around that carnival, and at home he stood in the corner of my bedroom since he was too big to sit up on my bed with my Cubby Comfortable Jr.)

Part of the reason competitions tended to run together for me was because they all tended to run the same way. Each time, in each location, hundreds of participants in all age-groups funneled through the doors and streamed toward the first match. We competed according to our age and weight. Boys paired off to fight on one set of mats, girls on mine. Most tournaments followed a format of double elimination or modified double elimination, though the elimination part never ended up concerning me much. By my second year of competition, I usually placed first and would be disappointed if I came in only second or third. I don't mean to sound cocky, that's not me—I was just hard on myself. Looking back, I know none of it would have been possible without my parents' full support, my coach's training, and a lot of hard work and practice. What skills God gave me I didn't bury but tried to use as best I could.

With eight tournament championships under my soon-to-be blue belt, my parents realized I was serious about the sport, serious enough to move to Scottsdale in 1981 to join a more competitive judo club. I kicked off the new year with a first-place win in Los Angeles. Ronald Reagan was sworn in as president, the American hostages over in Iran were freed, and Dad and I watched the Super Bowl. All this happened just in January.

What I'm saying is that, as dedicated as I was to training for judo and as dedicated as my family was in supporting that training, other things were happening in life. At the time, I was just a kid who also liked to play for fun if given the chance. When neighbor kids headed down to the field toward the back of our new apartment complex for a game of football, I joined them whenever I could. And when I say "kids," I mean boys. (Not my brother; he found friends his age to run around with.) Of course, girls lived there, too, but none of them were interested in playing football outside like the rest of us. I'd played a lot already at school in PE and at recess, mostly touch or flag football. These kids played tackle, and I was game for it. Turned out I was hard to tackle, though I was usually the smallest player. Maybe my judo training made a difference given all its focus on balance and on learning what a body needed to know to not be thrown down. I was the new kid, but in picking teams, I soon came to be the player picked first. Occasionally, I got to quarterback, but my favorite positions to play were receiver and running back.

So many things you don't realize as a kid. I was learning how to work through judo, and through play, I was learning what would become my most important work.

3

A STRICT REGIMEN

I was newly eleven when I received my first invitation to the Olympic Training Center (now known as the Olympic and Paralympic Training Center) in Colorado Springs. I'd be the youngest athlete in judo history to train there. No one else my age had ever won enough tournaments to qualify. For so long, I'd dreamed of going—though I get how that sounds, considering I was just a kid then, but that's how I felt. With all my training, I'd heard a lot about the place and had even seen some pictures, and now here I was at the entrance in front of the Olympic rings, and Mom was taking my picture.

Once inside, we found out those rings were everywhere. As you can imagine, the whole place was amazing—state of the art. You name it, they had it. The best part, besides the actual training, was being with peers who gave me the challenges I needed. The dojo here was bigger and brighter than any dojo I'd seen. You couldn't help but feel a flush of inspiration walking in wearing your gi hearing the *Rocky* soundtrack from the weight room playing in the background. That really pumped me up. To think I'd watched what judo matches I could in the Olympics just the year before, after competing in my first few tournaments, and now here I was, training at the center. I walked through the halls wearing a laminated badge with the Olympic crest on it, but that didn't mean I'd made the team or was a shoo-in for the next Olympics—women weren't even eligible to compete in the Olympics in judo when I attended. But I figured a lot could happen in the next few years.

Those two weeks in March up in the Colorado mountains flew by. Since it was colder that time of year, we spent more of our free time inside that first time I attended. I remember the game room and vying for the chance to play games not found in any arcades around me at home, games more fun than Pac-Man or Donkey Kong or the latest Atari. At the gift shop, I loaded up on clothes bearing the Olympic rings and counted on there being a next time. Of course, I still have one of those T-shirts.

On my return home, the Scottsdale Judo Club named me Outstanding Judoka of the Year, recognizing the level of intensity and discipline I brought to what I did as an athlete. I was on a mission to achieve perfection. Mom said that's what I needed to do if I wanted to make it.

Not everything was perfect, though. At both tournaments before and after attending the Olympic Training Center, I only came in third. Training took a lot out of me. I was all of sixty-five pounds and lived on tuna fish and eggs to make my weight class for competitions. I was eleven and growing and hungry all the time. All the time. The hunger caused so much pain I found it hard to sleep at night. Ice cream shared with Dad watching football became all the more important. Mom knew, too, what a treat ice cream was for me. So on occasion, she treated me, and I absolutely loved that.

One day coming home from practice, we stopped at Baskin-Robbins so I could get a scoop of Quarterback Crunch, my favorite of the thirty-one flavors. Maybe Mom wanted to recognize my recent Outstanding Judoka award, or maybe we stopped just because. Anyway, afterward, in the car I said something that upset her, and she got mad and grabbed my ice cream and threw it out her open window.

That absolutely crushed me.

The ice cream meant more than a treat then. It meant not being hungry. When Mom tossed it, she underscored the point that I was far from perfect. At church on Sunday, I struggled once again as I sat with that. As a child, I took everything so seriously and always wanted to do the right thing. It was hard to understand how I could be honored at judo for being so disciplined and yet have Mom plainly show me at times I wasn't.

Years later, I finally identified the simple truth that Mom and I handled frustration in different ways. Though we both went all in on my judo—at least we did then—we are different kinds of people. Mom is definitely more free-spirited, a flower-child type, and I am more even-keeled and focused. Even as a kid. My friends could see it with that question they asked: *What age are you today, Shannon?* But the diet I had to follow for judo was too hard even for a kid like me, who'd resolved to be as perfect as my fun-loving Mom expected. I was still a kid.

Like others my age, I snuck treats. I ate candy bars or slipped over to Thrifty to get a triple scoop of double-chocolate malted crunch. When I strayed, I paid for it by having to sit in a silver plastic suit in a sauna until the weight came off. At eleven, I was tall and thin for my age but hovered on the border between lightweight and heavyweight. If I couldn't get off those last stubborn ounces, I'd have to go up a class into the heavyweight division. Not the most ideal situation to have to fight a girl twenty to thirty pounds heavier.

Other challenges I didn't mind. Once tournament wins started coming more easily, I welcomed the chance to compete against older kids and use more of the advanced skills I'd learned. In my age-group—nine- to twelve-year-olds—you were limited to basic maneuvers, such as throwing and pinning. Wax on, wax off; at eleven, I was ready to move to the next level. If I competed in the age category for thirteen and up, I could use chokeholds, too. If I jumped to the senior division—those eighteen and older—even better.

Or so I thought—until I entered my first senior competition and my opponent put me in an arm bar. I can tell you I enthusiastically tapped out. I wasn't about to have my arm broken, nor could I ever break someone else's arm whether or not they tapped out. Although I'd spent a lot of time learning different choke techniques and how to escape from them, I'd failed to train for the arm bar—that other way to score a full (match-winning) point in the older age division. For this more sophisticated technique, you try to get your opponent's arm positioned so that the wrong move on their part could break a bone. You are essentially immobilizing that elbow.

It may seem obvious now that I should have learned that technique before going into that competition, but it caught all of us off guard—even my experienced coach. Mom didn't bother adding it to my list of the tournaments in which I competed. Signing up for that first match for seniors taught me some important lessons: Pay attention to what different rules apply to different age-groups. And keep that straight in my mind when going into a match. Going into my next practice, the arm bar was the first thing I focused on when I hit the mat. I would not be caught unprepared again, either physically or mentally.

In a way, that loss prepared me for an unexpected change in one tournament's format. For the Los Angeles Tenri Open Championships that year, tournament organizers didn't have enough entries in each age and weight division. So they decided to use the *kohaku*, or winner-stays-up format. Here's how that worked. We were lined up from lightest to heaviest, regardless of age. First, the two lightest girls fought each other. The winner fought the next person, and we continued that way until the last opponent remained. I had never competed in a tournament with such a format. At only eleven years old and sixty-five pounds, I was among the first to go.

From there, I would fight until I lost. I won match after match by a full point. Seven matches in a row like that, and I captured the title.

If I wanted to keep competing against older girls, my coaches wanted me stronger. They advised I start weight training, which would help not only with judo but with swimming as well. By that point, I had a growing number of state ribbons, medals, trophies, and plaques in my bedroom. Though I knew I should do what my coaches asked if I wanted to be the best, I confess that lifting weights wasn't my favorite thing. Mom had to stay on me to keep up with them. In the end, for both of our sakes, she found me a trainer. I got tired for sure (and even more sore) adding this to my regimen, but if this is what it took, I told myself, I shouldn't think about the pain. *No pain, no gain*, as Mom said, and my coaches, too. So I sucked it up and did what I had to.

That July, Mom drove me all the way up to San Francisco for the USJF Junior Nationals. With all the driving Mom was doing, she ended up buying a van and converting the inside to make it more comfortable for all the interstate travel we had ahead. The friends I made in my new judo club rode along, too. Mom liked chaperoning these trips, but I would have rather been one of the eleven-year-olds who occasionally went without a mom.

Racking up the miles seemed to dial up her enthusiasm cheering me on from the sidelines. People commented on how loud and "animated" she was. She'd yell and try coaching me from the side, too, not that I heard her. I was too focused; I tuned her out. I tuned everyone out.

Sometimes, in high-level competitions, people will bring their intensity but leave out good sportsmanship. They can get mean. I strived to be the complete opposite. Some might say I was kind to a fault. What happened at nationals is a perfect example of this. I threw a girl down as if she were a practice dummy and got her into a pin. Without much effort, I could have held her for the full time needed to win. But I would have felt bad to have beaten her so quickly. My heart got the best of me, so I let her up.

My coach threw up his hands. "You don't do that, Shannon!" he exclaimed. "This is nationals!"

I was in a zone. I shrugged him off. "It's okay, Coach," I said. "I can throw her down again and end it." That's exactly what I did. In that tournament, I went on to win first place, and I felt good about how I won it.

Fittingly, I finished out 1981 with a total of eleven first-place finishes out of fourteen tournaments. I was eleven and had won my first national championship. I'd been to the Olympic Training Center. Attending so many competitions meant missing out on being a kid sometimes. Mostly, it meant missing a lot of school. Mom pulled me out of class as early as Wednesday to drive to out-of-state tournaments and to make it in time for weigh-in, and my first match would be the following day. Mom started homeschooling me, which worked great. Acing the tests, I could whip through a year's worth of material in a couple of weeks. Homeschooling allowed me to remain focused on training.

My brother was focused on his competitive bowling by this point, so he and Dad held down the home front while Mom took me on the road. All our time together, and somehow she felt she had to give me more. She found a little stuffed monkey for me—she knew how much I loved stuffed animals. This little guy wasn't given for a birthday or holiday, and it wasn't a prize won at a carnival. This one, she made plain, I'd earned through all my hard work, and it was offered in honor of all I'd done. I put the monkey in a place of honor in my room, right next to my koala, my Cubby Comfortable Jr.

That first time I won at nationals, Mom and Dad gave me something else I've cherished ever since—a thank-you card—though I was the one who needed to thank them for all they'd sacrificed for me. Inside the card were two heartfelt poems.

Whenever I've needed an extra boost, I pull out this card and the poems again. The poem Mom gave me helps me remember to listen to that small, still voice inside when I'm not sure what to do. *Keep on listening to the right within,* hers advises. *For it's God leading the way.* We weren't a big churchgoing family—at least I wasn't then—but Mom talked about God being there for me, and that's given me great comfort through the years.

And it's inspired me to take action, too. Take the next lines, for example: *Your goals you'll reach, if you so seek. Let no man lead you astray.* As young as I was then, I still understood that though God might point out the path, I had to follow it. My action mattered.

The poem Dad gave me underscored this idea that no goal is out of reach if you try. Maybe because I'd had a bit of success, I understood what it meant: To unlock your chances at success, you need to turn the key. After all—

An idea is nothing but a thought, until action makes it real.

It's up to me to take action to realize my goals. To make them real. In doing the work, you get the satisfaction. Nothing and nobody can take what you've accomplished away from you.

And nothing beats the good feeling you get from a worthy achievement.

These words from my parents have helped me remember on my less-than-perfect days that losses won't sink you if you can step through them, past them, on your way to a success. Through action, you move forward.

My parents have given me many gifts over the years, presents ranging from the practical to the sometimes sentimental, from the economical to the extravagant. Yet these two poems, "smothered with lots of luck and love," are what have buoyed and sustained me through my most difficult times. Mom and Dad knew the power these words would hold for me: Listen for God's guidance and try those steps. It helps to remember that. When my parents gave me this card, they asked me explicitly to always keep these thoughts near. I am not one to save poems, but this old gift from my parents I plan to keep forever.

The monkey, too.

⌒

The next spring, Dad saw me win my second state championship since he could get to it and not miss any work. I wish he could have seen me win my second national championship, too. Only Mom and I got to fly to Hawaii that July. As usual, Mom kept a tight rein on me our first days there before the competition. One of the kids I met at the tourney was a guy named Cliff, who was very sweet. His two brothers competed, too. At first, I couldn't spend much time with him because Mom clamped down on all my free time to keep me focused. After I nailed the overall win, though, and the tournament was over, Mom set me free.

The post-tournament freedom she granted made all her rules leading up to the competition easier to bear. After breakfast the next day, I could disappear with Cliff and the others. We traveled in a pack, with energy from the tournament still coiled within us as we roamed the beaches and shopped for trinkets. At night we enjoyed the luau. Torchlight glowed on our sunburnt skin. We had a blast. The day we left, Cliff met us at the air-port. He brought a lei for me (and one for Mom, too), and we promised to stay in touch. For years, we did, writing letters in between times we'd run into each other at tournaments or the Olympic Training Center.

Fall of that year was my second time at the center in Colorado. Though I competed against only girls, I practiced with boys, too, like the year before. About fifty judokas had been invited to the camp, and we were pretty good athletes, but we weren't all necessarily that mature. One of the days there, as I was leaving the cafeteria with a group, this guy came up and bit me on the back of my bare leg. The guy wasn't another kid. He was in his twenties. I was twelve and didn't know what to make of it then. Honestly, I can't say I do now, either.

All I could do was put that moment aside. Instead, I focused on enjoying my three weeks there, especially any chance I had to hang out with Cliff. We lifted weights to "The Eye of the Tiger"—that new song from the latest *Rocky*—and felt the thrill of the fight pumping through each beat, pumping us up. That song by Survivor still brings me right back to those sessions every time. When we weren't rising up to the challenges of the weight room, we hit the mats, building ourselves up to compete against the team from Scotland, one of many competitions that have all blurred together for me now.

For breaks, we'd venture out into the September mountain sunshine and drape ourselves over the pole vault landing mat to hang out and watch track and field practice. Other times, we all hung out in the game room, and some claimed top scorer for these competitions, too.

Mom lingered around the edges of my days there, though now that I was a bit older, I really wanted to be on my own. One thing we did do together was get a petition going for the Olympic Committee to permit women to compete in judo in the next Olympics, not merely showcase it as a demonstration. Mom was gung ho with that petition, but even there, at the Olympic center—even with me in pigtails, looking equal parts hopeful and serious, even with Mom at my side, looking like someone famous— the two of us couldn't get enough signatures to bring the petition to the committee.

Back at home, the paper ran an article about my time at the training center. The reporter interviewed my coach for it. "Shannon is relentless," Coach Samuels gushed. "One time she had a permanent tooth knocked out in a match, and she wouldn't quit. She never complains; she doesn't stop. You have to scream at her to stop. Sometimes I have to send her to bed for a day and a half, she works so hard."[1]

Only I don't remember ever getting a tooth knocked out.

What I do remember was that, from that second national championship on, I welcomed the challenge to enter two different age divisions for any tournament I could. I competed as a junior, which was my actual age division, and as a senior, which was for women eighteen and older. Though I enjoyed competing in both, I actually preferred the senior division. It's fun to compete with people who are supposed to, through their age and rank, be better than you. My overall win percentage ended up being higher when I competed in the senior divisions compared to my own age and weight class. At the age of twelve, I won five of the six senior tourneys, whereas I won (only) eleven of the fourteen tournaments in which I competed in my own age and weight. The few times I didn't take first I came in second, except for that one third-place finish I got in a senior championship.

Not only did I start competing in the senior division, I also managed to talk Mom into letting me travel with the team without her to San Diego at the end of that September. We got there a couple of days early to prep for the competition. At night, the team took a trip out to the beach. It was nearing high tide, and we walked along a pier, looking out into the ocean. We were having a great time. I remember the coach's son, Bruce, being one of older judokas in the group—meaning he was maybe fifteen. I was with friends, doing exactly what I wanted to be doing, for once without my mom hovering nearby. When we all reached the end of the pier, I stood right up on the edge to feel the spray from the waves crashing up against the pilings, against the pier. The tide was still coming in, with wave after wave rising, then collapsing.

I stood up there so long that I had spray all up my legs, my toes soaked, until a huge wave swelled before me, rising up, reaching over the pier, and the strength of it lifted me up and pulled me back into the water.

I was terrified. The wave dropped, thrashing me up against the rocks under the pier. There was nothing I could do. I was a competitive swimmer, but the tide was too strong. It was all I could do to catch my breath when I could.

Next thing I knew, someone was in the roiling water with me by the rocks as the tide tried to pull me under. He held onto me, holding me up as best he could while others reached down to pull me out. Salt water was in my eyes as ocean-slick hands grabbed hold of me, pulling me up, pulling me out across the rocks, and I was gasping for air.

I didn't have to scramble for something to hold onto to breathe anymore. I was safe.

But my teammates were still reaching down into the water, reaching for the one who'd jumped in to help me—Bruce. The coach's son.

We were lucky that day. They managed to pull Bruce out, too, eventually. Thankfully. You can imagine the phone call to my mom, letting her know what happened. How likely would it be that she'd let me go on my own again anytime soon?

For the record, at that tournament, I did still take first place in the seniors division. I'm not saying that what happened wasn't serious. What I'm saying is that, even with a scare like that, I still did what I came to do once I stepped on that mat.

I was still looking for enough competition to keep me challenged. That fall, I moved up another rank to purple belt. In tournaments, I competed against older judokas as much as I could. At our freestyle practices—that is, during randori—I continued to spar with the boys. I had an older brother; I'd sparred with boys all my life. I was used to tackling with all the football I played after school with the neighbor kids. At twelve, I knew full well how hard boys played. I could play hard, too.

Mom had seen the gamut of stunts kids pull while watching us practice. The parents all sat on a bench pushed back against the wall and did what parents do while kids learn to be kids on their way to becoming grown-ups. One afternoon, the class was doing our usual mat work, and neither my opponent nor I was able to gain an advantage for some time.

That's when he bit me. On the inner thigh.

Adrenaline rocketed through my body. I grabbed him and put him into a headlock at the edge of the mat, near a brick wall, cranking his neck back as hard as I could. You bet I was angry.

Took time to form words through clenched teeth. "Don't you dare bite me again," I said, getting his head as close to the wall as possible without touching it. I held him there.

When I felt he got the message, I let go, and I stood and brushed off and stalked off the mat. Mom could tell I'd gotten the better of him, but from the other side of the room, she hadn't seen what he'd done. While the kid was walking it out, I stripped down to the shorts I had on under my gi. I showed Mom the teeth marks on my leg.

"Should have slammed his head into the wall," Mom said, and all the other moms, being moms, agreed.

During tournaments, judges kept a close eye on what was fair and what wasn't. Sometimes, when you're evenly matched with an opponent, no one will score, and then it's up to the judges as to who will win. Once you reach the championship match, it can feel like everyone in the entire building is watching, but you've got to block all that out to maintain the focus needed to win. By this point, I'd been on a mat surrounded by a big crowd plenty of times before. I knew what it took to edge out a competitor and knew the feeling I'd had in those matches when I'd fallen short. At the end of four years of competitions, I could still count the tournaments I'd come in second or third on two hands. Everything else I'd won, and I was at first confident I'd won this match, too, though the judges hadn't yet granted any points. The two side judges had split the decision, which meant the lead judge ultimately decided the winner. He gave it to my competitor. The room didn't agree. My mom and my coach did a lot of complaining about that ruling, but it didn't change anything. Later, we found out the lead judge was my competitor's dad. Hard to believe. Ultimately, though, it'd been on me to win regardless of the judging. And I hadn't.

After the awards ceremony that night, there was a dance that tournaments like this often held. It ended up being a good way to unwind. And it was super fun to let loose with other judokas. What wasn't so fun was Mom being right there, chaperoning, especially now that I was getting older and turning a bit boy crazy. These dances had begun interesting me in new ways, giving me the chance to see guys I knew from before, like Cliff, and to connect with other young men from all over the country and sometimes the world. None of these early relationships ever got too serious, I should say. Remember, I was twelve.

That October, I managed to win double firsts in my age-group and in the senior division for the first time. A month later, I won double firsts again in both junior and senior divisions, this time in the Fiesta Bowl Judo Championships. Those wins meant even more to me because Dad was there to watch. Every competition he came to, he made it extra special by buying me a tournament pin for my Levi's jacket. Tournament pins were big then. The tradition for judokas was to trade pins with other judokas from different states and even other countries, but I never traded the ones my dad gave me.

After the November tournament in Vegas, Mom treated me to Circus Circus for our postseason celebration, as had become our tradition. Every year my arm got better, or the games got easier, and every year I continued to bring home a heap of stuffed animals. Mom and I had to find room in the car for all my winnings. I had to fit in there, too. As we drove away, I remember lining up a dozen monkeys I'd won in the back window. I handed them out to my friends, saving one or two for myself. It's a tradition that keeps on giving. I still come home from my trips to Vegas with a car full of stuffed animals to give away.

Whenever we returned home from a tournament, Mom took care of my collection of ribbons and medals and trophies and plaques. She kept that running list of all my tournaments and my wins, and she tracked my camp invitations and honors, too. Each January, she rolled a new sheet into the typewriter to list all my awards that year. Any newspaper articles that popped up about me she slid into cellophane sleeves in a scrapbook. She fit medals into a display case, put plaques on my wall, and found a spot for each trophy. The chore she assigned me was dusting all the trophies overtaking my room. You can imagine how many I already had in my judo collection. I'd racked up several swimming and diving trophies and tennis trophies, too. All my awards came in all different sizes, though some from judo were ridiculously tall—with several taller than I was. Mom made it my duty to take care of my trophy population. I'd won them, I needed to tend them. "Make sure you dust in between all the arms and legs," Mom said, so I spent hours trying to get them looking perfect. I hated dusting all those trophies.

On top of all that recognition, Mom and Dad awarded me in other ways. Their gifts grew more extravagant as the years went on. As with the monkey and the poems, I think my parents just wanted to show me they were proud of all I'd managed to achieve. Maybe, too, their gifts merely reflected the times. It was the 1980s, *Dallas* topped the TV charts, and a lot of people believed greed was good even before Gordon Gekko told us so in *Wall Street*. Excess was the language of success, and my parents wanted to speak to the sacrifices made as well as the discipline I demonstrated as a judoka. I never felt I needed or even wanted a fur coat or a diamond ring or their other lavish gifts. I was twelve, competing in two worlds, and I was winning as an adult. But I was still just a kid.

4

SIDELINED

At the beginning of 1983, I had to take a break from judo. Not by choice. At thirteen, I'd messed up my neck and back so bad that I couldn't rotate my head all the way around. Mom booked me at the chiropractor. For several months, I had three appointments a week there instead of getting to spend time on a judo mat. In fixing my neck, they found I'd lost the curvature in my spine, too, so I needed that realigned before I could return to practice. Mom booked those appointments at the same time as my favorite TV show, *Days of Our Lives*. So I brought along my portable TV and watched it while the chiropractor worked on me. (I still try not to miss the show.)

That spring I spent in a regular classroom for the first time in a few years. I was still swimming, but without judo, I was a fish out of water. I couldn't wait to get back to the dojo, my home away from home.

Without judo, I needed other ways to soak up my energy. After school, I spent time at the Boys & Girls Club, picking up basketball. I ended up shooting hotshot basketball there for Coach Russ, who welcomed me and provided a much-needed sports connection at a time when I missed practicing and competing with my judokas.

When I finally could resume judo full-time, Mom wanted me to switch clubs again, so that spring, I did. I couldn't wait to get back at it and hit the mat again. The coaches I'd had through the years had offered what I needed when I needed it, building on my skill set at the time. Similarly, my new coach at the Shin-Gi-Tai Judo Club continued to teach me what I needed to know. Coach Rennick had been a member of the Polish National Team until he defected to the United States in the 1970s. What I remember most about him was how he lit up when talking about how much he loved being in America. The thought still makes me smile, as do my memories of all he did to prepare us for competitions. When we met up at tournaments—and there were three in Southern California within a week at the beginning of that summer—he was even particular about what restaurants we'd go to as a team. He wouldn't give the okay for us to eat until he physically checked out the kitchen to make sure it was clean first. I don't know if this concern of his came from living behind the Iron Curtain or from learning the hard way what you're willing to overlook when you're hungry from trying to make weight. I know that hunger. A lot of us did.

That summer, I was so eager to jump back into competing that by the week after Memorial Day, I'd nailed first place in all three tournaments I'd entered. For two of them, I'd competed in and won the senior division as well.

It was easy to make friends at this new club. Coach Rennick incorporated games as part of practice, though we didn't realize how unusual his tactics could be. A few times in class, he had us remove our belts, fold them up a bit, and chase our team members around. You could hear the cracking of belts around the room. My gi flapped over my T-shirt as I tried to hit teammates' backs with my purple belt before they could whack me. That hurt. Coach Rennick took his belt off, too, and joined the chase. We were all old enough at this point that parents didn't stick around much for practice, but the ones who caught wind of this took the time to express some concerns. Apparently, this kind of game had been part of how he'd been trained back in Poland. He didn't understand his tactics were unacceptable here in the States. Over time, he made adjustments and throughout my time with him was truly a phenomenal coach.

Coach Rennick asked us to work hard, and we did. That summer, my mornings started with an intense swim practice, and then I'd head off to the dojo. In the evening, I followed the same routine. You can imagine why I got so hungry. Each practice was tough and exhausting, like the time Coach Rennick took our judo team up to what is now called Piestewa Peak to run the summit trail.

The path isn't as steep as Camelback, but it's still a challenge, especially the closer you get to the top. There were maybe about ten of us altogether. Some I already counted as friends, but we were all teammates running up the rocky path to the top, passing other climbers. (And, no, it wasn't as busy then as it is now.) Running up it meant we had to concentrate on our climbing strategy, especially in the steeper parts, though we weren't likely to use any of the handrails installed along the way. Arizona heat shimmered around the mountain. I pushed up the trail. At the top, we barely took in the expansive view before we tapped the designated spot—besides, we'd seen the view before—and turned around to run back down. Down down down the stone steps. My legs acted as if they considered giving out. Which was strange.

Back at the bottom, along a wide-enough stretch, the coach made us run short sprints. Then he said, "Mountain, one more time."

During sprints, I'd had to press my hand hard into a cramp in my side. That wasn't enough to take care of the pain, so I also kept having to stretch and then shake out my legs. I hadn't said anything since I was only thirteen and couldn't name what I felt.

Everyone else headed back up the trail. Coach Rennick gave me a look.

I could have tried to explain it. I shook my head. "I'll do it," I said, "but you'll probably have to take me to the hospital when I'm done."

He didn't believe I was serious. Other kids complained sometimes about all we had to do. Not me. Maybe I was new to him, but I wasn't new to training. I knew what the stitch in my side was telling me, though it'd never spoken so harshly before. I looked up the trail at the growing distance between me and my friends. I looked back at my coach. *No pain, no gain.* Okay. I hit the trail.

When I finished, I could not take another step. Literally. The cramp that had started in my side doubled me over by the end. I couldn't move.

The ER doctor said it was a muscle spasm. With a muscle relaxer, the pain went away, and I got to go home. With that much running and jumping, that's how my body reacts, apparently. Now I know what to do whenever I feel that come on—stop running but keep moving, stretching as tall as possible while walking. If I don't catch it early enough, I have to take a muscle relaxer. So, *no pain, no gain* doesn't always apply, not for me, as the doctors explained to me and my coach and my mom. I would have to recognize my limits if the spasms started again and know my body couldn't push through the moment no matter how I tried. In that case, the adults in the room would have to let me call the shots.

The middle of that year I spent in the middle of the country. Junior nationals were held in Decatur, Illinois, in 1983. For the third year in a row, I won in my age and weight class, though one of my championship matches proved more of a challenge than the others. When I tried to get my opponent into a position on the mat so I could pin her, she suddenly drove her teeth into my arm, clamping down on my skin, and wouldn't let go. I screamed at the top of my lungs. You can imagine my mom went on high alert. Later, Mom told me she thought for certain I had broken my arm. The referee stopped the match. "What's wrong?" he asked.

"She bit me." I yanked up the sleeve of my gi to show him. In judo, intentionally trying to hurt an opponent can result in an automatic win for the one injured. She hadn't broken a bone, but she broke skin. There was blood.

He gave her a half-point penalty. I pulled down my sleeve, and the match continued. Better to earn a win through what I did instead of merely through the unsportsmanlike actions she did to me. I took first place. I was still bleeding.

Later that month, I spent a week in Kentucky at Camp Bushido, learning the ways of the warrior. Those ways lived in me every time I fought to win. Early the next year, an opponent tried to put me in a pin by grabbing my gi to pull me over. Somehow, the fabric raked across my left eye, scratching my cornea. The only way to relieve the pain was to shut my eyes. I kept both eyes closed to pin her to end the match. At that point, I was pulled aside, and a doctor was called in to treat me. He patched over my eyes and wrapped my head with gauze.

I pulled away from the doctor. I'd won my first event and was charged up at the thought of winning double gold medals. Competing blindfolded didn't seem a problem. "I've got to go," I said.

"No way," the doctor ruled.

Later, my coach guided me up to the second-place position on the podium next to the winner and the third-place finisher, and there I stood, both eyes wrapped, when Mom snapped a photo.

I'd been so sure I could have done more that day. I'm the kind of person who fights to the end. I play to win. That's how I've played ever since I was a little girl. I can't remember a time in my life that I didn't want to compete. To achieve the goals I set required a lot of hard work, which I was willing to do. I set my sights high. Why not the Olympics? My coaches gave me all the guidance I needed, and I had Mom and Dad cheering me on and could draw on strength given by God.

Knowing I always had that power behind me and within me gave me the confidence to overcome the challenges faced along the way. Things like getting bit or having muscle spasms wouldn't stop me. Don't get me wrong; those moments hurt. Yet I knew I could look past those parts and give myself another push to work through to a victory.

What I wasn't sure I could overcome, though, was my daily struggle to not gain weight in order to maintain my weight class. I faced that battle every single day from my first competition at age eight to when I hung up my gi at fifteen. My stomach hurt so much from hunger that it made it hard to fall asleep at night. Except for the few times I went off my strict protein diet, I was that hungry all the time, but I stuck to it. If I didn't make weight, I'd be back in that silver plastic suit, sitting in the sauna until the weight came off. On weigh-in day, I wouldn't eat all day. Or drink water. I didn't even brush my teeth—I couldn't afford any extra ounces. Not one. As I got older, I found tournament days were not the best time to get your period. Wearing a white gi was hard enough. The cravings, though—I didn't know my hunger pains could get worse.

Sometimes, I stripped down to a bathing suit to weigh in. If I still didn't make weight, I took it off. One way or another, I'd make weight to compete as I wanted.

My fourth junior national championship I won down in Texas the summer before eighth grade. I came back to more practice and summer movies like *Sixteen Candles* and *Ghostbusters* and my favorite, *The Karate Kid*. What should have also followed for me that summer was the Olympics. I wasn't set to compete or to demonstrate, but I had been asked to volunteer in a locker room. Unfortunately, the organizers didn't figure out until too late that the location would have been inappropriate for a fourteen-year-old female volunteer, even one with her mother.

Instead, I watched from home the relay of runners carrying the torch from New York to Los Angeles, with Carl Lewis's granddaughter running the final leg into Memorial Stadium, where the Rams played. Disappointing, sure, to not be there. Yet something about the 1984 games felt different, considering I had two stays under my belt at the Olympic Training Center and considering the competitions were being held where I'd competed before. Coach Rennick was such a fount of information, and yet we didn't think to ask about any insights he might have had about what all happened in his training behind the Iron Curtain, especially with his Eastern bloc country being among those boycotting the 1984 games. What I cared about then was cheering on Mary Lou Retton as she became the first U.S. woman to win the gold in the all-around for gymnastics. I cheered for the U.S. men medaling in silver and bronze in judo, too, though both were at least ten years older than me. No women to cheer on in judo that year. Not until the next Olympics would women get to demonstrate the sport. I hoped I was on track to be among them. In those days, tennis took up the national stage in women's sports,[1] and at the Olympics, Steffi Graf from Germany took the women's gold.

My grandma back in Massachusetts thought I should forget about judo and play more tennis, as if I could take on Graf, as if it'd be a breeze for me to qualify at that level. I'd played it competitively a few years at that point, and from my earliest tournaments in tennis, too, I'd been bumped up to compete against eighteen-year-olds. I'd forgotten all about that until looking back through some old albums recently. The things I've been so proud of in judo didn't stick in my memory with regard to tennis. The game never did draw me in as much as judo did. Or football. When I wasn't in one of Coach Rennick's training sessions or in the pool, you could find me out in the field having fun playing football with the kids in my neighborhood. I played a lot in junior high.

With both football and judo, I felt sure I belonged, out of everything I had done. My judo team felt like family. I'd even been invited to Coach Rennick's wedding. The whole judo club had been, too. His fiancée was a Chinese woman we'd come to know from all the time we spent together. Of all places, they held their ceremony—guess where?—on a judo mat, with both of them in a bright new gi. Since we were his students, we wore ours, too. Fitting for them to marry that way. It felt perfect.

In all I did, I kept trying to be as perfect as Mom told me I had to be. If we didn't live close to perfect, there would ultimately be a price to pay. We'd end up in hell. We didn't go to church that often, but it counted when we went. She put the fear of God in me that I might not be in line with the entrance requirements for heaven. Once, when I lied to help keep my brother out of trouble, I heard Mom's warning afterward in my head.

I tried to make amends. At church, at the end of the service, when there was an altar call, I stood and skirted around Mom and my brother and walked up the aisle to give my heart to the Lord. I wanted to do the right thing for Mom, for God, for my soul.

∾

In eighth grade, I tried more school. By only doing tournaments in San Diego in September and Vegas in November, I could try out for the junior high basketball team. Basketball *almost* made enduring school worth it, but it was hard to sit in class when I could whip through a year's worth of a subject at home in just a few weeks.

My first scheduled tournament of 1985 came after my fifteenth birthday. My time off served me well, if you can say that I had time off while training. That March, I had a good month, winning both the USJF and USJA nationals in the senior division. Just as important for me was receiving the Senior Sportsmanship award at the Pacific Northwest Open.

The best part: With my first-place finishes and multidivisional championship wins, I'd qualified to stay and train at the Olympic Training Center again, and not just for a couple of weeks. Getting back there had been my dream, exactly what I'd worked toward for years. Yet I was too young, by their standards, to live there permanently. Mom didn't want my age getting in the way of my dream. She knew I'd gone toe-to-toe with adults since I started judo, she knew I knew how to handle being the youngest. And didn't my recent Senior Sportsmanship award prove not only that I fit in with older competitors but also that I could stand on my own among them? Mom petitioned the Olympic Training Center committee, swearing her fifteen-year-old daughter had what it took to take up residence at the center. Mom knew how to persuade people. She had been my loudest fan from my first fight, and she intended to be heard. You can imagine that, if that show *Dance Moms* had been on back then and if they made a version for judo moms, my mom could have starred in it. At the least, she knew how to make her point.

When the Olympic Training Center committee extended their invitation to me this third time, it was for me to live there. Permanently.

Mom drove me to Colorado, and there I made myself at home. This place I knew well already: the same gift shop, the same state-of-the-art weight room, the same arcade games, the same great food in the cafeteria (unlike a lot of other cafeterias). And there, right there, was where I stood when that immature guy bit me on the leg.

Much was the same as before. We stayed in the same dorms, very much like ones at a university. I knew the routine of training all day. The training was hard, though that was the easy part. The hard part for me was what happened at night.

During the day, I focused on what I knew. I worked hard in the dojo and in the weight room. I saw friends I knew from before. Though my friend Cliff wasn't there, his brother was. Not every future contender trained there, and not every sport used that particular facility for training. That may explain why I don't remember ever seeing Matt Biondi or Janet Evans or other swimmers I would have looked for there. But also athletes from certain sports tended to hang out with athletes of similar sports. There ended up being cliques at the training center not so different from the cliques you see in high school. Since the judokas hung out a lot with the boxers, I got to have some fun with a two-time Olympian named Robert

Shannon. When he was my age, he'd already won a world championship in boxing but had to sit out his first Olympics because of the Moscow boycott. Everyone at the center had a story about how they started their sport so young. For Robert, he'd started fighting young because he wasn't white enough in one neighborhood and wasn't black enough in another. He was a good guy and an impressive talent. I still have on my jeans jacket the Golden Gloves patch he gave me. I remember his great sense of humor and how he kidded me about my name when we met. "If we ever got married, you'd be Shannon Shannon," he said. Robert made me smile.

I can't say I always get the sense of humor some guys have, but I've always gotten along well with them. I've been around them all my life, starting with my brother. I'd sought out boys instead of girls to play with at recess, at PE, and in junior high. Guys had picked me first on their teams for as long as I could remember. But at the training center, I had to start thinking twice about being around some guys. Certain ones gave me the distinct impression they weren't interested in having me step onto a mat to train with them—but they were plenty interested in having me there for after-hours fun.

I didn't know what to make of this. All the times I'd hung around boys, and this was the first I'd encountered sexism. What made it worse was the drinking—and so much of it, every night. Drinking was different back then. In Colorado in 1985, eighteen-year-olds could legally drink beer. Most everyone I hung out with there was eighteen or older. Not all athletes who trained at the center partied every night. But many of the ones in judo did back then. One night I could handle. Another night was pushing it. Every night became too many nights, too quickly.

I'd always been old for my age, and I'd always been strong, but I wasn't old enough or strong enough to power through training all day and drinking all night. Whatever combination that took I didn't have. I knew my limits and knew I had to listen to what my body told me ever since running up Piestewa Peak a second time. I knew my body couldn't take this.

I called my mom. I'm not sure she could understand me through the crying.

I'd lived my dream in Colorado for only a week. A dream looks different, though, when played out in real life. I thought I'd found a way free from Mom's constant pressure for perfection, I thought I was finally on a road of my own, and yet here I was, asking Mom to come and get me. My parents drove all night from Phoenix to Colorado Springs to pick me up and take me home. I was packed by the time they pulled up. I piled in with them. I was going home.

5

SUBSTITUTION

I wasn't done with judo, not while in the midst of tournament season. Within the week, I'd won the award for Outstanding Junior Female Competitor and took first place in the senior's division at Caesar's Palace, and by the end of that month, I was in Hawaii for nationals, and Cliff was greeting me and my mom at the airport with a lei in each hand as if he'd been there since seeing us off from the same spot a few years before. Nothing had changed, and everything had changed.

Mom kept her usual tabs on me before the competition. But when I won first place there in Honolulu in the women's division, Mom didn't even congratulate me. My sixth consecutive national title, and she didn't even say, *Nice job*. It was as if a national win was the least I could do. I was expected to win.

So I took off. Which I usually did, anyway, after tournaments—I went shopping. I went to luaus. I went everywhere I could, flying solo without my mother, enjoying my independence. A bunch of us went out on a catamaran and got to know the captain sailing it. He was good-looking, with a wide white smile and a sun-bronzed face. My friends and I thought it'd be fun to ride the net. The captain hesitated at first, pulling on the red bandana around his neck, but we talked him into it. We crawled out onto it with him glancing over at us nervously, the net bowing under our weight. I settled into the space I claimed and spread out. Under the Hawaiian sun, we sailed on, suspended in time, suspended by that net, skimming over waves, the ocean spraying us from underneath.

Back onshore, I filled Mom in on what it was like, out on the ocean, with the blue horizon stretching out on one side of the water and the island nestled up against it on the other. Maybe I oversold the experience because she wanted to come along the next time.

Not such a great idea in hindsight. As soon as she saw the catamaran dipping in the water, with me out in the middle of the net, she freaked out.

"Get my baby off that net!" she shrieked. "Off! Now!" She was yelling into the wind.

I exchanged a look with the friend next to me on that swaying net, and I shrugged. I'd been the one who'd brought my mother into this. Slowly, I climbed back over to the side, where Mom was clinging to hold on.

Needless to say, I didn't take her on any more rides.

Later, I went back on the water with my friends. We all rented a big clear-bottom inner tube instead of going out on the catamaran again. For this adventure, we didn't need a captain. We soaked up more sun, squeezing the last of the Hawaiian Tropic out of the bottle. My shoulders were peeling again. Sometimes, we had to brace ourselves as the tube crested a wave. Sometimes, a wave caught us off guard, and as the tube slid down into the trough, we'd fall into whoever sat on the other side. I forget what we talked about. It was important and not important, and before we knew it, we'd drifted all the way out past where we were supposed to be. The people on the beach looked impossibly small. I remember thinking it was going to be a long haul back. And then a wave hit and flipped us over. All seven of us grabbed onto the inner tube, one by one climbing back aboard—as if there'd been some invisible string tying us together so we wouldn't lose anyone. The moment jolted us into action. We were fully charged and frantically paddling back to shore.

We were not in a good place.

I didn't notice the surfer cruising over until he was practically on top of us. He dropped down on his board to get closer.

A cold, slick weight settled in my stomach. I knew why he'd come before he said a word. Then he said it.

"Hey," he said. "There a Shannon out here?"

I tried to brush the sun's heat off my shoulders. "Yeah," I said.

He looked as uncomfortable as I was. "Your mom wants me to bring you back," he said.

If I looked hard enough, I was sure I could have picked my mother out from all the colorful dots there on the beach. Yes, I was annoyed she was at it again. And yet a part of me was relieved, too, that she'd sent him. We were a bunch of kids stranded too far out in the ocean, and this had all the makings of one of those bad after-school specials that people talked about and I never saw. I was scared to death.

I could have climbed onto his board and ridden the next waves back to shore. Sure would have been easier. But my friends were there, at my shoulder. I had climbed off the net when Mom called me back, but I couldn't climb out now. We were having a hard enough time as it was, inching back to shore. All hands were needed.

"I'm going to stay right here," I told him.

He sat a second, looking at me, then at each of us, before giving a nod and turning away. No one said anything. It seemed that the string connecting all of us knotted more tightly. I bent closer to the water, digging in.

For as long as I could remember, I'd focused on being the best at judo. Centering myself on that goal had anchored me for years. But what did that mean now for me? I was starting to wonder. For the first time, the next steps being laid out gave me pause.

Like when the Kodokan in Japan notified me that fall that, in recognition of my accomplishments, they were awarding me a Shodan black belt. They had tried and they had tried to get me to test for my black belt, and now they were just giving it to me.

Trust me, this wasn't their standard practice. Their testing process was actually quite scripted and required candidates (except, apparently, for me) to demonstrate proper technique and execution of Nage-no-Kata, a type of randori that employed different forms of throwing techniques. Demonstrating knowledge of the technique was the key to the test, not the effectiveness of your response to the opponent's resistance. Defense skills weren't even considered. In fact, at testing, your partner wasn't supposed to give any resistance at all. With this being the case, the test to me seemed less of an accurate measure of whether a certain level of mastery of competition-style judo had been achieved and more of a box to check.

But you had to check that box to get that belt. For the Kodokan to grant me a black belt without making me clear all the hurdles of taking the test was such a surprise; it left me honored—but hesitant—to wear it. I had only my record as proof I'd earned the ranking. I did not feel ready.

Mom tried to convince me I was.

Coach Rennick did, too. "You should wear it," he said.

Still, I left it in my drawer. If I had to be honest, a part of me didn't want to be in danger of losing to anyone wearing a lower-degree belt.

Then the National Judo Center came calling. Mom handed the phone to me. She waited for me to finish the call. There's only one reason a place like that contacts you by phone: to offer the chance to train at their prestigious center.

"Congratulations," she cooed when I hung up, then caught my expression. "You know," she said, shifting her tone, "that's a good thing they called."

"But I *don't* know that's so."

She bristled, not understanding why I wasn't sure about going. What did I think I was doing in judo all those years?

I didn't want to repeat what I'd gone through at the Olympic Training Center. The only reason to take the spot was to continue my path to the Olympics. I didn't know whether I wanted to chase that shadow anymore.

At that point, I'd started my freshman year of high school, taking classes with kids my age again. I tried out for basketball since I liked it so much and had done well in it in junior high. And after just the first practice, the coach had wanted to move me up to the junior varsity team.

Which seemed like great news. Mom was not as excited when she heard it. "That'll just distract you from judo," she said.

I wasn't going to say more at that point. I decided not to continue on the basketball team. But everything felt different—or at least not right.

Even competing in Vegas felt different that year, though I still won first place in my age and weight class. Afterward, I roamed the games at Circus Circus and told myself I didn't have to be in another tournament to come back to Vegas again.

What if I *was* done with judo? The question that had been going around and around in my head now felt more like an answer.

Mom didn't think so. "What do you mean, you think you're done with judo?"

She had other thoughts to share with me about the thoughts I'd been having. What did I think all that money she and Dad put into judo was for? Did I think money just grew on trees?

I knew they'd spent a lot of money on hotel rooms, gas for the van, food, uniforms, airline tickets, you name it. I knew they paid a lot for all the training I'd had at all of my judo clubs.

It should not have been news to me that she did not want me to quit.

She pulled Dad into it. Actually, she pulled me to the couch he was sitting on, another one on which we enjoyed watching the Patriots. Mom told him what we'd been talking about. "And what do you think of your little girl?"

Dad stroked his mustache and looked from me to Mom before putting his arm across the back of the couch. He just wanted me to be happy, he said.

"And if moving on from judo is what Shannon wants," he said, "I'm okay with that."

∾

Basketball was moving on without me, but that didn't mean I couldn't blaze other new trails my freshman year. I found Mom outside smoking and went out to join her, sitting on her lap as I used to all the time. We started talking while I swiped the air, clearing the smoke away from my face, and I joked I should try out for wrestling.

You should have seen her eyes light up as she set down her coffee. "You should," she said. "You should."

I tried to play down the idea. Really, I shouldn't have even brought it up as a joke. Already, she had latched onto the idea. I couldn't bear to tell her I wouldn't try.

So the next day at wrestling practice, as boys warmed up on the mats, I threaded my way through to the coach. The guys looked at each other, and they looked at me. *What, are you lost?* one funny guy said. *This is the wrestling room,* said another. *Girls' basketball is over in the gym.*

But I knew where I was. I knew what I was doing.

"You're here for what?" the coach asked.

I had to explain again I wanted to try out.

"Well, this is a first." He sized me up a moment, and I stood, feet planted. "Alright," the coach said finally and called a boy over.

At first my soon-to-be-opponent didn't seem so thrilled. But he pulled himself to his feet and sauntered over. Some of his teammates had some comments peppering his way.

I was already focused, like at the start of any match. I was ready. At the shrill of the whistle, I grabbed him and threw him to the ground.

I was made for this sport, too.

The rest of practice wasn't much different than judo. *All right, then,* the guys on the team seemed to think after they saw what I could do. At the end of the day, though, the coach wasn't sure what to do with me. Managing to include me in one practice was one thing. Managing how to include me on the team was another. Title IX had been the law of the land for more than a decade. How it worked in practice was still being worked out.

Mom knew how to get it to work. Before I knew it, she'd talked me into carrying around another petition—this time so that girls could be on the boys wrestling team.

Word got out about me even before I started carrying a clipboard around for people to sign. At home, the phone started ringing again—a lot. The first call came from a local paper, the next from a local TV news affiliate. The coach went on record saying I'd be great. Mom fielded all those calls. She'd been the one to pay attention to the sports articles about me. I paid attention to the sport.

The kids in my class knew about me. They knew that when I wasn't in class, I was off at another judo competition. They'd seen their share of news stories about me. A bunch of kids knew me from beyond the sports pages, either from living in our apartment complex or from playing hotshot basketball with me through the Boys & Girls Club.

So the circle of girls clustered around a locker knew what I wanted when I walked up with my clipboard.

But when I had that petition in hand, standing in front of these kids, I realized I didn't want to push this paper around school for everyone to sign.

I'd asked for signatures before, over at the Olympic Training Center. But I believed in what I pushed for then. I loved judo. I'd wanted to compete in it at the Olympics. I didn't want to be on the wrestling team.

That's what Mom wanted for me. *You can show them that girls can do what boys have always done,* she'd said. *You know you'd be good at it.*

If I committed to practicing wrestling, sure. But I had to admit to myself and to my mom I didn't want to go down that road.

You can imagine Mom wasn't happy as someone who was still pushing me to do, do, do. I wasn't sure what to do, but I was sure of this: It wasn't God's will for me to jump right into another sport so much like judo.

Realizing that helped me discern the right next step in judo, too. Though I'd bowed to the pressure my coach and my mom put on me to wear the new black belt, it never felt right the few times I wore it, not even with the official certificate from Japan. I realized I didn't need either a belt or a certificate to know what I could do. In six years of tournament competition, I'd stood on the winners' podium for sixty-two first-place finishes, fourteen second-place finishes, and ten third-place finishes. I'd been the youngest athlete invited to attend the Olympic Training Center, and I'd been invited back two other times.

I couldn't do much more than I'd already done, winning a national title six years in a row. Even if I became the best in the world, I couldn't compete in the next Olympics. Women's judo would become at most a demonstration sport in Seoul. No woman could medal in it until Barcelona. Another seven years. Half my life again.

I folded my belt into thirds as I'd once done for a game at the dojo. This offering I slid deep into a dresser drawer with the kanji—the Japanese lettering—at the end of the belt still facing up. And I pushed the drawer shut.

God had to have something more in store for me. I was willing to put in more hard work and to find those who could coach and guide me through to what I was meant to do. I just had more discerning to do in deciding what should come next.

Later that month, I settled in next to Dad on the couch to watch the Super Bowl. The Patriots had made it to the big game as a wild card that year. They were playing the Chicago Bears down in New Orleans. We'd barely started on our ice cream when the Patriots put the first points up on the board. But they didn't score much more than that.

Dad said it was a painful loss at the end of a great season. We grumbled over the referee's error that allowed Chicago to score in the final seconds of the first half, when technically there should not have been any time left on the clock. In the end, that didn't matter, though, with the final score 46–10. All those points scored by Chicago and none by Walter Payton, though he'd been hyped up enough before the game. We didn't know yet that would be the Hall of Famer's only Super Bowl appearance. What we did know was we both liked the way the referee called out each "first doooowwwwn." Saying it that way, the sound filled my mouth. We took to saying it that way, even when that referee named Red Cashion wasn't the one working the game.

"First doooowwwwn." How I liked the sound and the way it meant a fresh start.

❧

For a spring sport, I tried tennis to finish out my freshman year of high school. These were the years the names Navratilova, Evert, and Shriver dominated the majors. I tried to fit in, I tried playing a girls' game. I did well. Tennis came easy to me.

At the end of the season, our coaches had the bright idea to pit the girls' team against the guys'. Maybe they were trying to re-create the Battle of the Sexes played between Billie Jean King and Bobby Riggs ten years before. I'm not sure.

We started with the lowest seed on the girls' team facing off against the lowest seed on the boys', then worked our way up. I'd been ranked first among the freshmen girls, so I knew I wouldn't play for a while. We all sat on a hot metal bench by the court to watch and wait our turn. I kept my Prince Pro racquet at my side. As it went, the girls won one, then the boys did. Any time one side got ahead, the other pulled even. I was beginning to see what was coming. The last match was going to be a tiebreaker.

My turn. I got up and brushed off the back of my white tennis shorts. It'd be up to me to bring it home for the girls, and I did, beating the guys' number one seed with a good share of aces, the tennis equivalent of throwing a judo opponent down like a rag doll at the outset of a match. I wasn't as close with the girls on the tennis team as I'd been with my friends in judo. But the girls loved that I'd given them bragging rights at being the best.

Afterward, my coach approached me to ask if I wanted to play on the varsity team that year since their season came right after ours. "Between you and me, you'll end up seeded number one for that team as well," she said.

Honestly, though, one season of tennis was enough.

My grandma back in Massachusetts liked that I'd landed on this sport, and she liked that I'd beat that freshman boy. She liked the drama of tennis, the Connors and McEnroe stories, the rivalry between Evert and Navratilova. She tried to talk me into sticking with tennis. She really tried.

But I knew in my heart tennis wasn't for me. I was waiting for the next big thing in my life, and I resolved that whatever it was wouldn't be defined by anyone but me.

"You're nuts, honey," my mother's mother told me, in her strong, plainspoken East Coast voice. "You could make so much money in tennis."

That's what I needed to hear to know for sure that what I needed would have nothing to do with money and everything to do with what was in my heart.

6

THE PLAYBOOK

One afternoon, the church came to me—literally. The youth pastor stopped by to welcome me to Praise Fellowship Church now that we'd officially joined the congregation. I knew who Bryan was. Praise Fellowship was a small congregation that celebrated services at a storefront plaza. It was hard not to notice him when he sang lead for the worship team at Sunday service. His voice was such a rich baritone. I loved listening to him.

And now here he sat on our couch. Bryan was even better looking this close up, with those blue-green eyes and his neatly trimmed beard. Already I'd asked as many questions as I could think of, trying to ignore Mom hovering nearby in the kitchen. At least I didn't have to worry about my brother now that he'd grown past teasing me and married and moved out of the house. It was easy to get caught up in Bryan's passion for the church, which came across so clearly in his answers. There was so much I wanted to know. I kept thinking of questions.

All his answers were so thoughtful and thorough. And kind. He looked at me. "I have to take off," he said, almost apologetically. Both hands were on his knees. "I have another place to be." He was on his way to play basketball with other guys from the church, as he explained when he showed up in shorts and not a tie, as he wore for Sunday services.

"Or I could join you on the court?"

I'd just eaten and was completely stuffed, and the idea of running around was enough to give me stomach cramps. But I was not going to pass up the opportunity to hang out with him more. Besides, I've never been shy, especially when opportunity comes knocking and is about to walk out the door.

Bryan would remember that first visit with me. He would remember how I played basketball that day, how I could compete at his level. I would remember how he didn't let down as if he were playing with a girl. And that day, I noticed how his chestnut hair glowed with auburn highlights in the Arizona sun.

I signed up for all the church youth activities that fall. Since I'd returned to homeschooling, I had the time. I was plowing through course material just as fast as before. The hours I'd once put into judo I now put into the church.

Wednesday nights, we had youth meetings. There, I got to know more people in the church, and I got to know Bryan, too. I noticed that the way he spoke to the youth group was different than how he spoke in front of the whole church. He made the effort to be relatable without making it look like an effort. With the way he brought the group together, you could see his work was clearly his calling. When meetings ended, a bunch of us would cross the parking lot from the church to an arcade on the other side, or we'd grab a bite to eat over at the Wendy's across the street. No one wanted the meeting to end. It was nice to have the time to just hang out.

On Saturdays, we met for Bible Quiz practice, where Bryan served as moderator, or question reader. The year I started, we concentrated on the Gospel of John. Over time, we also studied the book of Hebrews and Peter 1 and 2. We studied these assigned books of the New Testament to prepare for competitions against other churches.

To give an example of how Bible Quiz worked, a question would be asked based on a verse from the selected book of the Bible. You listened for key words to anticipate the rest of the question and be the first to buzz in. If the question reader asked, "What would the thief . . ." (and if you studied enough), you'd buzz in on the key word *thief.* You'd have to state the complete question and give the correct answer by stating the full verse from the King James Bible. To give the right answer here, you'd quote John 10:10. *The thief cometh not, but for to steal, and to kill, and to destroy: I am come that they might have life, and that they might have it more abundantly.*

That verse I still remember. Though I can't remember every chapter and verse anymore, I studied hard and knew them well back then. The competition I enjoyed, and I ended up rising in the ranks among other quizzers in the state. I remember facing off with a guy from Tempe First Assembly for first place. Bible Quiz allowed me to practice my faith in a way I hadn't had the chance to before. I was also developing other skills— learning to recognize patterns, to recognize them earlier than anyone else, and to make a call.

It was good to be a part of a team again. What was interesting was that, on the way home from competitions with other churches, the other girls all clamored for Bryan to drop them off last. It was fun to see them play the "Bryan take me home last" game so they could vie for more one-on-one time with him. He was twenty-six and had a girlfriend, but that didn't stop any of them from having a crush on him. I figured he'd pick the route he'd pick anyway, so I never pleaded like the other girls did. Somehow, he still usually picked me as the last team member to bring home. He claimed it was simply a matter of geographical consideration.

Not all youth activities were as competitive. We did mission trips to border towns in Mexico, and we played a lot of wallyball together. When the church moved from the storefront location into a more traditional church building in Phoenix, we helped move a few boxes. We had fun as a group, going to movies like *Home Alone*. Afterward, we'd grab something to eat. And that Thanksgiving, Bryan challenged another church to a game of football we called the Turkey Bowl. Not many girls showed up for either team. When Bryan saw the opposing team use a girl to guard me, he shot me a smile. He knew from our talks that I played a lot of football as a kid. I didn't talk too much about all the sports training I'd had with people at church, so I'm not sure the rest of the team knew what to expect before I scored my first touchdown. At that point, the other team put a guy on me. Even then, I scored again. I wasn't fast, but I knew how to get open. My teammates learned that if they could get the ball close to me, I'd catch it, even if it meant sacrificing my body to do so. Judo had taught me how to take a fall.

I was falling in other ways, too. That winter, after I turned seventeen, I could no longer deny the feelings I'd developed for Bryan, though I couldn't do much about it. Later, he would tell me he'd felt the same way. For obvious reasons, he still resisted his feelings. We didn't know then that we were both holding back feelings we shared.

In those months, I paid attention to how deliberate he was in all he did, how he always seemed under control. I enjoyed his sense of humor and his sense of seriousness, too. Much later, he would tell me that, in turn, he noticed I was more mature than others my age. I had felt that way a long time, long before I ever met him, maybe because of how I've competed and all I have done. From an early age, I've felt more at ease around those who are older.

That spring, I looked for ways to get even more involved in the church. It was a bonus that I'd get to be near him more. When I heard that the worship team he sang for needed a drummer, I taught myself enough on the drums to get by. Let's just say he was a better singer than I was a drummer. Once a week, we practiced in the new worship space, the sound of the strings and the sax and the piano bouncing off the walls with no one there. My favorite song had a great drum solo in the middle of it, and I tried to do it justice.

The Sunday morning we played, I was practiced and ready for Bryan to sing the refrain leading up to my solo. When he turned it over to me, I was in a groove, drumming away, having a great time, and then one of my sticks went flying.

I can't say I recovered well in the middle of that song. Bryan turned to see why I'd stopped playing. My problem was I couldn't stop laughing. Neither could the entire congregation.

For a long time, I wanted to believe he'd been fighting feelings for me as I had been for him. Months went by before I began to understand how hard of a fight he'd had. One night, it was late when he pulled up to my apartment building. We were deep in conversation, and the light by the door made the rearview mirror cast a shadow over part of his face. He shifted into park. "It feels," he said, "like this is more than it probably should be."

I told him it was for me, too. We talked honestly, finally, about our feelings for each other, and then he leaned over and kissed me.

I have always said you can tell a lot about someone from a first kiss, and at that moment, this told me everything I needed to know. The passion we felt for each other was clear. We resolved to keep our dates secret at first. That way, we could be sure we were both serious. We could be sure this was deeper than a mutual crush.

We did our best to look as if we were merely friends. When the opportunity to sneak away presented itself, we'd do something simple like hang out at the local park or even grab a cheese crisp at Ricardo's. I'm not sure we fooled many people.

Another complication at the time was that Bryan had been taking out the senior pastor's daughter whenever she visited from California. At first, he wasn't sure what to do the next time she came to town. Ultimately, though, Bryan decided he couldn't continue seeing her as before. It wouldn't be fair to her or to me.

When he told her he couldn't see her anymore because he had feelings for someone else, she wasn't surprised. "Let me guess," she said.

"No," he told her.

"Oh, come on. Let me guess."

"Please don't." He didn't want to lie, and at that time, he did not want to confirm what she already suspected.

Bryan decided he needed to tell the senior pastor—the father of the woman he'd just broken up with. Fortunately, the pastor graciously accepted the news.

Mom was excited for us—she really liked Bryan and knew he was a good man. Once our parents knew, we took our relationship public. All we had to do was sit together in church and have Bryan put his arm around me. News of our relationship spread, and, surprisingly, despite our age difference, we received an outpouring of support.

Our relationship moved quickly at that point. We hadn't dated more than six months yet saw no reason to wait; we were in love. We talked about getting married, but nothing was official until Bryan took me to San Diego. Out on the beach, the sun was setting, and our life together was just beginning. In a picture-perfect moment, Bryan dropped to one knee and said he loved me. He asked if I'd marry him. I was eighteen.

That seems so young now, but I truly felt ready to be married. Maybe what I wasn't ready for was being married to a pastor. Maybe I didn't fully understand what that meant for me and for our marriage. The senior pastor's wife let Bryan know she had some guidance she thought would help. "I've got to get hold of her," she said, "and make her the perfect pastor's wife."

Bryan let her know politely that wasn't going to happen. He loved me for who I was.

And I loved him so much that I didn't take a hard enough look at the signs I see now were there. One of the women who I'd asked to be in my wedding noted that Bryan always seemed as if he had so many things going on. "But you aren't a priority," she said. "He loves you, but you're overlooked." I was surprised my friend would say something like this but didn't give much thought to the remark beyond that. I was so looking forward to being married.

We held the wedding at our church, and the senior pastor married us. Our reception was lovely but a bit different than I'd grown up imagining since the Assembly of God doesn't permit drinking or dancing. Now, I never had been much of a drinker—in Colorado, I'd done it only to be with all the others. Not having alcohol at the reception didn't bother me. But I had wanted to dance with my husband at our wedding. The music was nonetheless beautiful. I remember the violinist, the guitar, and the saxophone playing. The best part of the ceremony, though, had been Bryan's song for me. He'd recorded it because he didn't trust he could get through it if he sang it in front of all our family and friends. I remember the lyrics, his smooth, clear baritone trembling as he sang, *I love you my lady, my love, my lady forever.*

At the end of the night, this lady changed into her going-away clothes, and we drove off together in a limo toward what we thought would be our forever after.

∽

Starting out, we lived at his dad's place. It was a full house, considering his sister and his brother-in-law and their two kids lived there, too. Still, Bryan and I had enough space to spread out a bit, with our own bathroom and an office right off our bedroom. All my trophies I stuffed into the office. They had a way of overpowering the room, especially while Bryan worked there.

We did the things that newlyweds do, which means that, at first, we tried to do everything together. Almost every day of the week, we were fully immersed in the church and all it had to offer. Sundays we committed to attending morning and evening services. Youth ministry took up Wednesday nights, and we hosted youth activities on Fridays or Saturdays as well. We also had obligations beyond Praise Fellowship; we served as campus pastors for Chi Alpha Christian Ministries at Arizona State University (ASU), so our Tuesdays were full, too. The days that Bryan wasn't on church property or leading a youth activity, he worked on something for the church from home. He was committed to the good work of the church.

We were so busy then, and changes were happening.

The first thing to change wasn't what I expected. Shortly after we married, my parents divorced. I felt bad for my dad because he provided my mom with everything and then some. They did not have the best connection in terms of things they liked to do, though. He mostly worked, and she mostly spent money. I'd hoped they could both be happy together, but that wasn't meant to be.

What was meant to be, I thought, was for Bryan and I to get a dog. A lady from our church gave us a roly-poly Shar-Pei puppy. It got complicated when the woman who'd been promised the pick of the litter decided that the pup she really wanted wasn't what she'd picked but the one we got. We had to give our puppy back. The breeder felt so bad that she gave us two dogs, a boy and a girl, and those two proved to be a handful. They chewed through everything, starting with the bedframe of our waterbed. (Yes, really, a waterbed—one of those purchases that seemed so fancy at the time and now just sounds so dated.) And speaking of water, our boy dog had a way of marking Bryan's side of the bed—and only Bryan's side. Bryan wouldn't find the wet spot until sliding his feet in at night. "*Toby*," he'd say. Toby wouldn't be allowed on the bed that night. But in the morning, as soon as Bryan left for work, Toby jumped up on the waterbed to lay all stretched out, his back warm against mine. Those were the days the house and our hearts were full.

My schedule was full, too. Right when we were married, I started attending Scottsdale Community College. I wanted to become a PE teacher and inspire kids as Mr. T, my favorite teacher, had inspired me. For my public speaking class at college, I remember giving a speech about judo and being comfortable right away while speaking in front of people. Who could have imagined then that someday I'd make and announce decisions that could change the outcome of a game—or not—in front of thousands?

What was hard enough to imagine then was how judo already seemed so long ago and yet remained so much a part of me. My trophies still crowded the shelves Bryan had put up along all the walls in our office. They took up so much space, and I didn't need them. And I still didn't like dusting them. So, one day while he was gone, with the help of our two well-intended Shar-Peis, I cleared them all out and donated them to the Special Olympics. Bryan hadn't expected that at all. I haven't missed any of those awards, except maybe for that marble one from the Fiesta Bowl.

About that time, I met my best friend Jennifer—not through school but through my continuing activities in the church. She and her family began attending after I'd married Bryan. I'm lucky we became friends. She's the sweetest person you could ever meet. She's so kind and thoughtful and super go-with-the-flow, which I try to be, too. I started hanging out with her at her house, at her mom's house, and at her nana's house. They all have the same great smile, which they share as easily as their words. Jen and I always have so much fun chatting. Whenever her nana was around, she'd be cooking up something great, like my favorite, a chili-cheese rice dish. Often, the four of us would end up playing card games like rummy or another version with tiles called Rummikub. Time flew by with them.

When Bryan and I moved into our first house and Jen needed a place to stay, she lived with us for a while. We had room, and it was great having my best friend close when my husband worked such long hours. Our new home even had enough space for the dogs to have a room of their own, with a doggie door to the outside—which, of course, the girl dog chewed through. So we nailed scrap metal on the back of the door to keep Jazzy from chewing it. Jazzy gnawed through the scrap metal, too.

Then Toby died suddenly, and Jazzy was so distraught without her brother. Bryan found a shepherd/lab mix at the Humane Society to offer her comfort. But Jazzy could not be comforted. Instead, she turned so vicious that we had to find her another home. We kept Dudley.

Life was hard those days in more than one way. Jen had moved out by this point, so it became more apparent how often my husband chose to sit at his desk instead of sitting with me. I've been told relationships with leaders of the church can sometimes be some of the hardest to survive. I knew from the start the order of his priorities—God, our family, and then the church family. The problem was that the church family kept taking priority over me. Bryan saw it instead as a way to uphold his promise and obligation to God.

I tried to stay occupied while Bryan dove deeper into the church, into serving the congregation. In 1990, I started working at a sports cards and memorabilia shop called The Batter's Box. I sold sports cards and signed memorabilia on the side as well. At first, the card market was great, but the industry got a little flooded, and it became harder to make money at it. While in the business, I paid special attention to anything coming through the door that had to do with football or with any pro sports in Boston. One day, someone walked in with a 1986 commemorative Super Bowl ball with the final score embossed on it. I remembered watching that game with my dad and wishing our Patriots had outplayed the Bears. Once I had that white-paneled ball in hand, I knew I needed to get Walter Payton's signature on it and not just because it'd make the football that much more valuable.

Years later, when I finally handed the ball to the Hall of Famer for his signature, I had no idea that I'd end up working on an NFL field myself. Nor could I imagine what I'd have to go through to make that happen and what I'd have to give up. Then again, it can be hard to fully see God's plans.

7

PREGAME

As much as I tried to prevent it, my relationship with Bryan steered in the direction my bridesmaid had predicted it would. I was wildly in love with this man, but I couldn't help feeling a little ignored. In my head, I knew I was significant and mattered to him, but I worried I could not feel it in my heart. God forbid our anniversary fell on a Sunday because we would be in church instead of somewhere else together.

I began to resent the lack of attention and looked for excuses to miss church. It was not for a lack of loving God but rather a disconnect I felt with the very thing that was pulling my husband away from me. I felt lost.

I tried to tell him and tried not to start a fight.

"You don't mean always," he said after I accused him of always being at the church or some such inaccuracy. He lived life very much under control, and I learned to be better at it, too.

A nearby school needed an after-school director, so I applied and got the job. My work at Hopi Elementary was fine but not quite what I wanted to do. This was the point in life where everything was supposed to be getting better, but it wasn't. It seemed I'd somehow climbed aboard a boat without oars and was drifting farther and farther away.

Things weren't right between Bryan and me, and his mother knew it. As much as she thought Bryan was the greatest, she also felt sympathetic to what I was going through. She and I were hanging out a lot those days. We'd grab a bite at Luby's or go shopping. We were on the constant lookout for Beanie Babies, which were big back then. One afternoon I stopped by her place, and she showed me the latest ones she'd found—a unicorn, a platypus, and a little monkey.

I picked up the monkey as we were talking. "Oh, I love this."

"Here, take it."

"I can't take it."

I couldn't take it.

"Just take it."

This was her way, to be so selfless and giving. It didn't matter who walked into her house—before they walked out the door, it turned out she'd been keeping the perfect gift for them in some closet or drawer. Except in those days, what I needed most she couldn't give.

Memorial Day was coming up, the time of year where Bryan usually planned a tubing trip down the Salt River for ASU students involved in campus ministries. Because girls in that group tended to be shy about the boys seeing them in their swimsuits, the adventure tended to turn into mainly a boys' outing. For that year's event, only three guys signed up. No girls.

While Bryan had always been so busy working, I had been incredibly busy lately, too, with my new job. For Memorial Day, though, I had the day off. Considering I couldn't remember a time over the past year when we had spent a whole day together, just the two of us, and considering how small the group was that was going, I thought there might be a way for us to reconnect that holiday.

I pleaded my case to Bryan. "Leadership can handle this trip without you," I said. "Please let one of your team members take those guys. I'd like us to have a day to ourselves."

He didn't agree on the spot, but he didn't say no, either. A few days later, during Tuesday night Bible study at ASU, I was sitting next to Jen as Bryan made the meeting announcements.

"I'll be chaperoning the tubing trip," he said.

I dropped my head. The one time I had asked him to take some time off to be with me, and he couldn't do it. I tried to hide my tears.

I was completely brokenhearted. I tried to talk to him about it later back at home.

"I asked you for one day," I said. "In an entire year, have I asked you for one day?"

I was coming to understand that my husband was what I considered a workaholic. I kept trying to tell him to take a breather, maybe spend some time with me, but he wasn't listening. Others did, too. Once, when we were over at Jen's parents' place, her mother took Bryan aside. "You need to start paying attention to your wife," she said, though I had not asked her to say a thing to him.

"My wife is fine," Bryan had told her.

We had been married for seven years at this point. We were not fine, and Bryan didn't see it. I was going to have to say it outright, or he never would. So, one night over dinner, I finally said it aloud. I said, "Bryan, we have a problem."

He was shocked. "We do?" he asked. "What's the problem?" He truly hadn't seen it.

I shared how I was feeling and that I felt our relationship had suffered a break a few months before, back when he had insisted on chaperoning the tubing trip down the Salt River.

In the moment, I felt that he was listening, that I was heard. I brought up what I hadn't before. "We need a date night," I said.

Bryan gave a small nod but did not agree. "That's just one more thing I'd have to do."

I know he didn't mean it in the way that it came out of his mouth. At the time, it was apparent to me that we needed more than a planned date night. We needed counseling. Bryan agreed, though he wanted us to start by speaking with the senior pastor. We started with the senior pastor. Eventually, we moved to work with a female couples' counselor.

In our first session, she asked for a history of our relationship. I summed it up for her, ending with what I'd suggested we do to reconnect. She agreed that a date night sounded like a good first step.

I glanced at Bryan. "Well, let me tell you what Bryan said."

I told her.

The therapist turned to him. "You said that?"

"Yes," he admitted. "But that's not what I meant. It's not that I don't want to spend time with my wife."

His argument was that he didn't want to have to block out time to be with me. My point was that if he didn't, it wasn't going to happen. It didn't happen. We never were able to progress any further than that.

One day, after many years of struggling, I woke up not wanting to be with this man anymore. I didn't want to believe I'd reached this point. In the end, I had to face the truth. Our relationship was over.

Asking for a divorce was extremely difficult for me. And agreeing to one was hard for him, though he'd seemed to me so absent from our life together. Not every relationship can last forever, as much as I had believed and hoped and prayed it would and as much as we tried to make it happen. I never wanted to make a life choice that wasn't pleasing to God. We tried and we tried, yet we never could seem to make things work.

It's still hard for me to comprehend. I'd loved him madly, and for many reasons, being a divorced woman was not a statistic that had ever been in my plans. Or Bryan's. Though we had failed as partners, I know, for me, our marriage had been a learning and growing experience.

Every step along the way of the divorce process was a struggle for me to figure out. Through much praying and soul-searching, I deliberated what to do. At night, I couldn't sleep, wondering whether I had done the right thing and where to go from there. I didn't have my dog anymore, a car, much money, or a place to live. For us to divide any assets, we would have had to sell the house, and I didn't want to do that to Bryan. I was hurting him enough. I would have to figure out life on my own, without Bryan and without Dudley.

Maybe part of the reason I struggled so much during this time was that after the divorce, I didn't go to church for a long while. I never stopped loving God; I just felt out of sorts as to where to go. I felt as if I'd let God down. I stepped away from the church, from all our friends—except for Jen. I felt I had to since almost everyone I'd come to know over the years had been involved in the life Bryan and I had together.

When the marriage ended, my friend Jen offered me a place on her couch. I started there, then spent some time at Dad's house. From there, I went to sleeping at the hotel where I'd started working as a night audit manager. I didn't get a lot of sleep those days. I picked up the 3 to 11 p.m. shift when I could, then worked my regular shift until seven in the morning. I'd catch some sleep and do it all over again. Although my work at the Hospitality Suites helped me get on my feet financially, I knew I wasn't meant to pursue working in the hotel industry in the long run. I thought about returning to college to finish my degree but knew that school was not an option at that time. I wasn't going to find my calling by sitting in a classroom. I thought it'd take a long time for me to discern what I should do. But that summer following my divorce, I found my calling waiting for me at a camp.

∾

God and faith remained important to me, but I wasn't attending church those days. I looked to remain connected in different ways. So, even though I was working double shifts at the hotel all that summer, I also took on a job with Christian Athlete Ministries. Dad had given me his old maroon Honda, and that helped me get to my summer job. After grabbing some sleep in my room at the Hospitality Suites, I'd head over to help coach their youth basketball camps.

My time on the court with the kids was my favorite part of the day. I felt at home taking the preteens and high school freshmen through shooting, dribbling, and passing drills as Coach Russ had done for me when I was about the same age. Helping these kids play sports felt right given my background and given how much I'd enjoyed the game during the months I hadn't been able to compete in judo. It was so satisfying to help a young person who knew nothing of basketball transform into a rebound king after just a week of camp. Witnessing that progress was certainly rewarding.

But I didn't realize how draining the work could be. Coaching basketball wasn't simply a matter of teaching kids the game. It also involved managing their emotional state. If they weren't progressing as fast as they thought they should, they'd get down on themselves. At the other end of the spectrum, if they excelled, some could get overly confident, and then it became a challenge to keep them levelheaded.

In between the sessions I coached, I had to take my turn filling in as referee as the camp required of us. Some coaches there didn't feel as comfortable in this other role on the court. As for me, I loved blowing the whistle. The work felt easy. As an official, I found I didn't have to get emotionally involved. I didn't have to think about who won or lost. I just had to make the call as I saw it.

Right away, a lightbulb went off in my head. I hadn't thought about it as an option for me before—I hadn't known I could—but officiating was what I wanted to do. I could do it. And I could be good at it.

In a classroom at a local high school, about twenty men milled around the student desks, all handshakes and smiles. I got in line to check in. The guy standing with a clipboard was older, maybe around my dad's age, but this man was buff. He talked with his hands to the men in line in front of me.

The men in the room were all different ages, and you could guess their different reasons for being there. Athletes just out of school. Young dads. Men who loved the game. Several who'd checked in already kept glancing over at me, trying to look as if they weren't. Maybe I imagined it. A lot of conversations those days focused on the bombing at the Olympics down in Atlanta, so they might have just been talking about that. But I remembered all too clearly how it felt walking into that wrestling practice, and it seemed once again that these boys wanted to make sure I knew where I was.

I knew perfectly well where I was.

After I got the bug to officiate, I'd asked around and found out that the Arizona Interscholastic Association (AIA) ran the training program I needed. Through the AIA, I'd already signed up to officiate high school basketball that year, but the winter sports season seemed eons away. I was ready to begin the rest of my life now. The football season was around the corner, and that was the sport I'd rather officiate anyway. That's why I'd stepped into this classroom—to train for that.

It didn't matter to me that women didn't play the game professionally back then. Women weren't yet playing in the WNBA, either, and Violet Palmer wouldn't be named one of the first two female refs for the NBA until the next year. None of this mattered to me.

Sure, not everybody was going to be thrilled about my presence at these meetings or on the field, but that didn't—it couldn't—matter as much as getting the chance to step out on the field. And I was about to discover my chances. I'd reached the front of the line.

"I have to ask," I said, "but would it be crazy for me to officiate football?"

The older guy with the muscles and the clipboard broke out in a broad smile. "That would be great!" he said, without hesitation—without knowing how many games I'd watched with my dad and without knowing all the times I'd been picked first when playing football as a kid.

So I took a seat. Once he checked everyone else in, he moved in a stiff-muscled walk to the front of the room. His biceps were so massive that his short sleeves strained around them.

He introduced himself as Larry Kindred. From his opening line and from the way he spoke with his hands to accentuate his points, it was clear Larry was passionate about his subject. His talk might have been a little all over the place, but I appreciated how he didn't hold back. He even made a point of telling the group that, in Arizona, a couple of women were already officiating football at the high school level.

If anyone crammed into one of those student desks glanced back at me as Larry said that, I didn't notice.

After Larry, a few other experienced AIA officials spoke, then people asked questions about the nuts and bolts of the job. The thing you need to know about these training classes is everyone thinks they can officiate, but sometimes the questions asked made even an enthusiastic guy like Larry pause a moment. They say there are no stupid questions—but sometimes there are.

I had a few questions, too. I don't remember exactly what I asked, but I do remember how the attitude in the room shifted after I spoke. Which proves you don't need to walk into a room knowing the answers, but it does help when you ask the right questions. Before I left, Larry waved me over to meet an instructor named Tom Frazier. Though this Tom seemed more on the reserved side at first, I'd also noticed how others in the room had gravitated toward him before the meeting started and again as it ended.

With me right there, Larry asked Tom what he thought of my last question. "What do you think? Think she might know a little about football?" His hand was on my shoulder. "You want to bring her onto your crew?" He meant for the freshman and junior varsity football season.

It was hard to tell what Tom Frazier was thinking beneath his Tom Selleck mustache.

"She won't disappoint you," Larry promised, which was hard to believe considering he just met me. "Tell you what, though, if she does, I'll buy you a beer."

Neither of them knew how competitive I was by nature or that since I was eleven I'd played out of my league, above my age division, and won. What mattered then, what mattered now, was proving myself when going to the mat. Or on the field. I found myself straightening.

The chance to be in the game meant more than the price of a beer to me, though it was clear even then that the path ahead wouldn't be a cakewalk. I might not have known that this trainer named Larry was pulling me toward one of the top high school referees in our state, but I understood well enough that Larry was making sure I wouldn't get lost in the shuffle. He was giving me a chance, and I would have to deliver.

For the first time since the divorce, I believed things were going to work out.

8

THE KICKOFF

The way I saw it, I couldn't scrimp on the essentials needed to be an official even if money was tight that first summer on my own. Back in the 1990s, Arizona didn't require the fingerprint clearance card they do today. All I had to do was register with the AIA, get all the equipment, and find a uniform either online or from the vendor at the AIA kickoff meeting. Better, I thought, for me to actually try the knickers on for size. I remember bringing a pair into the girls' restroom at the school and frowning in the mirror while bunching up the fistful of loose material in the crotch area. Seriously. Those knickers were not made for the female body.

I had to buy knickers two sizes too big and spend about a hundred dollars at the tailor to get them to fit right. I wouldn't need that taken care of until I worked my first varsity game. For youth games, we wore shorts.

That August night, I brought home a pair of white shorts and a collared, striped short-sleeve shirt and tucked them away among my things. I also found a place for my new whistle and a lanyard and the other officiating equipment: a down indicator, a plastic chain clip, a yellow flag, and a white bean bag. (These days, the bean bags are mostly blue or black.) The knickers I set aside to bring to the tailor. At Target, I would find a good sports watch with a timer that counted down. Last but not least, I pulled out of the bag a fitted black hat with white piping. I curved the bill before tucking it inside a storage case and zipping it shut.

There, that was everything. For now.

What I didn't get at that kickoff meeting was a white hat. To wear one, you had to work your way up through the ranks, officiating as many games as possible (and receiving a lot of good evaluations in the process). Though I already hoped to be a varsity crew chief one day, that seemed a long way off.

With everything checked off my list, I signed up for all the games I could—and not just to earn back all the money I put into equipment. I couldn't wait to get started. I looked forward to the games.

First, I started with high school scrimmages. I left home plenty early to make sure I wouldn't be late in case I had trouble finding the field or if I ran into traffic. I pulled into the lot with plenty of time to spare and my choice of parking spots. I popped open the car door. The afternoon's heat pressed in. Over a hundred degrees, and it would only get hotter. I tucked my ponytail up into my hat and grabbed my water bottle.

The high school stands stretched out empty, the metal benches soaking up the sun. The field below lay open and inviting with its freshly painted white lines. I couldn't wait to get out there.

Before long, other cars pulled into the lot. A man in the white hat climbed out of a maroon Nissan truck. That would be Tom, the ref for the day. He waited as another man gathered what he needed from his car. The two seemed to talk easily the whole time it took to reach me, the give-and-take of what had to be longtime friends.

Once they got close enough, Tom called out to me. "You're early!" His words felt like a stamp of approval. "You ready?"

"Ready to go," I said.

Tom led the way toward the sidelines. "Have you two met?" He introduced me to the other official, who happened to be new as well. Turned out that Tom was easygoing with everybody.

Larry was right behind them. I'd recognized his walk as soon as he got out of his pickup. I hoped to greet him before we started, but he and another official stopped short of us, deep in conversation, and by then, I was chatting with Tom and the other new official.

For the scrimmage that day, there would be eight to twelve people rotating in as officials. Besides Tom's crew of five and some newbies, there were a few others there at Tom's invitation since they couldn't make the scrimmage to which their crew had been assigned. As Tom gathered together all the folks in stripes, he advised those of us who were new to limit our focus to one or two things at first. Master that, he said, then we move on to something else. "There's a lot to officiating, and you can't try to take on everything to start." Try to do everything at once, and you won't be able to do anything.

Finally, it was time. New officials often begin on the wing, and that's the position I took, my toes on the sideline, brushing the edge of the freshly painted four-inch line. I looked across the crown—that is, the arc in the middle of the field—to the line judge on the other side. We straddled the line of scrimmage. All I was supposed to focus on to start was making sure there weren't more than eleven offensive players on the field. How hard could it be to count to eleven?

To start, counting eleven players can feel like a challenge since they're all clumped together in a huddle. Before the first play, I didn't count them all in time. For the second and third plays, I barely did and finally figured out to count in groups as they broke the huddle. There—three, six, nine, eleven. Got them. Easy.

Now I could move on to something that had a little more to do with the game, like focusing on the line of scrimmage, ensuring that everything was legal before the snap. No false starts by the offense. No encroachment by the defense.

Right around then, I saw one of the veteran officials on the sideline grab the fabric at the back of a new official's shirt and talk him through something. Not long after, the same thing happened to me. It was as if Coach Rennick had grabbed at the extra fabric at the small of my back again. But another trainer stood behind me now, his voice friendly and helpful. "Here, watch those happy feet. Don't move until the runner goes beyond the line of scrimmage," he said. "Let the play come to you." And with that, he let go.

I got it then. In officiating, as in judo, it helps to keep your feet steady. You need to get comfortable waiting before trailing the play up the sideline to get a good progress spot. No more happy feet for me from that point on.

When the scrimmage was over, Tom gathered us together again, and we took turns talking about the challenges we faced and going over what we learned. Veteran officials shared what they saw. One pointed out that some newbies just needed to get comfortable blowing the whistle. Tom closed with some words of encouragement and a few helpful, really practical tips. I was beginning to understand why folks gravitated toward him. There was a calm assuredness about Tom that modeled to us the makings of a good referee.

A late afternoon sun smothered the field with a blanket of heat as the teams packed up, and the boys and their families—who all had filtered in throughout the scrimmage—left one by one. I wanted to start everything all over again. I was so stoked. Others must have felt it, too. They talked about where to get a drink and a bite to eat.

But Tom pulled out his keys. "Have to pass this time, sorry," he said.

"Oh, come on," Larry insisted.

"No, I've been gone a lot these days, between work and officiating," he said. "Haven't spent enough time with my wife lately. I'm heading home to take her to dinner and a movie."

The guys all sounded a response, all of them different. A groan of disappointment, a smart-aleck comment about going home to the wife.

I remember watching him go. Thinking, what a great guy.

❧

For my first paid assignment, I was scheduled to work a whole day of Pop Warner games, at all levels of play—from six- to fourteen-year-olds.[1] I left super early again to make sure I'd be set and found Larry already there, ready to go. He liked that I was an early bird, too.

We got to talking as we waited for the others. At one point, he leaned over, as if telling me a secret. "You know how impressed instructors were at the meeting with the questions you asked," he said, though I hadn't known. "That's why Tom's willing to have you shadow his varsity crew."

I'd received the same kind of praise as a kid. It'd been a while, but I wasn't any more comfortable with getting it. I was just doing what I was meant to do.

Larry must have seen the expression on my face. "You'll do great today," he said. He was such a Papa Bear. He wanted to fill me in on the day ahead and who else was joining us. "You'll like working with Donithan," he said. Donithan proved to be a big linebacker of a man, and Larry proved true to his word. I enjoyed working with the fourth official who joined us, too, of course. I came to count Donithan and Larry as friends. We'd look for each other at later meetings and trainings and often sat together.

That Saturday (and on so many other Saturdays), Larry acted as a mentor, teaching me through what he did and what he said, and I listened. From judo, I'd learned to pay attention to the basics, so I knew to pay attention to even the simplest practices Larry talked about. I listened to how he never rejected an assignment and to how he showed up for every game prepared to work hard. Over the years, I've put these basics into practice, and it's proved invaluable to me. So simple and yet so important to say yes to every opportunity—and to show up and work for it.

With Pop Warner serving as a form of training grounds for officials as well as for kids, we officials rotated positions on those Saturdays, so no one wore a white hat. That approach helped me learn the different responsibilities of each position and how all interrelated. All my life, I'd focused only on a single opponent while on the mat. Now I had to pay attention to several players on the field—and my fellow officials. I would not only learn from each crew member, but also I'd learn how to communicate with each one while on (and off) the field.

That first Saturday, the ice in my cooler had melted by noon, and I kept drinking in every lesson I could learn. I learned how you need to be aggressive on pass plays without a back judge in place, I learned how you need to get ahead of the runner at the goal line (the only time to get ahead of him), and I learned how much running you need to do in each game, even with happy feet well under control. Officiating several games in a row also helped me see what worked and what I could do better. I worked on getting good progress spots without getting caught too close to the runner who might get hit and be driven back out of bounds. (Later, I would learn a great technique called cross-field mechanics, which would make this kind of play a lot easier to officiate.) Another skill I learned was how to be more aware of not just the runner but also the blocks happening around the runner.

Before each of the five games played that day, we met a new set of coaches. One of them might do a double take on meeting me, but usually all I had to do was show I was competent and a hard worker, and the day would go smoothly for the most part. I figured the problems anyone had with my calls would most often have been the same problems people have with any official. Usually, it's a parent up in the stands who thinks they can see better from where they sit than we can. And sometimes it's just someone who thinks they know the game better because of all the pro games they've watched. Parents get like that in part because they're looking out for the kid they're bringing home after the game. When coaches get red in the face, it's because they're making a point about the rules and the facts they think they know. When a coach is yelling, it's not the emotions I pay attention to, it's the rules of the game. More often than not, he just wants to know he's being heard, and a simple *I hear you, Coach* is enough.

Sometimes they need a bit more. When Larry dropped a flag on a play during one of the games, I was running past the coach. "But he's out of the pocket," the coach yelled at me, "he's out of the pocket," his voice rising with conviction that it wasn't intentional grounding, as if he was sure he was right. And he would have been—in an NFL game.

After the play, I made a point of going back to the coach. "Yes, the quarterback was where you saw him," I admitted. "But in youth games," I pointed out, "there's no such thing as being out of the pocket." That's not a rule on Saturday, as we put it then. (The rule has since changed.)

Larry seemed to be veering toward us, but I didn't need rescuing. The look of understanding was already crossing the coach's face. I waved Larry off. "I got it," I said, "we're good."

Getting yelled at from the sidelines has never bugged me. I have found you need to be able to let comments roll off your back and keep your head in the game.

That said, I haven't always known the right response to give coaches, but sometimes it helps to start by agreeing on what we're both seeing. Once we establish this, I can point out something more that I saw or considered that led me to apply a different philosophy than the coach did. That approach can help foster respect if not agreement.

It might have been early in my experience, and I certainly didn't know all the rules, but from my first games, I did everything I could to not get caught off guard not knowing rule distinctions between games for younger players and those for older ones.

At the quick break between games, Larry wanted the details of my exchange with the coach. He nodded as I told him. "Yeah, you did right," he said. He liked that I not only knew the rule but also came across as even-keeled while the coach was getting all over me. "That will serve you well," he said.

~

I loved officiating from the start, and from the start, I got to officiate a lot of games. In addition to the Pop Warner games that I worked on Saturdays with Larry, I covered freshman football on Wednesdays and junior varsity on Thursdays. Tom split the freshman/JV schedule with another longtime ref. So many of these officials on those crews were highly regarded and well experienced. In working games with these officials, I got to see what was common practice and what differed as a matter of style.

One of the assignments I enjoyed most that first season was the chance to shadow Tom's varsity crew. Following them on Friday nights, I got a bird's-eye view of the action. Observing a great crew like this was as helpful in learning how to officiate as actually working a game. It's a bit like driving—you learn where to go if you're behind the wheel, but when you're a passenger, you get a wider view of everything along the way.

A couple hours before kickoff, I sat in on the pregame meeting Tom held in the locker room. He walked through different scenarios the crew could face in that evening's game—everything from kick coverage to fourth-down measurements to how the ball is relayed after a long pass play to how to communicate when a flag is thrown. A lot to keep in mind considering I'd recently learned how to count to eleven just before the snap. At the varsity level, every step of the game requires a little more attention to a little more detail, just as you'd expect. No surprise that there's a similar step up when progressing to the next level, junior college. That happens again while rising up through to Division I. And you can imagine there's another level altogether when stepping up to the NFL.

Following Tom's crew provided an ideal introduction to the world of officiating. Not only were they good with rules knowledge—earning them the honor of officiating several championships—they also made me feel welcome as a part of the crew even though I wasn't an on-field official. Mostly, I helped on the sidelines with whatever was needed. I charted penalties, helped with the chains, and acted as a ball girl. I did what I could to stay close to the action and absorbed all I could by watching the officials.

Because I wasn't working the game, I had the luxury to see the positions each official took and how they fed into the other. I watched what they watched, how they handled themselves, and how they communicated not only with each other but also with the players and the coaches. This made for quintessential on-the-job training, and I learned so much.

My new friends Donithan and Larry were on Tom's Friday night crew, with Donithan as umpire and Larry as back judge, a position we didn't have the luxury of having on Saturdays. As back judge, Larry set up about twenty-five yards deep in the defensive backfield before the snap, as he made sure there weren't more than eleven players on defense (a task I could now appreciate in itself). His job then was to keep an eye on long passes, runs, and kickoffs, which meant he was often running, especially as he made sure the goal line would be covered on long running or pass plays. And he ran sixty yards after every touchdown, too, to set up the ball. I think he liked all the running he had to do for passing teams, considering he'd tell you that games with running teams turned his position into "somewhat of a sleeper."

Those weeks shadowing the crew, I also appreciated observing Tom's work as referee. Some officials like to say this is the easiest position on the field. I am not confirming or denying that—and when you do a job well, it makes the work seem easy—but know that the one wearing the white hat sets the tone for the game. As the one in charge, the crew chief handles the coin toss, counts the players on offense, and calls for chains if a measurement is needed. A ref will be stationed in the backfield, twelve to fifteen yards off the quarterback's throwing arm to tell whether a ball's release counts as a forward pass or a fumble. The ref also looks for false starts, holds, and illegal blocks. But most important, he—or she—must protect the quarterback from hits considered unnecessary or a form of roughing. In addition, a ref is the one who announces all the penalties and ensures that they're properly enforced.

Tom made a great referee. He always treated me fairly as I shadowed his crew. I never got the sense he was put off by the fact I was a woman.

After the game, the crew made a point of including me as they headed over to a place called Native New Yorker. An essential part of their post-game ritual turned out to include hashing over the game while enjoying some beer and wings. I went but didn't drink.

It was clear from the start that these guys loved what they were doing, especially with the way Larry and Donithan worked varsity every Friday night only to jump in again early on Saturday to go all day for Pop Warner. It was also clear to me how much these guys enjoyed hanging out together. I wish you could have seen them in that restaurant booth, with Larry so animated, Donithan a little more reserved, and Tom so outgoing. I didn't know if every crew bonded like this, but I knew I wanted to be doing what they did.

To learn as much as I could as quickly as I could, I joined them those Friday nights. I had moved up the ranks in judo, and I'd figure out how to do that as a football official, too. Sitting with that crew my first fall season, I knew I wanted to be a ref and knew I wanted more beyond that. Even then, I was thinking that someday I wanted to officiate in the NFL.

9

THE OPENING DRIVE

Since deciding to become an official, I committed to doing everything I could to become the best. I read the rule book. I read it again closely. When the NFL season started, I watched (or taped and then watched) all the NFL games I could, especially if the Patriots were playing. I paid special attention to the officials—where they positioned themselves on the field and where they seemed to focus their attention. And I noticed how their movement differed on pass plays compared to run plays.

Following Larry's lead, I'd taken on all the assignments I could throughout the season. On Wednesdays, I officiated freshman football. On Thursdays, it was junior varsity. On Fridays, I followed Tom's crew, and every Saturday, I worked five Pop Warner games with Donithan and Larry. And yet, as full as my first-year schedule was shaping up to be, all this didn't seem enough.

If only there was a way to speed up the process to be eligible to work Friday nights, not just shadow a crew. But this took time. The AIA's rating system starts everyone as a 4. It takes a year to move up to a 3 and another year to reach level 2. That's the typical progression, with opportunities to work increasing as you advance. Once you became a 2, though, you aren't guaranteed to be promoted to be certified level 1 the next year. And yet, to work regularly, you're more likely to receive a full schedule if you're certified level 1.

I'd already run across some folks who weren't getting the evaluations needed to rise to a 1. I confess I was not interested in getting stuck as a 2. Fortunately, I caught a break in the yearslong process of certification. The head linesman on Tom's varsity crew had a conflict for one of the games and needed a substitute, and Larry suggested I might fill in, as Tom put it when he called. So was I interested?

You bet. Stepping onto any varsity crew as a first-year would have been an honor, and here I was being asked by one of the top crew chiefs among high school officials. It had to have helped that Tom saw what I could do while working on his crew for the freshman and JV games.

That first game was a west-side rivalry, Maryvale vs. Trevor Browne. The Friday night lights shining on the field somehow made the other side-line seem farther away. The crown of the field felt somehow higher, too, and I had to resist the urge to stand on my tiptoes to get a clearer view. I was nervous, and I wanted to do a good job.

I must have done okay. I don't remember the details of that first varsity game, but I do remember the coaches didn't have any complaints, and the crew assured me that I did a good job. As a first-year official, I'd just officiated a varsity game. That meant something. So we all went to our favorite hangout afterward, where the crew ordered their usual (a pitcher of beer and a plate of wings) and I ordered mine (water and cheesy bread and a dinner salad).

All my work on the field left little time for a night out with Jen or time for any dates. It hadn't escaped me that my personal life had become secondary to my career. I had asked for a divorce because I'd never felt as important to my youth pastor husband as his job—now, ironically, little was more important to me than mine.

Like so many officials, I loved what I did. That explains why the work is called not a job but an avocation. The better I got to know what it meant to officiate, the more I liked it, even on long-haul assignments. Like Larry and Donithan, I enjoyed working varsity on Friday nights and Pop Warner on Saturdays. And my favorite Saturdays were the ones spent in Buckeye, though we'd be out late the night before and have to be on the road by 6:15 a.m. for the hour-long trip. What made those days great was the way the host association offered us what felt like VIP treatment, feeding us throughout the day. Larry and Donithan knew them all, and both made a point of bringing me in and making me feel a part of the group during our quick breaks between games. By the fifth game, I was tired mentally as well as physically, but I had it in me to push through. The red-carpet rollout continued at the end of the day. We were invited to their after-party at someone's house. Normally, I don't recommend socializing like this with those for whom you work—officials buddying up with one association's coaches and parents can create a sense of impropriety. But Donithan and Larry were such legends. We got home around midnight. Days like that I wouldn't have changed a single moment.

❧

Within a year, I had changed my life around, and I felt as if I was on the right track. I felt so at home on the field.

Late one Friday, after Larry and everyone else had left, Tom and I were standing by his truck, saying goodnight. The next day was going to be another early one, with five more Pop Warner games lined up, but I wasn't in a hurry for the conversation to end.

And then Tom moved in closer. "I've been thinking about you a lot," he said, and he kissed me.

Whoa. That had never even been a consideration for me. I hadn't been kissed like that since—since Bryan. But wasn't Tom still married?

Both of us agreed that it couldn't happen again. It just couldn't.

But before long, pretty much what couldn't happen and shouldn't be happening was in fact happening whenever we could find the time and opportunity. We both knew it wasn't right.

When basketball season started up, I had the chance to change focus. Finally, I was working what I'd first signed up for, starting with everything from kids' basketball to high school games to men's rec leagues. With basketball, it was clear from the start that I could officiate higher-level games sooner than I ever would for football. Women were already officiating basketball at all levels of play up to the pros. Only I didn't feel as connected to the game. The simple truth was that I loved football more, and I hadn't expected to love it so much.

With my mom out East, I spent the first holidays after my divorce with my friend Jen and all her family. Her two brothers cracked me up. Her nana cooked a huge spread for Christmas, making the lasagna everyone loved. I filled up on everything, piling up on sides because I don't eat meat. Jen could tell I had something on my mind; she'd noticed it before. She thought she better finally ask.

That night, my friend took me aside to see what was going on. She was the only person I could tell the truth about what was happening in my life.

I took a deep breath. "You know that guy, Tom?"

Although Jen disapproved and didn't think the relationship was healthy for me, she was through it all my friend. For my birthday celebration a few months later, she made a point of inviting him to Eli's, one of our favorite places to hang out.

What a great time we had, joking around together. Tom saw that Jen and I were partners in fun. Jen was my deputy, and I was the sheriff, as someone at the bar that night put it—nicknames we still joke about today. Jen's bringing us all together felt like such a gift.

I'd wanted to believe I'd found the right someone. But I realized I'd somehow moved into another relationship with a man who couldn't fully commit. At night, I'd lie awake, trying to find a way to make peace within myself over that, but eventually, I couldn't be at peace when I was with him, either. I knew it was displeasing to God.

I had to end it for good. I finally planned to while saying good-bye outside my apartment door. "I can't go on this way," I said and braced myself for what came next.

I hadn't expected him to answer by taking me into his arms. "I love you," he said.

But when you really love someone, you shouldn't have to keep your love for them a secret. You shouldn't have to wait until you threaten to pull away before they pull you closer. Of course, it's so much easier to see all that clearly now from a distance.

10

THE RED ZONE

Stepping on the field provided a much-needed escape for me. Out on the gridiron, I could forget my personal life and simply focus on the game. After my first season, my level had jumped up from a 4 to a 2, skipping a whole level. As a 2, I could fill in regularly on Friday nights if a crew requested me.

And every Friday night in my second year of officiating, I was fortunate enough to have different high school crews requesting me. Working with different officials was the best learning experience I could imagine. There were so many great officials, and each one of them brought something good to the game. One could give advice about rules applications, one his perspective on positioning, and another his philosophy to why he threw a flag or passed on a potential foul. I learned something from each person and became a better official because of those guys. And—I'm going to be honest here—I also worked with some officials who were subpar. Not everyone was at the same level of officiating. Some, like me, were new, and others were past their prime. Some failed to progress due to lack of ambition, and others simply didn't care to do better.

Working with different crews broadened my knowledge and overall skill set, and it also bought me time to wait for a good crew to have an opening. At the end of my second season, the AIA commissioner spoke to referee Scott Williams about putting me on his crew, and Scott was up for it.

I joined Scott's crew my third season. Although he was a top-notch official, his crew was not. Scott had been working high school football for more than a decade at that point and was already regularly working postseason assignments. Scott's crew was made up of a bunch of good guys who enjoyed hanging out with each other while sharing drinks and dinner after Friday night games or while swapping stories during poker once a month. I was glad to join them that year. But I was ambitious, and they were operating at a lower level than where I was hoping to advance. Not only were they not going anywhere, but they were not striving for more. Scott was, but his crew wasn't. Still, we managed to be selected to work a low-level semifinal game that year. The energy that Scott brought to the group carried it.

At the end of that season, I began thinking about the bigger picture—what I needed to keep doing and what I needed to change. As much as rosters change for football teams, officiating crews change constantly, too. Older guys retired or quit, and some refs would transfer to other crews or get promoted to the college ranks. Who you knew mattered, too.

So Scott and I started talking again to the AIA commissioner. As it turned out, the commissioner knew of a good crew that needed both wing positions filled. If Scott was okay with not being a referee, the commissioner could recommend us both. Scott was willing to make the move.

Scott had been working ten years as an official by then. His situation got me thinking whether working with a good crew from this point on was going to be enough—did I need something more to advance as far as I wanted to go? While I was working through this, basketball season started. I'd been working these games at the high school level, and that year, I was hired to officiate at the junior college level, too. As much as I liked the challenge of officiating at a higher level, I still loved the game of football more. It was time for me to take control of what I could. It was time to make an investment in some training.

❧

Under the California sun, on one of UCLA's practice fields, I worked the line for an intrasquad scrimmage under the watchful eyes of a couple of clinicians. My first training had been led by the best officials in Arizona. Now I was attending a camp led by the best in the country—officials and supervisors for Division I as well as for the NFL. While camps like this do offer training, it's really more a place to showcase what you can do as an official: The supervisors who come to camp are the ones who make hiring decisions for their conferences.

Access to camps with this level of experience and expertise comes at a cost. The Personal Touch camp was not a cheap training option, but it was the best training available, taught by legends like Red Cashion. He's the official with the signature "first doooowwwwn" call, which my dad and I heard as the Bears did a Super Bowl shuffle over our Patriots in Super Bowl XX. When I signed up for the camp, I thought it might give me a chance to approach him. I never dreamed he'd be the one to approach me.

I was lucky Red was still working camps like this, though he'd retired the year I began officiating. Another official I looked forward to seeing there was Chuck Stewart, who was in the midst of his twenty-year career working as an NFL line judge. Also attending the camp was Ron Botchan, a former linebacker who came to be known as NFL's best umpire. During his career, Ron would officiate a total of five Super Bowls, a record shared with other luminaries like Jack Fette (who'd been on Cashion's crew for two years of regular-season play) and Al Jury (who'd been on Cashion's crew for Super Bowl XX and for the 1990 season). Ron was laser focused when he officiated. The story goes that he was knocked to the ground during a game and suffered a cut on his head but kept going, not missing a play, though afterward he needed eight stitches.

This was the caliber of people leading this camp designed to help develop and mentor up-and-coming officials. I would be a sponge learning everything I could from these legends. Running up and down UCLA's fields, I'd discover how useful cross-field mechanics could be as a head linesman in getting good progress spots, in avoiding being in harm's way, and in getting a crew to work better together. All these things were amazingly helpful to learn, and yet I'd come for more. I hoped to be rec-ommended to the supervisor of officials who managed a junior college conference near me in Arizona; I hoped that would prompt him to ask me to work his conference.

Truth be told, ultimately, I wanted to get noticed for even bigger things than that. I had made that intention public during interviews the year before when I became the first woman in Arizona to officiate a Pop Warner state championship game.[1] "It may sound crazy to some people," I admitted to one reporter, "but I think I can be in the NFL someday."[2] It wasn't crazy to me. The path forward seemed clear and even doable. If I caught the attention of the junior college supervisor and he hired me, I could gain the experience needed to work my way up to Division I. From there, I might even need to work as an official in NFL Europe a few years, but I was willing to do that if that's what it would take.

Some in the media were making a big deal about my being a female official, but what I hoped to do would be hard for any official, male or female. And for the most part, my gender hadn't been a factor, pro or con, in dealing with players or coaches. They just wanted to know I knew what I was doing. Coaches will try to work you whether you're a man or a woman. That's just what they do—but they will usually let you know when you're right as well. Those moments were great to hear.

With big plans, it's sometimes the small decisions that set you on your way. Even before stepping onto the field, I had to position myself right. In signing up, I'd checked "wing" as my preferred position. Everyone I talked to advised that I'd have a better chance to move up as a wing than as a referee. By this point, I'd been working as a ref for freshman and junior varsity games for a while, and I liked that position more. That's what I'd rather do. But I listened to advice and marked the box for "ref" as my second choice.

Others must have received the same advice because more people wanted wing than referee at camp. I ended up being pulled in to work as crew chief. My big chance! A clinician shadowed me as I refereed from about five feet away—close enough to give feedback between plays. We all worked close together.

We had to, given the number participating at the camp. UCLA has expansive facilities—eight practice fields and a main field—but we were a big group, including not only the scrimmaging teams but also about forty clinicians and a hundred of us campers/officials. With so many on the gridiron, each crew, mine among them, worked only half of a field.

In this smaller space, I had a big job. I wanted the clinicians to notice I could make sharp calls and was willing to work hard. Others might have already noticed I was the only woman on the field, but I wanted to be noticed for the right thing—not for being different but for being better. In my experience as a woman official, you needed to be in better shape, know the rules better, and communicate on a higher level. Mistakes by men tend to be more forgivable. When the official is a woman, the simplest mistake can be interpreted as proof that you don't know what you are doing and shouldn't be on the field. And in some instances, when something goes wrong, it's easiest to pin that on the one woman on the field. More about that later.

That part comes later because this camp was about giving those with potential the tools to move forward. I didn't hear anyone making derogatory comments about my presence at this camp. I didn't pay attention to that sort of thing anyway. In judo, I learned to tune out everything except for the opponent in front of me, and I did much the same while working as an official. Over the years, I did catch a couple of insults from the sidelines about how women don't belong on the field. One actually made me laugh. "Go back to the kitchen!" some guy once yelled at me. It's funny because I didn't cook, at least not until the pandemic.

So I took my place on the field, believing it shouldn't matter if I was a woman. And, at that UCLA camp, it didn't. I kept getting positive feedback from clinicians, and I had a good crew—all campers put forth their level best. One clinician even said I had good field presence. *Good presence*, another told me.

I'm not sure how I managed to get it—maybe from all those years competing in different sports. For those who don't have it, it's hard to figure out what to do to get it. Some find it hard to define, but it comes down to this: When you have presence, you appear confident. You appear as if you're in control. It's as important for an official to have it as it is for a player. Some say it borders on cocky, though that's never been me.

If you'd ever had the chance to talk to Red, he would have told you about the change he experienced when he started acting as if he had confidence. He would have pointed out how, at the beginning of his time as an NFL official, it was simply an act. If that was true when he started, it sure didn't seem so by the end. In his time as an NFL referee, he was considered the best, the most consistent, and the fairest. And he was also considered a really, really nice guy.

So I didn't need to take a second look to know who'd joined the clinician nearest me during one of the plays on that UCLA field. That was Red Cashion standing there. Out of more than a hundred people there for the camp, he'd sought me out. I am sure he talked to other campers there as well, but the living legend had a way of making you feel as if you were the only one who mattered when he extended his hand and introduced himself. There was obviously no need for introductions; I knew who Red Cashion was. I was in awe of him and was honored he took it upon himself to meet me.

Red was surprised to hear I'd been officiating for only a few years considering how comfortable I seemed on the field. Not everyone can carry themselves with such presence, he noted. Not even a lot of men. "If you ever need anything, don't hesitate to ask," he said.

It's still so hard to believe that Red extended that offer. This was huge for me. At least I had the presence to take him up on his generosity. Whatever knowledge or expertise he was willing to share, I was willing to listen.

Before I left camp, Chuck Stewart and Ron Botchan also offered their assistance. All of them, including Red, offered to actually connect that fall, when they would be in town for an Arizona Cardinals game. They said they'd come in an extra day early to observe me officiate at a high school football game. Maybe grab dinner afterward.

Maybe the closest I'd been to someone in the NFL before this was the time I'd stood in line two hours to meet Walter Payton—worth every minute—to get his signature on a white paneled commemorative football from Super Bowl XX, when the Bears played the Patriots. I thought it'd been a big deal back then just to get a quick picture with Payton. This was so much better than getting a picture. Red was promising to watch my whole game. I was beyond excited. I had no idea he'd be the first of many NFL officials to do so. And I had no idea the disaster awaiting me at my next camp, where I'd work for the first time as a clinician.

11

ILLEGAL USE OF HANDS

Later that spring, I had another opportunity. I'd been asked to work at the Round Valley officiating camp, one of Arizona's top in-state training opportunities about three hours from home. What an honor to work alongside Arizona's best officials as a fellow clinician my first time taking on that role. I looked forward to being on the field, working with brand-new recruits as well as those with a little more experience. I especially looked forward to passing along some tips I picked up at the Personal Touch camp.

I put a lot into preparing for Round Valley. In addition to teaching, I'd helped organize the event. Since I was still working as an assistant manager for a resort, it seemed natural to be picked to help coordinate the room block and conference space needed. We're lucky to have Round Valley Ensphere nearby. It's a high school facility, shaped in a beautiful dome—apparently the only one in the country for a secondary school. The interior space allowed us to run all-day intensives without worrying about desert summer heat.

I might not have thought twice about helping to organize the event, but I did wonder whether the hotel manager seemed a little too friendly when I reserved all the rooms. And, pulling into the hotel, it was hard to miss the message splashed across the marquee. It read, *Welcome, Football Officials! And Happy Birthday, Shannon!*

No, it wasn't my birthday. Sure, wasn't he hilarious.

I didn't let it bug me. I couldn't. We had between seventy and seventy-five campers coming, and I had a session to lead at camp, so I dug in and led it.

Afterward, we caravanned back to the hotel for dinner. Nothing fancy—most of us were still in shorts. Between campers and clinicians, we filled the room. We'd had a good day. All the sessions had gone smoothly. I was in my element, and I felt as if I'd made a difference. As dinner finished, people floated from the dining room into the lobby. The people from my table did, too. One of the campers was new to officiating, and I was intent on making him feel welcome as I answered questions on some rules and logistics covered that day. I enjoyed chatting with him and with all of them.

In the lobby, some folks had clumped together. Officials are a social group. Newbies might have clung to the people they'd come to know on the field, but most were mingling all around. I'd gotten to know a lot of them. Some of the guys in the lobby were debating whether to go to a nearby bar for a drink. If anyone asked, I wasn't up for it. I was wiped out from the day and planned to head up to my room. The others who'd been at my table had a few more questions, so I lingered a while, leaning up against the back of a couch and talking about what went right and what we could do better, when who came through the lobby straight for me but the commissioner of officials for a local association.

You might not know him, but you've run into this kind of guy before, a guy who sets standards for others he doesn't live up to. Who berates others for being overweight as his belly hangs over his belt loop. Who by the end of the night is the loudest in the room. This particular guy was in his mid-sixties, and he was my boss.

Maybe I'm being too hard on this guy. Maybe he just rubbed me the wrong way, so to speak. But if that was it, I could have handled him. I'd managed my dealings with him just fine until that moment in the lobby when he came up and grabbed my arm and the back of my neck and forced me over the back of the couch.

I hadn't expected it at all. This wasn't judo. My boss was a big man, and he pressed my nose against the backrest, the crown of my head brushing the seat. I fought to lift my head, first instinctively, then deliberately, but the more I did, the more it hurt, and I knew pushing harder could damage my neck. So I stayed down, shorts riding up, with my butt over the top of the couch.

Then this guy who was my boss held me down and slapped my behind—hard—three times in front of everyone there in the lobby. Only then did he let go, letting me up. "Your birthday spankings," he explained. And he started laughing.

I had to straighten my shirt since it'd ridden up too as he held me over the couch. He'd caught me so off guard. He actually thought this was okay?

I shook my head to clear it. "*What* are you doing?"

My words echoed through the lobby. Everyone had quieted. Everyone there was looking at us. At me.

I couldn't bear it. I couldn't bear to stay. I practically ran over to the stairs, straight up to my room, and I shut the door and locked it, and I pressed myself against the door. I was shaking all over. The way he yanked me over the back of that couch replayed in my mind again and again. I was devastated, humiliated, and shamed. And where he slapped me still smarted. I wiped the tears from my face, and as I blew my nose, absolute anger seeped in.

I started pacing around my bed.

I should have decked him.

Someone knocked gently on my door. As if I wanted to talk to anyone. But Tom stood on the other side.

I undid the chain and pulled open the door.

Some of the guys had told him about the "birthday spankings." They were all stunned down there, he told me. "You okay?" he asked, though plainly I was upset. He saw the red handprint still on my neck. I pulled at the elastic on my waistband. My boss's handprint remained stinging red under my shorts too.

"That's it," Tom said. One quick look had been enough for him, and he stalked out of my room. I knew what he was going to do, and I didn't want him to do it. Before long, he was back knocking on the door, this time with the commissioner in tow.

Would I let them to come in and talk to me, Tom wanted to know.

The commissioner was the last man I wanted to see. My skin still burned from where he'd hit me. I didn't want to, but I let them enter.

My boss said he was sorry, then said the so-called spanking—that's what he called it, the "so-called spanking"—sounded worse than it was because of the nylon shorts I was wearing.

A lot of thoughts ran through my head. Number one, hearing and feeling are two very different senses, not to mention being held down against one's will in front of one's peers. And number two, I had to ask, *This is your apology? Are you kidding me?*

"If I'm going to stay for the rest of this camp," I told Tom, "just keep him away from me."

The rest of that night, I stayed in the room and didn't let anyone else in. I didn't get much sleep. I definitely considered leaving before anyone showed up in the lobby the next morning, but in the end, I decided to stay. Longtime officials had trusted me enough to train others. I told myself I had good reason to stay.

The next morning, I went back out and worked as I'd said I would. Being in that group again was as awkward as you can imagine. At breakfast and during the course of the morning, the campers who had been with me and watched the attack each made a point of coming up to me one by one to talk about what had happened. All of them were almost as stunned as I was, especially the new official I'd been talking to when I was assaulted. I don't remember exactly what the camper said other than he was totally shocked at what he witnessed. The guys who spoke to me about it all said it had happened so fast and out of the blue that none of them could react until it was over. One guy was upset he had allowed it to happen, another felt terrible he didn't stop it.

Out on the field that day, I could feel when people were talking about me and about what had happened. I focused on what I could and mostly on the fact that I was on a field, doing what I loved. When I got another chance to talk to Tom, though, I did. I had to tell him that if the commissioner came anywhere near me again, there was going to be a problem. Tom made sure the guy didn't speak to me for the rest of the event.

I've never been one to hold a grudge or stay stuck in a bad incident, but when I tried to put that episode out of my mind, I couldn't.

Once camp wound down, rumors ramped up. Back at home, a bunch of stories had begun flying around about "the spanking incident." The only person I told was my friend Jen and only because I had to tell someone. I didn't want to talk about it otherwise. I didn't want others talking about it, either. I couldn't let the story or whatever embellishments had started continue. I had no choice but to call the local association that the commissioner headed. Although I left a couple of messages, no one returned my calls.

Not until the camper who'd just started officiating, the one who'd been at my table and by my side when the incident happened, sent in a note to the association. He detailed all that he witnessed. (It hadn't been pretty to watch, either, apparently.) When the note was shared with me, I couldn't help but notice the point he made at the end: If this was what the association was about, he wanted nothing to do with the organization.

A full investigation finally ensued. They interviewed me and the officials who'd witnessed the event. A matter of time, the association told me, before they could gather all the information. But I knew these facts already: The guy who hurt me was the commissioner. And it would be up to his board of directors to decide whether he needed to be held accountable.

In the midst of all this, I had another camp to attend. This time, it was for basketball. This time, a woman who'd broken the gender barrier was the featured speaker and core instructor. Violet Palmer had been hired by the NBA along with Dee Kantner a few years before. By the start of the new millennium, the NBA had had two female officials working a few years already, while the NFL's first female officials still seemed an impossibly long time away.

I had yet to get an assignment at the junior college level in football, and in basketball, I was working on getting into even more Division I basketball conferences. This camp was exactly what I needed.

Palmer watched us work and offered great advice throughout the camp. She was full of energy and was a fun and positive person to be around. And she had the experience at the professional level in basketball that I hoped for someday in football. Just counting her first season officiating for the NBA, she'd worked fifty-four games. She would become the first woman to officiate an NBA game in the postseason, too. In her almost twenty-year career officiating for the NBA, she'd work almost a thousand games, including several in the postseason.

She'd heard her share of derogatory comments about women officiating, sure, and then talked about how she realized she couldn't control what others said about her and what they felt about her. It couldn't have been easy, with players like Michael Jordan and Dennis Rodman making plain they weren't happy about her being on the court. "This is a man's game, and it should stay that way," Charles Barkley then insisted.[1] I could imagine some of the hurdles this hardworking woman had to overcome.

I listened to what Palmer had to say about what it took to be successful as an NBA referee. Some of what she said I knew. Some I hadn't thought about before. What I found inspiring in particular were the insights she offered as to what she learned as one of the first two female officials in the league.

At other times, she's mentioned that one of the problems was that coaches and players didn't know how to act around her: "They wondered, *Can we cuss at her, can we yell at her, can we argue with her?* [emphasis in original]."[2]

She found she could model how others might respond to her through her own words and actions. While she might not be able to control what others thought of her, she could control what she did and how she did it. The way she communicated would be a way to demonstrate that she belonged.

She did her best to communicate as effectively as possible. And she passed it on. Through the clinics, she and other instructors offered feedback for us to be able to do the first part: to be better officials. In her talk, she offered suggestions on ways to put her technique to work. She spoke of the importance of the process of mirroring, which she used when dealing with coaches.[3] Simply put, mirroring is consciously adopting the gestures or speech patterns (including pace and volume of speech) of another person to create connection and trust. If one person ends a statement with a question, you do the same. If someone laughs a lot, you laugh.

Violet Palmer was the first person I had heard make mention of this term. Of all the speeches I listened to about officiating and things we could do to better ourselves or our endeavors, this was probably at the top of the list of the most helpful tips I received. Thanks to her, I immediately began using mirroring in my own interactions with coaches. I think my doing so made others more comfortable with me, but equally important, it made me more comfortable with those around me by using this great technique. Later, I learned that all kinds of studies had been done on the power of mirroring. Servers increased their tips. Sales clerks gained higher sales and better evaluations. More students agreed to write essays for other students. Researchers found that when someone mirrors your behavior, the areas of your brain that activate are the same ones that process rewards and make you feel good. It's not a matter of coldly manipulating another for personal gain. To mirror effectively, you must feel a connection with the person you mirror. You need to establish empathy for them, or none of it works.[4]

Violet Palmer found that the hard work she put in proved even more effective once she began mirroring the behavior of coaches. If a coach liked to joke a bit, she joked with him. If he was strictly business, so was she.

Ultimately, what mattered most in her work was doing it well. She figured if she managed to do that, the NBA would hire another female ref.[5] And now the league has eight.

If the technique worked for Violet, I thought it might work for me. Of course, putting something into practice doesn't always make things perfect.

∽

In the meantime, the association was completing their investigation of the commissioner. In the end, the board ruled that my boss's actions called for his termination. So it looked as if I could put the whole incident behind me.

Time came for me to walk back into those airy executive offices for the director to meet with me to apologize on behalf of the association. This was supposed to mark the end of the process, but I know what can happen when you complain. And I knew the commissioner wouldn't let them reach this decision without putting up a fight. His livelihood had been on the line.

During the second-floor meeting where the director apologized, I specifically asked for reassurances that our crew not be punished for this man's firing. On the flip side, I didn't want to be appeased with a championship game as some sort of compensation, either. The executive director sat back in his desk chair and promised nothing would happen. There would be no retribution.

I believed and trusted him and felt he was a man of integrity. In the past, our crew had worked at least two games each postseason. With his assurances, I had every reason to believe we'd get a similar assignments that year, too.

But after the regular season, when the playoff assignments came out, we were left off the list. We got nothing. I was told, based on inside information from a person who worked in the office, that for one of his last duties in his position, the commissioner had been permitted to assign all the playoff games even after he was fired.

I immediately called the executive director and told him what I had heard about the assignments.

"Do you know who my referee is?" I said emphatically. "He has been a mainstay in the classroom for many years and has dedicated numerous hours mentoring officials. He is a great man and a person of integrity!" I couldn't believe what they'd let happen to him. "I don't care about me, but the crew should not be punished because of what happened to me."

I had trusted the executive director, and he had looked in my eyes and lied to me. I couldn't let them do that to such a dedicated crew. The association would be hearing from my lawyer.

We ended up coming to an agreement, but I would rather have worked a postseason game with the amazing crew I belonged to. They weren't only great officials, they were great men.

The only other time I ran into my old boss was years later after a football officials kickoff meeting. He walked into a bar and sat at another table. We did not speak to one another.

After he was fired, he still went to games and talked to officials on the field. I can tell you I was shocked to look up while working a game and see him there. Later, I found out that if he wasn't there representing the association, he could show up as a spectator at any high school event.

He's dead now. Toward the end, one of my fellow officials saw the guy working at a car wash—taking tickets, not actually washing the cars.

I still don't have the answers to why that man did what he did and why he thought it was okay. Still, sometimes, when I can't sleep at night, I relive that moment and question whether I did the right thing. Maybe I would have felt better in the moment had I decked him. But then I would have been no better than he was.

Some actions you don't ever want to mirror.

12

DELAY OF GAME

Another Friday night, another varsity game, and I can tell you I was nervous. That's the way it was going into every game, no matter the level, but this time standing under the lights of the field was a little different. Red Cashion and Chuck Stewart were in the stands, watching. So I was glad for the butterflies keeping me alert and at my best.

Red and Chuck were in town for a Cardinals game. They'd come in an extra day early to see me work since they'd seen me take only a few snaps at the UCLA camp and wanted to see what I could do over the course of a game. Red was one of those guys who had mentoring in his blood, and Chuck had seen something in me that prompted him to do what he could to help, too.

Jen had brought them from their hotel to the high school. They'd started the night on the sideline, and by halftime, they'd moved up to the bleachers. Of course, given who they were, they were welcome to make themselves at home pretty much wherever they wanted.

It'd been so unreal when Red's name showed up in my in-box, yet it should have been no surprise. Red was known as a man of his word. In the e-mails that followed, it'd been fun to find that Chuck and I had a similar sense of humor. I'd looked forward to seeing them both again at my game.

Now they were here. I was glad to be on a crew with Scott on the other side of the line of scrimmage from me. We stayed on our toes the entire game—the whole crew did (figuratively speaking). We counted ourselves as lucky to have Red and Chuck there watching. Getting to enjoy dinner with them afterward was another thing entirely. Since all us officials had to get cleaned up after working the game, Jen, Red, and Chuck went ahead to the Native New Yorker to scope out some tables. They pulled a few together for us so we could all sit as a group. I'd known that Jen would be up for taking them around; she's got such an ease about her that she can make even a shy stranger feel comfortable—though these two NFL superstars were anything but shy. Anyone who loved football, of course, wanted to be near. By the time I walked in, I wasn't surprised to find the seat closest to Red already taken by my crew chief, who was practically clinging to the famous ref all night.

Red was such a good sport. In those days, he was missing his wife Lou, who'd died in her sleep the year before. He still worked with the NFL as a trainer in charge of all the white hats, though he'd been retired a few years by that point. Each week, he traveled to different NFL venues to watch the referees and give insight where needed. When the waitress brought wings for the table (salad and cheesy bread for me), Red was telling us stories. I liked the one about all the places he'd been where people came up to him out of nowhere, yelling, "First doooowwwwn!"[1] Red said he loved meeting every single person. That was his way.

Before the night ended, both Red and Chuck made a point of saying what a great job I'd done and what a good crew we had. That fall marked the beginning of many similar visits whenever any of those guys came to town for an NFL game. Ron Botchan even set up a time to come observe the crew, too. With Ron being known as the NFL's best umpire, I was expecting the others to be just as excited to meet him, considering Botchan had five Super Bowls under his belt and Red had worked two. But there was only one Red.

At the end of the season, when Jen came over to give me the scoop on her recent engagement, she stopped in front of one of the Christmas photos I had out. *Is that a card from Red? Red Cashion?* Red was wearing a Santa hat and holding up a golf club. He wasn't just an icon to me anymore. I was glad to count him as a friend. So much had changed within just a year. So much more could happen for me in the new millennium.

~

Word about me started getting out. In the spring of 2001, I was floored to get an e-mail from Johnny Grier. He'd been an NFL official a dozen years already and was the first Black NFL referee ever named. At the time, he also served as the supervisor of officials for the Mid-Eastern Athletic Conference (MEAC). Johnny wanted to know if I'd be interested in working the spring game at Florida A&M. Of course I would! Another NFL line judge would come to the scrimmage to take a look at me, too.

A referee for the MEAC coordinated the assignments for the scrimmage. That referee, like many others, held down a day job in addition to his work as a football official. Some officials I'd met were personal trainers, some were in insurance, and some were lawyers, just to name a few examples. Dan Evans, the referee coordinating the assignments for that spring game, happened to work for NASA as a project engineer for shuttle program activities—as if proving that the kind of day jobs football officials held ran the gamut. Dan asked if I had worked other positions besides head linesman or line judge, more specifically, referee. So many times, people had told me to not focus on being a referee if I wanted to advance, but here he was asking if I had that experience. He was asking if I'd want the chance to be crew chief.

As a matter of fact, I'd love that.

"I might use you in that capacity as well," he said.

Honestly, the highest level I'd ever refereed outside of that UCLA camp was a high school junior varsity game. But I couldn't wait to get on the field to prove myself. Three high-level officials—two from the NFL and one from the MEAC—would be evaluating my football aptitude. Opportunity was calling. I was ready.

The afternoon began with me slated in a short wing spot. I'd had about five snaps at that position when Dan Evans approached me. The man who worked for NASA by day was now wearing the white hat as referee, his usual position while officiating.

He said, "The referee position is yours to take if you want it."

Yes! I was completely flattered he'd give me his spot. I gladly wore the white hat for the rest of the scrimmage.

Apparently, my refereeing caught Johnny Grier by surprise. He knew I could work the wing, but he didn't realize I could wear the white hat as well. I guess he was impressed because a short time later when I was attending an NFLRA clinic in Dallas, several of his NFL buddies approached me.

"I don't know what you did at Florida A&M," one of them said, "but Johnny can't stop talking about how good you were at referee."

I was floored. And I was honored to receive such support. Both Johnny and the other NFL official from the Florida A&M scrimmage called Doug Toole, Big Sky's supervisor of officials, to endorse my application to officiate in that college conference. NFL scout John Alderton recommended me, too. And Red Cashion—*Red Cashion*—said he'd be honored to reach out on my behalf. Both Ron Botchan and Chuck Stewart recommended me as well.

Chuck recognized that I might face some resistance in the hiring process, even with all this weight behind my application. For starters, for me to go from officiating high school football straight into a Division I conference would be a leap, even with the UCLA and MEAC scrimmages under my belt. However, the several NFL officials who had observed me felt confident I could successfully make that transition. Chuck also may have wanted to preemptively address the elephant who walked into the room when my application crossed the supervisor's desk. When Chuck sent an e-mail to Doug—a fellow NFL official—my new friend wrote, "She is the perfect person to be the Jackie Robinson of collegiate football officiating. I know you are aware of her, but I felt she deserved me mentioning her name to you."[2]

To be honest, I never thought of myself in that context. Technically, Johnny Grier was the Jackie Robinson of football officiating, with Grier being named the first Black referee more than ten years earlier. But I understood what Chuck meant—that the first female official in college football would face pushback and that whoever hired the first would need to be assured she was ready. Chuck meant what he wrote as the ultimate compliment. I've held onto that.

Despite all the backing I received, Doug didn't end up hiring me. The Big Sky wouldn't be the break for me that the Dodgers gave Robinson.

At the time, I sent out other applications, too. I recognized the more logical progression would have been for me to officiate at the junior college level next. The Arizona Community College Athletic Conference was a good geographic fit for me, and the supervisor of officials there was Tom Scarduzio. He was the one whose attention I'd hoped to catch by attending that UCLA camp. Scarduzio happened to be quite progressive in his thinking, never discriminating against anyone. Still, he denied my application, even with all my powerhouse references. No woman had yet been hired to work football at the junior college level in Arizona. Only one other besides me had been interested, though she wasn't getting any backing. And the rest of the women officials in Arizona at the time weren't interested in going beyond the high school level.

So the traditional paths hadn't yet opened up for me. I was still figuring out what other options I might have to take a step forward when a man I hadn't met before handed me his card as I stepped off the field. I'd just finished officiating as a white hat for a JV game at Scottsdale Christian.

"You did a great job," he said. "If you ever need anything, please let me know."

The logo on his card was for the Arena Football League. He happened to be vice president of administration for the Arizona Rattlers.

So that spring, I reached out to Gene Nudo, the vice president who'd handed me his card at Scottsdale Christian. In turn, he reached out to the vice president of football operations for the Arena Football League. Nudo went to great lengths, complimenting my "excellent [football] knowledge, athletic ability and most important, a 'field presence.'" Along with this letter, I also had recommendations from a side judge for the Big Sky Conference and from Hank Mancini, the commissioner of officials for the Arizona Football League, a semipro league for which I also officiated. These last two were highly respected among officials in the state; in time, both would be inducted into the Arizona Football Officials Association Hall of Fame. Both had been my crew chief for various high school games the past five years. All had forwarded to me what they'd sent to the league office in Chicago. In vouching for me, the Arizona Football League commissioner made a point of noting the respect my work garnered from officials even at the Pac-10[3] level: "Not one, I repeat, no one, patronizes her for gender," he wrote. Still, I wasn't hired.

Let me just say this: I believe that if any man had the references I did, he would have shot straight to the top.

What could I do? I did what I could. That's all you can do. Maybe they truly had no openings. But they had my name now at least.

Frankly, at times, it was a challenge for me to stay positive. I did the best I could, but I am human, and with that comes emotions that I could not always hide. I was determined not to let those moments of disappointment break me. I continued going to camps and working everywhere I could. Around this time, I was even invited to serve on the Advisory Committee for the Arizona Football Officials Association. The committee discussed rules and positional mechanics, examining the duties of each official during a game and clarifying which players—that is, which keys—each official should focus on at the start of a play.

I was applying wherever I could and wasn't getting anywhere. It was frustrating. I am not going to lie about that. I felt stuck. Yet I kept going.

∾

The next year, I filled out more applications, filling out my job experiences, listing the camps I attended, and providing all the same references. I worked some junior college scrimmages, rotating in whenever I could. It was a good experience, though I didn't get the usual welcome whenever

I ran into one guy who was known as one of the top officials working in the Pac-10. Word was this man flat-out didn't think women should be officiating since women didn't play the game, and he didn't try to hide that's what he thought.

Fortunately, Scarduzio seemed to be cut from a different cloth, one that didn't pull against me. And Scarduzio took my application for a second year in a row. If he refused me again, I intended to just keep coming back. Back on the field, I kept giving it my all. Then, in 2002, the second year I applied, Scarduzio took another look at me.

Tom Scarduzio was known among football officials. Over his career, he'd officiate three high school state championship games and two all-star games. Fifteen years earlier, he and Hank Mancini (who went on to become the Arizona Football League commissioner) had put together the first training film for officials made exclusively from coverage of local high school football games.

Scarduzio called me into his office to talk details. But before I came in, he said he'd need to talk to one of my references.

When I met Scarduzio, I shook his hand and sat on the other side of his desk. My application file was opened up before him. He sat back in his chair with a serious look on his face. He'd talked to Red, he said, and let his words hang in the air.

Maybe he was looking for some reaction from me, but I had my game face on.

"Red gave an enthusiastic recommendation," he said.

That didn't surprise me. I knew the long list of NFL officials in that file were all willing to give me the green light. I also knew Red was willing to go above and beyond to help. That was his way.

So I understood what Scarduzio was really getting at. "You just wanted to talk to Red Cashion," I teased.

He laughed. It was true. But then he grew serious again. He said he'd been thinking about what would happen if he hired me. "Everyone is going to ignore your qualifications and say you got hired by sleeping your way to the top," he said. "And this will be the case, whatever level you achieve."

I leveled my gaze at him. We both knew that was not the case.

"Better for you to know up front," he said, so I could handle it.

I could handle it. The harsh reality was that, back then, too many still attributed that as the reason for a woman's advancement in too many businesses.

Scarduzio went on to say I was the Jackie Robinson of this step— echoing the same incredible compliment Chuck Stewart had given me in his recommendation. And he said I had the "stuff" to be the first one to stand against discrimination.

After all that, he hired me as a head linesman. I got the position!

I'd experienced success at the Pop Warner and high school levels, but this was a big step up. I was thrilled, even knowing I'd meet some resistance from fellow officials as well as from some coaches in Arizona. A female college football official was something new, it was a change. I couldn't expect everyone to be excited with the idea.

I knew I had to do everything I could to prove I belonged, starting with the first test I took on college rules. I was determined to get 100 percent. Never having taken this kind of test, I did not know what to expect, so I did everything I could to prepare. I studied night after night since so many rules at the college level were different than the ones for high school. For example, what constitutes a foul can vary between the two levels. In high school, the rule on blocking below the waist is pretty straightforward, but in college, many different factors determine if a low block is legal or illegal. Different levels of play can also have different penalty enforcements: In high school, a hold by the offense behind the line of scrimmage was then enforced from the spot of the foul. In college, it was enforced from the previous spot—that is, the line of scrimmage. (By the time you read this, both levels will enforce the penalty from the previous spot.) For the test, I had to know all those different factors and rules and enforcements then in place.

Each official and aspiring official takes the test every year. That year, we received our result by mail, along with a cover letter by the supervisor, Tom Scarduzio.[4] In the letter, he announced that one official in his conference was let go for failing the test. In contrast, another official got all the questions correct—including the bonus question. That official was me, and he shared my name with everyone. He didn't have to do that, but it instantly gave me credibility when I stepped on the field. For that I was grateful.

I quickly became the go-to if questions on the rules arose during games. It came in handy in resolving issues, though I can't say the ability to absolutely recall all the rules is the most important requirement in officiating. So, if a thorough knowledge of the rules is not the most important requirement in officiating, what is?

Field presence. From the moment you step on the field, you need to project a strong confidence, one that falls just shy of cocky. NFL referee Clete Blakeman has this quality down to a perfection, from his assurance in his signaling of penalties to the conviction in his voice in breaking down calls. You notice the way he has had to alter the sleeves on his uniform because of the girth of his biceps. Every detail about him signals he knows what's going on.

To have a strong field presence, you also need to be in complete control of your actions and emotions always. You should not be afraid to admit when you have made a mistake, and on the flip side, you need to be confident when you know you're right.

On the field, I had a game or two where a coach adamantly challenged me on a call when I knew I had nailed it. "If I'm wrong," I said, "I'll bring the team pizza to your next practice. Watch the film and let me know."

Needless to say, I have never had to deliver a pizza.

Sometimes it didn't matter what I said or didn't say. Some coaches only had to take one look at me to decide what I could or couldn't do. Before my first word, their mind was made up. Guys like this can be harder to win over. In those cases, I just had to let my good work on the field speak for me, hoping I might crack the hard shell formed around them. That's what I did the first time I officiated a game for Scottsdale Community College. The longtime coach for the Artichokes was an old-school guy who made clear how he felt about a woman calling his game. It didn't help that the entire chain crew was made up of women as well. This proved to be a bit much for Coach G, and he did not handle himself well. The lack of respect radiated in his words and actions so much that I moved the chain crew to the other side of the field while I remained on Coach G's sideline. It was my responsibility, not the volunteers' responsibility, to absorb the abuse.

All I could do the remainder of the game was do my best to communicate and keep my level of professionalism at its highest. I didn't blame Coach G for his behavior during the game. Again, I was the first woman ever to officiate at this level in the state. In the conference, he was known as a great coach and had served the Artichokes well for years. The change had to be difficult for him to take at face value at that point in his career.

So I was surprised the next day when the coach called me. Scarduzio had given him my phone number. Coach G said he wanted to come see me.

"That's not necessary," I told him.

"But I have to come see you," he said, "or I am going to kill myself!"

I knew he was in no way suicidal, but I also sensed his urgency. "All right," I said, unsure of what to expect. We set up a time for us to meet at the hotel where I worked.

He showed up at the front desk with chocolates and a written apology. Inside the card he'd written out a play with arrows showing routes and blocks and positions. He said he was an ass (an all-caps *A-S-S* actually) and acknowledged I could have thrown him out of the game. *Please, please, please find a way to forgive me,* he wrote. *You do an outstanding job as a college football official and can be on my sideline any time.*

In coming to my hotel lobby, Coach G had gone out of his way to make clear that from then on, I'd be a welcome guest—a welcome official—at his games. The gesture meant a lot. I knew right away I'd want to save his card, though I didn't know yet what the other note tucked inside would eventually come to mean.

13

ODDS-ON FAVORITE

I kept taking assignments at whatever level I could. My colleagues noticed the time and effort I gave during camps and scrimmages. At one camp, a Division I supervisor of the Western Athletic Conference even said, "Hey, superstar, I hear I need to hire you!" But he didn't.

I'd hoped to move up again after working a couple years at the junior college level, but that didn't happen. So I kept going to as many camps as I could—to be seen. Why else do singers and actors go to auditions? Why do baseball or basketball players go to tryouts? I spent thousands of dollars on plane tickets, hotel rooms, and camp registrations. I went to camps all over the United States. I knew a lot of high-ranking officials attended these camps to observe or work there as clinicians. I believed my work on the field would speak for itself, that I had what it took to get noticed.

For my preferred position at these camps, I kept following the advice to check wing, once again putting referee as my second choice, though that position remained my true preference. That's what I did in signing up for the Reno Football Officials Camp in 2004. This camp counted among the more well-respected (and more expensive) of the camps. It was run by Ken Rivera, the supervisor of officials for the Mountain West Conference in Division I. You can imagine how thrilled I was when the organizers assigned me as referee from the start. Throughout the camp, I got to work with the same crew. Each crew worked a scrimmage, then rotated fields so we could be observed by a variety of clinicians who'd critique us and offer advice. It was like an endless job interview that lasted a couple of days.

At the end of the camp, the clinicians voted to recognize the top crew. Most camps didn't typically give awards or recognize performances. An up-and-comer might receive a scholarship for a future camp, but ultimately, the award we're all there seeking is to be hired by a college conference.

To say everyone was working their butt off in the hopes of receiving this honor would be an understatement. Some might have found these days exhausting, but to me, it was exhilarating.

Then at the end of camp, out of all the crews, Rivera announced our crew had won the award!

My hands shot up in the air. I high-fived all my crew members, and they high-fived each other. What a huge nod of approval for the work I'd been doing as a referee. For all of us.

I was so ecstatic! I gave Ken and all the clinicians a big thank-you. So many of these guys I'd watched officiating on TV, and now in this surreal moment, these men had gathered everyone together to say they'd found something good and promising in our crew and in me. At that point, I'd worn the white hat only during sub-varsity high school games, besides the chance I'd been given at the UCLA camp and for the Florida A&M scrimmage. This recognition had to lead to other opportunities. It had to, right?

Rivera wasn't done handing out awards, though. Among the others handed out was one for top female official. That camp was unusual in that it had a total of six women attending. Usually, it was just me and one or two other women at these sites. After the votes came in, Rivera announced I had won it.

I was honored to have won another award, but I'd been perfectly content with being simply part of the top crew. Recognition like this strikes me as a bit odd in that they don't vote on which man deserves the top male official, but I'm sure that Ken and the clinicians had nothing but good intentions in wanting to make sure someone who deserved recognition didn't get overlooked.

Ken was being kind, but other times, I haven't known what to make about the special attention given me for being a woman. Like that one guy from another time and another place who'd barrel ahead of me whenever we approached a door just so he could hold it open. He did it every time. Every single time. *My ref, my ref,* he kept saying, like he was doing me a favor. It was so overdone. Weird.

The thing is, as a female official, I have tried not to focus on the fact that I am a woman. I just wanted to be the best official I can be. And I wanted the chance to move up the officiating ranks. After the camp in Reno, I hoped I would.

❧

I might have been hitting a wall trying to move up a level for my work on the field, but off the field, the opportunities were coming to me. Around this time, I was approached by the franchise owner and director of all sports for National Youth Sports (NYS). Shawn Connors was looking for someone to assign officials for their newly formed youth tackle football program. For the past few years, I'd been scheduling officials on a smaller level, for the Boys & Girls Clubs of Greater Scottsdale. I'd offered to help them more as a way to give back to the club, where I'd spent a lot of time as a kid. But Shawn's group was looking for something on a larger scale. As a brand-new league, its pool of teams was minor compared to the well-established Pop Warner, which had been around for years. It would be a challenge to draw officials to this new league. Pop Warner's officials were deeply rooted in its program. I knew what it was to buck tradition. I decided to help NYS.

Though I'd made many friends in all the officiating I'd done for six years, a lot of those guys were already booked. I'd have to find officials and train them from scratch. Finding enough people wasn't easy, but somehow, I'd get it to work out. That's when I realized how much I loved training new officials. I'd led one of the four-week-long beginners' courses for the AIA by that point. I could do it for NYS as well.

So I recruited people from all over. If I saw someone who appeared to be in good shape, I would approach them and ask if they would be interested in officiating. At work, at ASU intramural sports events, at restaurants—anywhere I happened to be—I would recruit. Although I don't drink, I spent some time with Tom at Four Peaks Brewing Co. (They offered a great spinach and artichoke dip.) We got to know a couple of the bartenders who worked there. They were young and looked athletic, so I thought they might have what it would take to do the job.

"Hey, are you interested in football officiating?" I asked.

And the answer was, "Yes."

I was always overjoyed when an opportunity like this would occur. It was fun to take these men who knew nothing about officiating and see what I could do with them.

I spent numerous hours and countless Saturdays training the recruits. I went to sites and stood behind them, teaching them as they worked games. Like many new officials, they suffered from happy feet. So for each, I held onto the back of his shirt and let go when it was the right time to move.

"Don't get overwhelmed doing too many things at once," I said. I was just a couple of years removed from learning all this myself and remembered how that felt. "Just focus on one thing at a time to start." That's how I learned. My first game, I told them, I had a hard time counting eleven players on offense before the ball was snapped. They'd find, as I did, that after a couple of plays that came easy. So then they could move on to something else—like making sure there's the right number of players on the line of scrimmage. (Over the years, that rule has changed.) From there, they'd learn how to not get ahead of the play—to let the runner go beyond the line of scrimmage, then trail the play and get a good forward-progress spot. Though, when the goal line is involved, they'd need to be ahead of the play, standing at the goal line, waiting for the play to come to them.

All this, much easier said than done, I know. Sometimes during a play, I had to tell them to just throw the flag and explain afterward why it had to be thrown. Other times, they'd see something they thought might be a foul, and I'd have to explain why they should pass on throwing a flag in that instance.

"It's okay, you're not supposed to know all this at once," I said. "Right now, you're at the stage where you really don't know what you're seeing or when to throw a flag. But eventually, you'll progress to where you begin to think you know everything and want to throw a flag all the time." This was the sort of thing we'd talk about over many games. This group showed a real willingness to learn and a seriousness about wanting to get better. I told them that eventually, they'd advance on to the next stage. "That's where you'll start seeing the play," I said, "and you'll start asking yourself questions like—was there any advantage gained from that potential foul you saw?"

Once you get new officials to think about the advantage/disadvantage of a play or call, you can talk more about the philosophy of officiating. In some instances, a call is black and white—like when someone grasps and twists a facemask. Easy. Flag. But sometimes you need to run through a series of questions before reacting and throwing a flag. *Was it a quick grasp and release?* Yes? Then ask this follow-up: *Did the grasp in any way cause the runner to break stride?* If no, then the flag stays in your waistband. That's philosophy. Sometimes your mind sees something and wants to react quickly. Philosophy slows the mind down and asks, "Are you sure you saw what you saw?"

Those Saturdays (and on some other days), they all put in a lot of time thinking about football while officiating it. "Again, to reinforce," I said, "one thing at a time. And before you know it, you're settling in and starting to officiate more by feel instead of having to think about everything you're supposed to do." That's when officiating becomes fun.

Those Four Peaks recruits were fast learners and picked up the rules and mechanics quickly. A couple of them, Nick Nelson and Graham Ensign, ended up being top-notch officials. When I needed additional help, the guys I knew who were already working Pop Warner games would come help out and work the NYS games too. Some officials are so into the game that, if given the chance, they will work all day if you let them. Hadn't I done the same thing when I first started youth football? All the great training I'd had I could now pass along.

∾

Through all this, Tom and I were still seeing each other off and on. I didn't want to love him, yet I did.

Twice I'd moved to make myself stop seeing him. I went to Texas. It was the right new place for me, I convinced myself. It would improve my college basketball schedule. But I was completely miserable there. I didn't last much beyond the season.

After that, I tried moving to New Mexico. This time, I didn't move for basketball, though I did work some games while I was there. I had every intention of planting roots, but my efforts didn't take that time, either. I kept driving back to Phoenix. After less than a year, I moved back home to Arizona.

Changing where I lived wasn't the change I needed. I knew what I wanted. Things weren't right, and things weren't getting any better.

Then his wife divorced him.

I felt I could take a deep breath and start all over. Our relationship would finally settle onto the right track.

And, more important, the recognition from the camp in Reno did seem to be making a difference. I'd recently added Division II football for the Rocky Mountain Conference to my résumé. At the end of 2005, my junior college crew worked the Valley of the Sun Bowl, which was not only a bowl game but also a National Junior College Athletic Association national championship game. Maybe I could now get on the roster for some higher-level scrimmages.

But not everything was falling into place—not with Tom. The divorce had not made everything right between us. Even after some time passed, I remained the outsider on holidays and special occasions. It was frustrating to still be kept separate. Guilt probably drove his actions—make that his lack of actions. "I forced her to do it," he said.

Which forced me to look hard at what we had together, to consider what I would need to do to stop loving him and if I even could.

∾

Had I married Tom the way I wanted to, when I wanted to, and had I reached every career goal of which I felt I was worthy and willing to work for, would I still have fallen in love with poker? I don't know.

Around this time, a group of high school and college football officials invited me to one of their poker nights. It sounded like a good distraction and a great way to hang out with my buddies. When I sat down at that poker table in my friend's dining room, I had no idea how to play. The guys talked me through the first few hands, and I gave it a shot.

We played a couple of rounds of Texas hold'em. I didn't fully understand the game and needed a few questions answered along the way. What they say about beginner's luck held for me that night—I ended up winning one of the two tournaments played. I was hooked.

I watched what poker I could on TV to better learn the game. After a couple of weeks, I decided I was ready for a casino and maybe a real tournament. Not far from me, there's an Indian reservation with a great poker room. One morning I headed down to the Talking Stick Resort and Casino and paid sixty bucks to register for their No-Limit Hold'em Tournament.

What strategies I'd learned in that short amount of time worked well for me. And with a little luck, too, I won the whole thing and left with eighteen hundred-dollar bills stuffed inside my pocket.

The next day, Tom wanted to know if I wanted to go up to the casino and play some cards. I wasn't about to pass up an opportunity to be with him. So back to the casino I went.

The money I'd won the day before had already settled nicely into my bank account, so it didn't seem prudent to take any big chances. I grabbed a seat at a table with a low-limit game. After about an hour, I found myself in a hand holding four aces. Everyone at the table started yelling, clapping, and high-fiving everyone. Frankly, I had no idea what was going on. They had to explain I'd just won, saying something about a "bad beat" jackpot. They explained this was what happened when a very good hand like aces full of jacks loses to an even better one like four aces, which is what I had. The house handed me a quarter of the $4,800 jackpot. The losing hand won half, and the rest was split among the others at the table. After more than fifteen years, I have yet to hit another jackpot like that one.

In just a few rounds of poker over just a few weeks, I'd gone from flying by the seat of my pants at a friend's house to winning a tournament at a casino to hitting a bad beat jackpot. I was up over three grand. To say I was hooked was an understatement.

Though I was winning, I had little idea what I was doing. I had so much to learn and couldn't learn it fast enough. Like anything else in my life, if I was interested in doing it, I wanted to be great if not the best. That spring, I spent hours of my spare time watching poker on TV and absorbing as many games and tournaments as I could. What I loved about the game from the start was all the strategies poker required, and strategies seem to come easy to me. Before long, I ventured away from the lower-limit tables at the casino up to where higher limits were offered. I played daily tournaments when my work schedule allowed.

Then I heard about the World Series of Poker (WSOP) in Las Vegas, which was held in the dead heat of summer—my off-season for officiating. My mind became set on going to Vegas. With the lowest entry fee amounting to a grand—more than my financial capacity in my work assigning officials—I knew I'd need to earn my seat at the table another way. One of the tournaments at Talking Stick offered a seat at a woman's event at the WSOP as one of its prizes, so I entered. And I won.

A month later, I headed to the 37th Annual WSOP. Tom came with me, and Jen came in from California, where she had moved with her husband. The plan was for them to hang out while I played. Over a thousand women had entered the No-Limit Hold'em event. The tables seemed to stretch in all directions on the floor of the Rio, and this wasn't even the main event. I was extremely excited—and incredibly nervous. I was about to play in one of the biggest poker tournaments in the world.

The first table I was assigned had two big-name competitors: a top female pro, Kristy Gazes, along with actress Jean Smart, whom I'd loved on *Designing Women*. I couldn't have asked for a better table.

As we played, my chips started piling up. On one hand, I raised with pocket kings. The pro pushed all in, and I called. She was holding an ace and a queen. My kings held, and I knocked her out. Jean Smart hung on a bit longer, but eventually she was knocked out, too.

What preparation I'd done paid off. Fortunately, over the course of the tournament, luck fell my way most of the time, when needed. I gained confidence.

Hours later, the tournament director announced we'd finally broken the money bubble. All the players turned more aggressive. After more than eight hours of play, the woman on the button—the best position in poker—raised all in. I was in the blind with ace-8. I sat for a moment, trying to get a read on her. My read was that she wasn't that strong. I called, and she turned over ace-5.

I had made the right call. With poker, it's sometimes better to be lucky than to be good. We both hit an ace on the flop, and she hit a five as well. That knocked me out, in 67th place. For the day, I'd made just over two thousand. The first-place winner took home over two hundred thousand—and a WSOP jewel-encrusted bracelet.

Jen and Tom were both thrilled for how far I'd made it, but I'd wanted to win.

14

ENCROACHMENT

If given the choice, I'd still rather step onto a sunny gridiron than into a dark casino. Even heading into the WSOP that year, football remained foremost on my mind. That was the spring I tried breaking into the scrimmage scene at ASU. The coordinator for those games was a great Pac-10 official who typically filled the seven spots needed with whatever D1 officials were available, then rotated in aspiring officials from the junior college level to see how they worked. What I had on my résumé should have put me in a good position, even with ASU being a higher-tier Division I school. Not only had I worked at the junior college level a few years at this point, but the previous season, I'd worked as a linesman, line judge, and side judge for D2 games. I was versatile and could be placed wherever needed.

But I had yet to be picked to fill in for any of these practices in Tempe.

I held out hope that a spot would open up and I would be rotated in. I felt I was a good candidate given my national championship experience. So I kept my phone close.

Tom Frazier was the one who got the call. He was sitting next to me at Four Peaks when he was buzzed. Tom was on a Division I crew and later that fall would be inducted into the Arizona Football Officials Association Hall of Fame. The coordinator was short an official and was calling to ask Tom for a name.

Tom gave me a look. "I can ask Shannon," he said. "I'm sure she would do it."

I could hear what the coordinator said next, loud and clear. "I'll go with six officials before putting a chick on the field," he said.

Tom laughed it off. I know he was in a tough spot and struggled at times with being caught between supporting me and fighting his peers, but

I did not find their conversation funny. Not at all. Tom should have said something to stand up for me. After he hung up, I told him so.

His point was that the coordinator was a friend of his.

My point was that the man sitting next to me was a friend of mine.

The situation was impossible, or it felt that way. The spot was filled with a high school guy. So that was frustrating.

I considered my other options. Tom happened to be in charge of assigning officials at another Division I school, Northern Arizona University, which was in the Football Championship Subdivision, not the higher-tier Football Bowl Subdivision, which included ASU. Maybe I could work those.

Then Ken Rivera called. He asked if I wanted to return to Fresno, this time as a clinician.

And that fall, referee Bob Sietsema called to say that he had an opening for a line-of-scrimmage official on his varsity crew, and I was his top choice. What a great opportunity—I felt as if I'd won the lottery! (In another win, officials got to upgrade to black pants that year. Good-bye, knickers!)

I couldn't believe my luck. Bob and his crew I counted among the best football officials at their positions in all of Arizona. In working as a linesman on his crew, I'd get to officiate alongside Umpire Dana Smith, Line Judge John "Jocko" Whitney, and Back Judge Pat Wishowski. All would work on a crew for at least one All-Star Game. Bob would eventually be among those inducted into the Arizona Football Officials Association Hall of Fame. All were good teachers, mentors, and friends.

I've found that an exceptional crew like Bob's works like a well-oiled machine. Calls are made, relayed, and administered, so you can easily move on to the next play. The more games you officiate, the more your knowledge of the rules broadens and deepens, and you're able to apply those rules and communicate a call more effectively. With that experience, any earlier tendency you had to operate on high alert and run ahead to catch the next infraction can then downshift into a cooler, calmer state. You no longer feel you have to hunt for the next violation. With experience, the plays open up, and the game comes to you. You learn how the stance of an offensive lineman at the snap can dictate pass or run. As field presence grows, it builds on itself, and the demeanor you carry is catching. When the whole crew is in this state of calm and cool, coaches and players know they're in good hands. That allows them to exhale and let go of any concerns about officiating so they can focus on what matters—playing the game.

It was great to work on Bob's crew for the high school season. I am not going to lie, I was not surprised when we found ourselves scheduled to work the postseason, including the 5A Division I high school championship game. Buzz that year centered around how the game would be held in the brand-new Cardinal stadium. Unfortunately, the schedule our crew was given for the quarterfinal turned out to be a bit of a problem for me. I had a Division I basketball game scheduled the same night. When this happens, you always work the higher-level game in officiating, so that's what I planned to do. But when Bob informed the commissioner that the crew needed a replacement on that one game for me, the commissioner informed my crew chief that we all needed to work that quarterfinal together, or he'd pull us from the championship game.

It seemed an untenable decision. For me, it was not. I couldn't let the crew down no matter the consequences I'd face. That was the last year I worked Division I basketball. I was not asked back, nor should I have been. I'd written my own ticket out.

I wasn't that upset. This was not the first time in seven years of working that I'd given back a basketball game for football. My priorities had been clear since I asked a stranger what he thought about me signing up to officiate—although Larry didn't know me yet, he already could somehow tell that he could vouch for me.

Ten years into officiating football, I worked my first high school championship. That was also the first time a woman worked the top high school game in the state. Before game time, I went up to the coach on my sideline to introduce myself. The stands at the Cardinal stadium were just beginning to fill—to the extent fans for a high school game could fill a stadium that size. It was a huge deal for those kids to be playing on a brand-new NFL field on fresh Bermuda grass.[1] I don't remember much about the game, but I do remember that when the coach shook my hand, all he said was, "Well, you must be good." And then he walked away.

Hamilton plowed through Mountain View to win the title that year. Our crew worked the game as seamlessly as we had throughout the season—though when a team wins 34–15, you sometimes have to work harder to remain focused.

Bob asked me back on his varsity crew for the next year, and I was glad to return. I would have loved to work many more seasons with those guys, but after that second year, other opportunities arose, making it impossible for me to stay.

∿

Sometimes you have to block a challenge to clear the way for your next opportunity. That spring, I ran into the Pac-10 official again, the one responsible for filling spots at scrimmages. This time, he and Tom were working as substitution officials in the Arena League for the Arizona Rattlers. A substitution official sits in the team box and tracks players going in and out of the game. The league has specific rules that could possibly disallow a player to reenter. Each team was to have a substitution official in its box. One game the Pac-10 official wasn't able to work, and neither were the regular backups. Tom knew I could do the job, so he asked me to fill in.

As substitution official, I'd be in the Rattlers' team box, where Gene Nudo was now the head coach. Nudo had been the gentleman who'd given me his card at the Scottsdale Christian game some years before. "Coach Nudo knows Shannon," Tom told the Pac-10 official. "And he'd be happy to see her."

I wouldn't be on the field at all. I was not even going to officiate. I was simply going to be doing paperwork, so to speak.

They went back and forth, and that escalated into an ultimatum. "Allow Shannon to work the game," the official warned, "and I will no longer support you in moving up in your career."

This man was part of an elite group of Pac-10 officials who'd worked a national championship, so he had pull, and Tom aspired to work in that higher-tier conference now that he'd been working in the Big Sky a few years. But I'm happy to say Tom did not give in to his demands, and I ended up working the Rattlers' game. Though as a substitution official I wasn't on the field, I was given a flag in case a player broke a substitution rule. These flags were mostly for show; they were rarely used. When a substitution infraction occurs, you just notify the coach. During that game, the Rattlers illegally subbed a player. I told Coach Nudo, and he balked, taking issue with the validity of what I'd tracked.

All right. I had been in this kind of situation before. I asked him to look at the film and to please let me know if I was wrong.

Afterward, Coach Nudo looked at the film. He realized he'd made a mistake. And at the next game, he found Tom and admitted his error. He wanted Tom to make sure I knew that I'd made the correct call. That's integrity at its finest.

That wasn't the last time Coach Nudo stood in my corner. And it wouldn't be the last time I bumped heads with an official who didn't want me there.

∾

That summer, I made it to the final six in a qualifying event at the Talking Stick Casino, and the winnings covered my seat in the 2007 WSOP $1,500 No-Limit Hold'em Tournament. This was the second most popular event in the WSOP, with more than 2,800 people—mostly men—throwing in their chips to compete.

This time, I decided to go it alone. I wasn't sure how long I wanted to stay, and besides, Tom and I were on and off again. I wanted to focus just on poker.

Once again, tables and tables of players filled the casino floor. I took my seat and played. At one point, I was sure I was done and stood to leave the table—only to find I'd won the hand. I was very low on chips and knew I had to start playing more aggressively. Pushing all in, I managed to double up. I went for it time and again. With that, I gained quite a few chips back, and at around five o'clock, everyone still in counted our stash and bagged it. All that time sitting in the padded chair, I'd felt fine, but now that I stood, I could feel the extent of the stiffness in my muscles. I walked it out on the way to dinner.

An hour later, and we were back at it. I was playing tight, and we were down to three tables when the two players before me each pushed all in. I checked my hand. Pocket aces.

"Oh my gosh!" I exclaimed and pushed all in.

My poker face had deserted me. The people behind me immediately folded. As for the remaining two players, one had ace-king, the other had ace-queen. I knocked them both out.

The tournament was down to its last two tables, and I was still in. The massage I had at the table helped work out the tension in my shoulders, but a charge of electricity still ran through my core. A couple of pros sat at my table, most notably Phil "The Poker Brat" Helmuth. I recognized him from all my TV viewing of poker. He was one of the greatest. His total live tournament winnings now exceed $28 million, which puts him about twentieth on the all-time money list. And here I was, two years removed from a friendly home game in Arizona, sitting across from a man who'd won ten of those WSOP bracelets when I was hoping for my first. This chance to play him was, in a word, surreal.

When I caught myself thinking that, I did my self-talk to bring myself back into the game. That's how I stay focused. If you're not paying attention to what's at hand, you can get caught off guard. Staying focused keeps you alert, on your toes. Ready.

As ready as I was, the cards weren't coming for me. I tried to be patient. Phil and another player at the table taunted each other, taking verbal jousts at each other's masculinity. Guy talk. Despite the posing, Phil, for the most part, was a conservative player. I'd been card dead for a while when he raised, and the other guy at the table pushed all in. I felt the guy who went all in was not strong at all but mostly trying to push Phil out of the hand. I looked down and saw ace-queen. I went all in. With Phil's conservative approach, I felt he would fold, leaving me with the best hand.

As I expected, Phil folded. I turned over ace-queen, and the other guy turned over king-jack. Phil folded pocket sevens. I now had the best hand. My opponent flopped a pair, then turned two pair. I had outs going to the river, but again luck was not on my side. I was knocked out at seventeenth place. Sixteen away from over purse of more than $600,000, not to mention the WSOP bracelet—both of which Phil pocketed in the end.

Still, I walked away with more than $24,000. Not a bad investment from a $1,500 start.

The main event was a few days away from being played. Getting *that* close to life-changing money and not getting it left me hurting mentally. Still, I considered laying down $10,000 to enter. In my current state of mind, it was probably not a good idea.

I found myself back at Circus Circus, taking a mental break from poker while trying to win more stuffed animals up on the second floor—and talk myself out of coughing up the ten-grand entrance fee. I'd just won more than twice that. But did I want to risk that amount of money?

Just as I was about to tell myself no, Tom called. I told him what I was thinking. Then he offered to put in a grand. A friend of his was willing to do the same. My part of the fee would be down to eight thousand. So I played.

And I was knocked out on the first day.

I was so upset with myself that I lost all that money. I decided to stay in Vegas and play cash games until I earned back the ten thousand I'd just lost. Often this kind of thinking can lead to trouble, I know. Especially with so many dynamics in play in Vegas during the WSOP. You should see it. Every guy who thinks he can play shows up for the showcase. You can often see them traveling together in packs. A good amount of drinking can get under way. The synergy of egos and liquor together tends to free up money during play—so find the right table of guys and sit back and be patient for the cash to come your way. Being a woman can be an advantage when guys underestimate us at the poker table.

The next few days, I took in an average of about eight thousand a night. I earned my money back and then some. I ended up leaving Las Vegas with more than forty thousand.

When I told my friend Scott about it, he wanted to know why I didn't stay longer. Like other guys I knew who officiated, he caught the bug to play every once in a while. He knew what it was to be at the table. "And you were doing so well," he said.

But in Vegas, I'd been playing most nights through the next morning, and I can go without sleep for only so long because that can intensify my headaches. As much as I love Vegas, it can wear on me. Poker is inherently a grinding game requiring so much patience. You have to know how to take the good with the bad. There can be streaks where it doesn't matter how good you get your money in; you still get outdrawn. As much as I like to be in control of my emotions at all times, some things about poker make that very challenging. My competitive nature doesn't help. For two years, poker blazed through my life, and then it was time to let the desire to play burn out.

∾

In the fall of 2007, I was back on Bob Sietsema's high school crew and working as many other assignments on all levels I could. And at the end of the season, I was selected to a junior college crew to officiate the Valley of the Sun Bowl again as line judge.

The bowl game that year wasn't deciding the Junior College National Championship as it had before but would mark the end of Scarduzio's role as supervisor of officials for that conference. I was going to miss him. Five years earlier, he'd taken a chance in hiring me. I always felt he had my back.

The new supervisor had come to watch the game. I knew the guy; we'd even worked a junior college game together. But now here he was, asking how many of these I'd worked.

I didn't like the feeling I was getting. "A few," I replied.

In my heart, I knew, with him now in charge, this junior college bowl game would be my last. It wasn't just about the way he asked that question. He had always been a nice enough guy, but his blatant lack of support was no secret. After he'd been supervisor a year, he sent an e-mail to several college supervisors and to some Pac-10 and other D1 officials. In the e-mail, he included a tier system he'd created to rank officials, his way of recommending those who should advance from his junior college division up to Division I. According to his standards, I belonged in the lowest tier.

Out of five head linesmen, he put me dead last. Not that he sent the e-mail to me: A friend I'd been in touch with through the years had forwarded it.

After reviewing his tier system, I called him and asked if he could tell me about the four guys who ranked higher than I did.

I don't think he expected my call or my question. He stumbled and said he didn't know but would have to look it up. I already knew the four guys, and one of them had no clue what to do on the line. He was an umpire trying to convert to head linesman. I had even tried to help him.

Five out of five. That burned me. I had worked the Junior College National Championship and another bowl assignment for two out of three years before he took over.

I wasn't the only one unfairly ranked. The guy right above my name in this bottom tier was Mearl Robinson. Mearl is now working as a deep official for the NFL. The new supervisor and his allies ended up treating Mearl the way they treated me. My guess is that they felt Mearl was moving too quickly up the chain for their comfort. And they felt, like me, that Mearl was going around them to get ahead.

As competitive as I am, I am also a realistic person. I am honest with what I can and cannot do. Play in the NFL I could not. But I've always known I had what it takes to be an NFL official. Unfortunately, having a woman officiating even at the junior college level ended up being too much, apparently, for many of these guys to handle. I don't get it. Why are some men so threatened by a woman who can competently and confidently referee a football game?

The frustration with men in power wore on me physically and emotionally. It affected how I looked back at my year. It didn't feel as if I was making any headway. So when I got a call from a fellow clinician I'd met that spring in Fresno asking for help, it brightened my spirits. I was only too glad to help.

Jim Corpora was a good guy and an ACC official. We got along from the moment we met. He liked to challenge me with rules questions, and I think I surprised him a little when I usually had the correct answers.

He'd recently taken over as the supervisor of officials for an arena league that held their games near me. Being from out East, he wasn't familiar with the work of some officials who'd applied. If I knew them, he wanted my opinion. In confidence, I offered honest yet diplomatic information. Some of those applying had Division I experience, so those résumés spoke for themselves.

The e-mails we exchanged weren't anything out of the ordinary— unless you're someone who might happen to take issue with a woman you think is getting a little too big for her knickers.

Ready to watch football with Dad.

Friends say Mom looks like Barbra Streisand.

With big brother on Misquamicut Beach, Rhode Island.

Tending to my collection of stuffed animals, with Cubby Comfortable Jr. in my lap and Smokey in the corner.

With early awards (a pain to dust).

On the road to another tournament.

From the first time I was invited to the Olympic Training Center, at age 11.

With catamaran captain on Waikiki Beach after the national championship.

Taking down an opponent at practice.

I always wanted to be Wonder Woman.

Eyes bandaged and accepting medals.

All smiles with Walter Payton.

Red Cashion took a swing at helping me rise to the NFL. *From Christmas card given Shannon by Red Cashion*

Making the call. *AP Photo/Denis Poroy*

The last Christmas gathering Riley and Cooper had with "Uncle" Larry before he died.

The newest crew member, Rosco.

15

PERSONAL FOUL

In the spring of 2008, it looked as if I'd hit the end of the line, that I'd reached the highest level I'd ever get to in officiating while working at the Division II level. So I looked to other avenues, looking for another way through (and up).

Thanks to the work that Jim Corpora saw me do at the camp in Fresno, I was one of five officials he hired that spring to work for the American Indoor Football Association (AIFA). I was glad to work with some longtime friends and respected officials like Tom, Scott, and Dana again. It also gave me the chance to work with a great Pac-10 official named Kevin Kieser.

Really, though, what I still hoped for was the chance to work Division I in the fall.

I remember feeling so down sitting in my apartment, thinking I wasn't going to get anywhere. By the end of July, I was sure I'd exhausted all my resources. At least I had Jen to talk to. It was such a blessing to have her friendship through times like this.

In the end, it was up to me to figure out what to do to get my foot in the door at a higher-level conference. I knew I had to be missing some opening. With the season so close to starting, most doors to get into any conference had already shut.

Then Dan Evans popped into my head. Something I'd heard through the grapevine clicked into place for me. I'd heard he was still with NASA but not a referee with the MEAC anymore. He'd gone on to become the supervisor of officials for the conference. It'd been seven years since we'd met, so when I heard what he was doing, it didn't occur to me at first to reach out to him. But I could. What did I have to lose?

I wasn't sure if Dan even remembered me, as I indicated in the opening of my e-mail. But if he did and if he needed any supplemental officials, I'd be willing to work in any capacity. I let him know what I'd been doing since I last saw him at that Florida A&M scrimmage.

It was a long shot, I knew. And my offer was all the more tenuous since, at the time, conferences tended to hire officials who lived in the geographic areas where their schools were located. All the schools in the MEAC are out East by the Atlantic, and I lived in Arizona.

To my surprise, Dan responded right away. "Yes, I remember you," he wrote, "and I need a referee."

I'd just wanted the chance to work Division I. I would have taken any position. And here he was offering a spot as a crew chief. Crew chief! It's hard to fully capture the feeling I had reading his e-mail. Every single *No* I'd heard up until then had been worth it, given this much-needed *Yes.* I'd so desperately wanted this. This was what I'd worked so hard for.

I was going to be a referee for a Division I football conference. The first woman in a white hat at this level! I would not be the first woman to officiate D1, though—that honor went to Annice Canady, who'd been hired by Johnny Grier back when he'd been supervisor of officials for the MEAC.[1]

I couldn't wait to call Tom. I knew he'd be happy for me. Truth be told, he might have been a little shocked, too, when I told him the invitation was not only to work in the conference but also to work as referee.

He knew about the collective wisdom shared by nearly every official or supervisor who'd crossed my path: *If you want to move up, Shannon, you need to stay away from working at the referee position.*

To be hired at the referee spot, male or female, was unheard of. General progression came from working wings (or any other position for that matter), and then, based on games worked and evaluations, you were promoted to wear the white hat. I could not believe this jaw-dropping opportunity Dan had granted me—especially with how much I absolutely loved working as referee.

Dan invited me to the MEAC preseason clinic, and, of course, I accepted. For as much praise and recognition I'd received working as ref at all the camps I'd attended, sub-varsity was still the highest level I'd worked in that spot for an actual game assignment. Whatever prep I could get I would take in order to be ready to ref for the MEAC that fall.

In further preparation, I shot off a note to the person coordinating scrimmages at ASU, requesting the chance to get some more experience under my belt in the scrimmages yet to be held. And now that I'd been hired as a referee to work in the MEAC, I was officially a Division I football official. If you remember, ASU and Northern Arizona University (NAU) scrimmages were open to all Division I officials. So this was the note I sent to the person in charge of coordinating those assignments:

> I know that you are in charge of ASU scrimmages. With my assign-ment in the MEAC, I was hoping that it would be okay for me to be included. I know that I could learn a lot from watching and getting some snaps as well. It is very important to me to do everything possible to prepare myself. If you have any concerns, I have worked scrimmages at UTEP, Air Force, Wyoming, Colorado State, Florida A&M, New Mexico, and NAU. Please let me know. Also, if you are in charge of the Wednesday night meetings, I would like to attend those when I am available. Thank you for your attention to this e-mail.
>
> Shannon

I didn't hear back, not for a while.

First, I heard from Dan again. He forwarded me an e-mail received from an official with whom I'd once worked. This guy wrote out of con-cern for Dan, he said, to make sure Dan knew I had no junior college experience—or varsity, either, for that matter—while wearing a white hat. Dan replied that I'd worked a scrimmage at UCLA in 2000. This he gave as shorthand for the time my refereeing caught Red Cashion's attention and was the reason Red and other NFL officials came scouting that fall, which my fellow official knew only too well. After making the point that he knew my work, Dan asked, "Are you telling me that she cannot handle the game?" Dan didn't need an answer.

A week had passed by this point, and I still hadn't heard back about working any ASU scrimmages.

I asked an NFL scout I knew what I should do. He advised to send it again. This time, ask overtly for a response. And copy others. "Don't back down," he told me.

Those tips helped—though the response I received four days later felt like a nonanswer. The official who'd been coordinating the assignments wrote that he'd been in San Francisco the past few days for a clinic and was on his way to another camp. He'd get back to me. I was quick to reply, saying I'd be at the NAU scrimmage that weekend and looked forward to hearing from him again.

Another ten days passed before I heard from him again. A friend shared with me what was taking so long. At a meeting with D1 officials, this man had passed out copies of the private e-mails I'd exchanged with Jim Corpora. Someone had apparently broken into my account and printed out several messages I'd sent.

What I understood from what I heard was that some people had taken issue with the professional assessments I'd provided Jim at his request about the hiring decisions for the Arena League, although nothing about my communication had been unethical. In fact, the exchange had even mirrored discussions I'd heard between other officials from time to time. The only difference I can see: This time it was a woman giving her opinion.

I suppose I shouldn't have been surprised by this official's final response, sent just two days before the ASU scrimmage. His e-mail read more like a court filing than a note to a colleague. He said that the D1 officials collectively wanted to "express [their] disappointment with the way [I] had handled getting assigned to the MEAC." He continued,

> We are trying to create a fair and equitable environment for our Arizona Officials [*sic*], devoid of politics and manipulation. The way you achieved your MEAC assignment completely flouted what we are working toward. We are trying to establish a meritocracy, where officials move up the ranks based on their talents and skills and not just on their networking skills. However, it seems that you are under the impression that you can manipulate the system, jump over other qualified officials, and are entitled to special treatment because of your networking.[2]

As I read it, it seemed he was referring to the support I'd received from people like Red Cashion and Johnny Grier, but both Red and Johnny got behind me right away based on the evidence of what I could do at the camps. If in doing my best work I happened to impress officials and clinicians—and the college supervisors there to hire—and if he wanted to call that networking, then, yes, absolutely, I networked my butt off!

For him to claim I flouted his meritocracy didn't ring true at all for me, considering I knew full well he'd rather "go with six officials before putting a chick on the field." How was his stance fair and equitable? How was his approach devoid of politics and manipulation? The integrity of the game starts with the officials. What kind of integrity is exhibited by passing around someone else's private e-mails?

The most devastating part for me at the time was reading his conclusion, this single-sentence paragraph: "At this time the PAC-10 Officials [*sic*] choose not to invite you to the ASU scrimmages."

It's still frustrating to think about.

If women couldn't qualify as officials because they'd never played a down of football, what about all the men who'd never played? It didn't matter all the times I played the game for fun as a kid, all the times I was the one picked first.

The tone of the e-mail bugged me, especially where he threw in that I must consider myself "the voice of Arizona Football Officials in regard to the hiring process of the AIFA." I was getting backlash for nothing more than offering my opinion to someone who had asked for it.

I sent a measured reply, offering to sit down with him to discuss his concerns. And I suggested he come to one of my games to decide if my work stood on its merits. He wasn't interested in my response. They were the ones who decided which officials worked what games or scrimmages. They had the power to influence decisions by bringing names of promising individuals to supervisors who wanted to hire for their conferences. A football official's professional life expectancy was based on how closely one followed and met the criteria established by these men. If someone chose to undermine them, they could hamstring that person's opportunities and prevent them from succeeding.

As exasperated as I was, my problems with guys like these were just beginning.

Dan Evans forwarded me some e-mails he'd received.[3] Some Arizona officials had apparently been firing them off to him, condemning him for hiring me. Dan let me know that their notes didn't affect my employment status but thought it might be something I'd want to know. Turned out those e-mails had been sent from a fake account. Dan had sent me what I needed to know for the next meeting of Division I officials.

The weekly meeting was held at the home of a Pac-10 official. The first hour the group dedicated to the review of D1 game films. For the second part of the meeting, the D1 officials rotated in a different junior college crew, to comment on that crew's game film and to offer advice on their officiating. Since I was a newly hired supplemental official for the MEAC, I'd started attending the meetings every week. I knew how a couple of guys felt about me, but I wasn't about to let them tell me I couldn't attend. With a couple of Pac-10 officials supporting me and a couple who were neutral, there was a good mix present every week.

If anyone had issues with my officiating, this was the place to share it. That's why we met, so those with experience could help others figure out ways to improve for their next assignment. But apparently, some guys thought it'd be better to send e-mails from some fake account behind my back instead and close me out of the feedback loop.

I had to say something. For years, I'd taken everything dished out at me. I'd never spoken up for myself, just kept my mouth shut and head down and continued to make my own way. But I couldn't do it anymore. I'd always known well enough I couldn't rely on anyone else to make my dreams happen. They were *my* dreams after all. But I wasn't interested in following anyone else's guidelines or time frames of making my dream come true—or in having someone else decide whether I was allowed to dream at all.

Time for me to stop worrying about what others thought and just do what I felt I had to do. I'd brought copies of the e-mails sent to Dan. I threw them down on the table so all who'd attended would know I was aware I wasn't being supported by the group as a whole. I wanted to hear what they'd have to say.

Instead, I heard what the Pac-10 official hosting the meeting thought about it all. He took over the discussion pretty quickly—the guy can make his voice heard when he wants to. So I let him say his piece but knew I needed to finish this conversation with him after the meeting.

Afterward, though, everyone was so slow moving out the door. I couldn't wait any longer. I asked the host if we could talk in private.

He led me out to his backyard, and standing there in the grass, I confronted him. I asked him about those e-mails sent to Dan trying to sabotage my working as a supplemental official for the MEAC that November.

He and I went back and forth a bit under the porch light. I wasn't getting what felt like an answer, so I kept pressing until he finally blurted, "Some of the guys have a problem with you," he said, "because you're a woman!"

That did it. "*Some* of the guys?" The gall he had. "You're f—ing one of them! At least have the balls to say it to my face!"

"Well, I've been discriminated against my whole life in officiating for being fat," he said.

I couldn't believe the stupidity of what he was saying. "There's nothing I can do to change my gender," I said, "but you can lose weight!"

His wife poked her head out the door. She frowned. "It's getting a bit loud out here," she said.

We lowered the volume, but our exchange remained heated. We went around and around, and I finally shook my head and headed back into the house. We were getting nowhere. But enough was enough, and I could no longer remain silent. Maybe I'd done so for too long.

∾

That fall, I bumped up against complications at the youth level, too. My work assigning officials for NYS had been going so well that I was asked to assign officials for the fledgling Charter Athletic Association (CAA) (now the Canyon Athletic Association). The CAA had been created to provide competitive athletic competition for junior high and high school students. The new executive director there had worked basketball games with me at a rec center on the Pima Indian Reservation, and he said I was the first person he thought of for the job. He knew about my work providing top-quality officials through NYS.

He's a good guy. He likes telling the story that when we met, I didn't think he was a good basketball official, which always makes me laugh. I can't say he's the best I've ever worked with, but he's not the worst, either.

When he hired me, the CAA was still in its infancy stage and had roughly fifty schools in the association. Although fifty may sound relatively small, the job was not. All most people know when their child has a football game is that four or five officials show up to work. Most don't think about other games scheduled that same night or about how many officials have canceled the night before or even the day of the game. When you're assigning officials, though, you're scrambling to fill all those spots. The constant juggling and overcommunication needed can at times become overwhelming—especially when four different sports are in motion at once. Cancellations, forfeits, turn-backs, traffic, car accidents, illness, wrong venues, wrong times, rules interpretations, and ejections get sprinkled in every week, along with issues arising from parents, coaches, and athletic directors. Nine to five? Not this job.

All these complications I expected, though. What I didn't expect was how the Arizona Football Officials Association started pressuring members working for both CAA and AIA to choose a side.[4] Their push that fall for exclusivity seemed unnecessary. Seemed to me that limiting assignments available to officials unnecessarily limited the experience they could gain. Besides, if being assured of commitments was a concern, I've always told officials that if you accept an assignment, you need to keep that commitment. You don't turn it back for a more attractive game regardless of the association for which you work. Do it once, and you risk not being assigned any more games. Them's the rules, as you learn from your first assignment. That's why I'd understood that turning back the D1 basketball game I'd accepted for a high school football assignment could possibly end my basketball career.

Money can drive this decision. Pay can range from $20 for a youth basketball game on a Saturday to more than hundred bucks for a high school football game to several thousand for a Division I college game. That fall, officials had to also factor in the pressure that the Arizona Football Officials Association placed on them in regard to youth football as well. Many officials who liked working all kinds of games now couldn't. Some came to me saying they didn't know what to do.

"You're an independent contractor," I said. "Do what feels right for you."

They felt that in some cases, if they chose to work for me, it would affect what high school games they'd be assigned even when there was no scheduling conflict between the associations. The organization appeared to penalize associates if their loyalty wasn't crystal clear.

It took a while, but the board figured out their position wouldn't serve them well in the long run. In the end, the pressure was lifted, and officials felt more at ease taking on as many assignments as they wanted.

I was relieved that reasoning prevailed. Issues like this could give me a headache.

∾

All that was happening was taking its toll on me. I kept waking up feeling as if I had a hangover even though I didn't drink. As I started the day, my head felt cloudy. Sometimes the symptoms improved as I worked, and other times the pain developed into a migraine.

This had been going on for years. My doctor had referred me to a neurologist who administered every test possible to see if there was something more serious going on. We tried several different medications, but nothing seemed to work. The doctors couldn't say why this was happening. To rule out some things, they wanted to try a spinal tap, but that's where I drew the line. I'll be honest, it sounded terrible, and the idea of it scared me.

I've almost always been able to work through the worst of my headaches. I just set them aside. But during one game, a migraine set in that I couldn't shake. My vision blurred, and I couldn't think. I had to take a seat on the sideline. As bad as the headache was, I hated just sitting there more. I went back into the game. That time, honestly, I probably shouldn't have. But that's how it is when you're on a crew. You want to be out there with them. And when you're not, you feel as if you're letting them down.

So as that November rolled around, I had a lot on my mind. On top of everything else, I was preparing for my biggest opportunity yet working my first D1 game. And as referee, no less. All the different crews I'd been on, all the camps I'd attended, and all the crews I'd led had given me insights into different styles of officiating. Over the years, I'd considered what worked, what didn't, and how different approaches set different tones. To start, for the pregame, I didn't want to be the only one among the crew talking. A pregame isn't a lecture. Get each official to play a part, and you can begin team building. With that in mind, I e-mailed an outline to the crew, and I assigned each position something in particular to talk about, starting with the line judge, who'd speak to goal line mechanics, cross-field mechanics, forward/backward passes, and so on.

Though I knew how to prep for the pregame and for refereeing and was confident about stepping out on the field, I wasn't as familiar with what to do for travel arrangements for the conference. I'd never been to Delaware before. I'd be flying into Philly, and I'd heard that no matter what time you arrive, it's always rush hour getting to and from the airport. The logistics part I needed to research more.

Then Johnny Grier gave me a call, offering to pick me up from baggage claim and escort me to Delaware. Not only did he know the area, he'd once been supervisor for the MEAC. What a relief to know I wouldn't have to find my way alone. Plus, it makes sense, knowing what he did for Annice Canady, that he would help me as he could then, too. Interestingly, Annice's first game officiating for the MEAC had also been with Delaware State.[5]

It was good to see him. We chatted the whole way down to the hotel where my crew was staying and where I was about to hold my first pregame meeting. Johnny planned to stay over until the next day to watch the game. To think that someone I admired and respected so much would be interested in seeing me work my first D1 game—I was blown away. There are no words to express what having him there meant to me.

I had enough on my plate with preparing for what I was about to do, and I was nervous. Not the kind of nervous that I didn't think I was ready, just the good kind of nervous that keeps you on your toes. The meeting with the crew the night before went as planned. The guys seemed like a good crew and were ready to present the part asked of them, as expected. A few might have had some reservations, as anyone would when a new crew chief steps in—maybe in part because there'd been a ref within the league who'd been available and could have subbed that day. Instead, Dan had taken a chance on me when he didn't have to.

We were all as ready as we were going to be for the next day—game day. Thirteen years after first donning a black and white top, I walked along the sideline in a white cap, umpire at my side, ready to meet my first D1 coach for a pregame conference.

Delaware State wasn't having a great season that year, but they squeaked past Winston-Salem that afternoon. And Johnny gave me great reviews. I was buoyed even further when Dan let me know he'd heard I'd done well and that the MEAC's neutral observer, who is there at games to observe and report on the crew, had been "very complimentary" as well.[6]

Thank goodness I hadn't let fear stop me from sending one last e-mail to a person I wasn't sure remembered me. Over the years, one *No* after another had almost buried me completely until Dan pulled me out with his singular *Yes*. I kept working at what I loved. I worked hard, I worked at getting better. And when one door wouldn't open, I kept looking for another way through. That's what made the difference. I'd been ready to give up, yet kept trying to think of one more way. One more chance. Once more.

Only I didn't know what a toll the effort had taken on me.

16

CHARGED TIME-OUT

One night in January 2009, I had such a terrible migraine that I couldn't drive myself to the emergency room. Jen's brother and sister-in-law ended up taking me—we lived a street apart then, so we'd been hanging out quite a bit together.

By the time I was checked in, I could barely stand. My blood pressure had dropped to such dangerously low levels that I was admitted.

The doctors ended up keeping me overnight. They administered some much-appreciated pain meds. The next day, when it became clear what I had was more than a bad headache, they started running tests on me. They ran so many tests. Dad stopped by to see how I was doing. Mom had moved back to the state around this time, so she visited, too. I wasn't getting better, and the doctors couldn't figure out what was going on. One day became another. One test led to another. If we did a spinal tap, the doctors finally said, they could rule out other possibilities.

I'd heard this before. That remained the one test I didn't want to try, but they kept pressing. The procedure had always been a last resort; they convinced me that we'd now landed on that shore. I finally gave in.

Mom came to sit in the waiting room to be there for support while I was in getting the spinal tap. The one good thing about their keeping me so drugged up was it helped ease my anxiety over the test a bit.

But not completely. The doctor or nurse performing the procedure hit a nerve in my back. One whole side of my body seared with pain, and I screamed. It felt as if I'd been electrocuted.

Later, Mom said she heard me from out in the waiting room. She knew my scream. Mom seriously considered breaking down the door to get to me.

A nurse next to me asked what was wrong. I managed to tell her about the charge I still felt all the way down my left side. "I thought if she felt it anywhere," another nurse whispered, "it would have been on her right."

I knew where I felt it; I was crying from the pain and felt super emotional. What I had worried might happen had now actually happened. Something had gone wrong with the procedure.

I was wheeled back to my room. The tears were still welling in my eyes. My situation wasn't looking good. I was almost forty, and I didn't have health insurance.

Mom came up as soon as they let her. She looked as if she could use another cigarette. She asked if I needed anything.

My body still held so much tension from the procedure that I couldn't move.

"Can you give Tom a call?" I asked my mom. "Can you let him know?"

Mom looked at me, then picked up the phone.

If I could just see him, I'd feel better. This is what I thought, though we weren't together at the time. I couldn't begin to say when exactly we'd broken up. We were on and off and on and off so often and for different reasons. I thought at least he'd want to know. I thought he might want to see me.

He wasn't answering. Mom tried him again another time but still no response.

I was heartbroken.

Those days I was in the hospital, everything made me emotional. I was so doped up and so frustrated that the doctors had no idea what was going on. And then the morning after the spinal tap, when I woke up to go to the bathroom, things took a turn for the worse.

My legs had gone numb. I couldn't get up to get to the bathroom. I had to call the nurse.

This development brought a doctor to my room again. As he examined me, I couldn't feel his hands checking my legs. I couldn't feel the pin pricks. The nerve that had been hit had been damaged, he said. That's why my legs didn't work. The nerve damage had not only affected my ability to walk but also caused tingling in my hands and arms.

How long was I going to be like this? I wanted to know. I had to get back to work. I had MEAC games scheduled for the fall. I had my dream.

"Most likely," the doctor said, "the damage isn't permanent. But it could be."

I was a mess, and Tom still hadn't come to see me.

Right after the doctor visit, the phone rang. It was Dad. "Hey, how you doing?" he asked.

"Not a good day, Dad," I said, barely holding myself together. "Please don't come see me."

Dad respected my wishes. All I did was cry and sleep. I'm not one to make deals with God, but I was praying a lot those days, especially since God is the one I can always count on to be there for me.

I had so much medication pumping through my IV that I pretty much felt like a vegetable most of the time. From time to time, I'd wake up and turn on my computer. My buddy Scott had run over to my place to bring it to me so I could—through my fog—try to fix the problems with officials or game assignments that cropped up for games played while I was in the hospital. At this point, I was assigning officials for up to 160 schools for the CAA, and my company was managing 250 officials overall for both the CAA and the NYS, but mine was still a lean organization—which is to say, I was the only employee. If I wasn't doing it, it didn't get done. The CAA ran lean, too, with only one other full-time employee at that point: the executive director. He did his best to help me out, but it was a stretch for him, as that was not part of his normal day-to-day operations. I just didn't want games canceled or kids shortchanged because of me. I struggled to ensure that didn't happen.

And through all this, Jen kept trying to call, but each time she did, I was asleep. Finally, for once, I was awake when the phone rang. When I picked up, I heard Jen's voice. She was crying; she was that frustrated that we hadn't yet talked. She so desperately had been trying to call for so many days. She hated that she lived so far away and couldn't be with me.

Many friends did come in to see me or called, but I don't remember a lot of that time. One guy, however, I did remember—Pete Corrado, who worked softball, volleyball, basketball, and football for me and is now on staff with the CAA. He stopped in daily to check on me and see what he could do to help. "What are they doing to you?" he asked. "You're getting worse every day. They're killing you."

His words hit a nerve. I felt trapped in a nightmare. I wanted to shake myself awake, and I couldn't. A week before, I'd checked in with a headache, and now I couldn't walk.

With all my IVs—more than twenty of them—my arm started swelling. Some had apparently not been inserted correctly. Once, while my mom was visiting, a nurse poked me, trying to find a new spot for another IV. The nurse got it in, but I started bleeding out of my arm. The nurse had to ask Mom for help to get the bleeding under control.

It sure felt like my care and treatment were not being handled right. I was moved to another floor where the nurses were given strict orders to take very good care of me. The nurses seemed to be trying to not say too much in front of me, but I overheard them at times talking about how shocked they were I was in this condition. The hospital administration was investigating what happened.

Staying in the hospital was exhausting not only because of the meds they gave but also because nurses awakened me each night about every two hours to draw blood or perform various tests. When the physical therapist started coming to my room, she urged me to push past my exhaustion. All the exercises she had me do to strengthen my legs were designed to be done in bed. "You need to wake up," she said, "so we can do your exercises."

"If you want me to be awake," I said, "they have to stop giving me so much medication."

We went through this exchange each time, and each time, I tried desperately to wake up. Most exercises I did with my eyes closed.

After a few days of this, it was time for me to start getting back on my feet. I started on a walker with assistance from a nurse. I did laps around the nurses' station along with all the elderly patients also doing laps.

The new nurses asked, "What happened?"

I'd checked into the hospital with a headache, I said, and spread my arms as if to add, *And look what happened.* All they could do was shake their heads.

Once I could move around, my old training habits kicked in. I pushed through rehab until I was able to walk with the help of crutches. At this point, finally, I was able to leave the hospital. It had been two weeks since I'd walked into the ER.

The hospital administrator found no fault of the hospital for anything I had gone through. However, they managed to make sure that the health care assistance program approved me immediately. Without this help, who knows what I would have done. The bills topped a hundred thousand, but my responsibility with this assistance amounted to less than $600. They never did figure out what brought me in in the first place. God helped see me through that terrible time.

After my release, I kept the crutches until I felt strong enough to get around without them, which is the point at which they are more of a hassle than a help when using them.

Soon enough, I was mobile enough to go shopping again, which has always been among my favorite things to do. While out at the mall, I passed a kiosk where a gentleman was doing a demonstration. I stopped to watch.

He had some magnetic bracelets he said could help with nerve damage. With everything that had happened to me with the spinal tap, I figured I'd give it a try. And I liked the bracelet. I got one.

What I noticed wearing it was that I started waking up without a headache. I went back to the mall and bought more bracelets. I sent a couple to Jen. A friend who'd suffered tingling in her fingers for years heard about what happened. "Give me one of those magic bracelets," she said. Within a half hour of putting it on, the tingling went away. She wears one all the time now.

I still don't know what put me in the hospital or what kept me there. Or what caused my migraines for all those years. Only God has those answers. As difficult as the hospitalization had been for me, the timing couldn't have been better. With the worst of it happening in January, I had several months to get back to full strength before the start of the football season, and a truly incredible season lay ahead for me.

I thought I had time to get prepared.

෴

After my medical scare, I went out to visit Jen in California. While gone, everything I had of value was stolen. Now, I've never been one to get attached to worldly possessions—you know me, I gave away all those judo trophies—but that 1986 Super Bowl ball that Walter Payton signed I'd wanted to pass down to my nephews. Unfortunately, that ball had been taken, along with all the sports memorabilia I'd collected while working at the Batter's Box in the early 1990s—including autographs from Warren Moon (my favorite quarterback at the time) and John Havlicek (a Celtics legend). When I told Havlicek he'd be the only one signing that basketball, he said he'd better make it good then, and he did, signing a big *J* in cursive and extending the line out long enough to write the rest of his name on it. I'd loved all that memorabilia so much. Having it all stolen turned out to be a great reminder why I don't get attached to things: It hurts when they're gone.

After that, all I wanted to do was focus my attention on officiating. So when Dan Evans extended an offer to me to work as a MEAC crew chief for the entire next season, I was all the more grateful to be so supported and encouraged. Officiating gave me something to look forward to, offering a break from what, at times, felt a bit hopeless. The focus needed during a football game forced me to set everything else aside if I were to have any success. While that level of intensity might be a challenge for some, for me, it served as a relief.

17

INTEGRITY OF THE GAME

For the first game of my first full season as referee, the crew planned to arrive dressed in our uniform. Usually, we changed at the stadium, but those on the crew who'd worked Bethune-Cookman before said it was better to avoid the locker room as much as you could. Especially when it rained, and the forecast called for rain.

I thought they were exaggerating until I walked through the locker room door. They were right—that locker room was worse than any I've ever had the privilege to use. It was super small, with nothing in there but a couple of old metal chairs. To make things worse, it did rain that day, and the rain leaked into puddles on the locker room floor and onto the chairs. There was no place to sit.

I wish I could tell you more of what I remember from that first game, but I cannot. My second game, however, was unforgettable, being played in the old Giants Stadium in the Meadowlands, where the Jets and the Giants then played. Every season, the MEAC has one or two games called classics in which select teams play in NFL stadiums. For this one, Morgan State was designated as the home team.

There's something about officiating in an NFL stadium. Just a couple of years before, I'd worked in a brand-new one, and here I was in an older one. Something shifted within me that day. I'd just started with the MEAC, but walking up that sideline as a Division I crew chief made me think about what next step I wanted to take for a dream I'd first given voice to a decade earlier.

Whatever thrill I felt in that moment had to be held down and pushed aside to remain focused. I had a job to do—I was stepping into a pregame conference with my umpire and the first of both coaches. Meeting a coach for the first time, you don't know what to expect. Often, they don't know what to expect on meeting me. The formalities of normal pregame protocol usually carry you through, starting with a hand respectfully extended during the introduction. I typically ask if the players were legally equipped and maybe inquire about any trick plays or if they had any questions for us.

It's a minor formality that takes place before every game, but for me, it's a way to learn a lot about a coach. What I found in other levels while officiating held true at the Division I level as well. Most coaches seemed perfectly fine with a female working their game, giving me the benefit of the doubt. So when a coach is open and appears comfortable, the meeting might last a bit longer. But when a coach thinks having a woman on the field is a tough pill to swallow, they can turn quiet and aloof, acting as if my presence at our meeting is a bother. They tended to direct their attention and all their questions toward the umpire. After all, what could I possibly know about their rules questions? In a situation like this, it's on me to be professional and show them what I can do. I make sure to answer their questions, even if they give me no eye contact. Other times, I'd encounter the kind of coach who fell in the middle of this spectrum, starting out all business—not rude but not welcoming, either, reserving judgment based on my performance.

Morgan State coach Donald Hill-Eley probably fell into this middle group. When we first met, he even seemed to test me a bit. Who could blame him? Not only was I the first female crew chief in Division I, but I was also a white female officiating in a college conference whose full members were historically black colleges and universities (HBCUs). Once he realized I knew what I was doing, his view of me seemed to evolve, and our relationship changed. Our pregame meetings became more open and welcoming. The respect was mutual—many of his players ended up on the all-MEAC team, and for several years, he'd have one named defensive player of the year.

What's worked for me in winning over a coach is communication. When asked a question, you need to answer it. You have to know the rules and be able to enforce penalties without lengthy discussions. Take the data given, sort it out, and administer as if it's another routine call, no matter how complex it may be.

At times, I've also gained credibility with coaches by finding ways to help them choose to accept or decline a penalty. A coach on the sideline might be signaling to decline the penalty, but when I know that wouldn't be advantageous, I'll simply say, using a controlled voice, "Coach, I am not going to decline it. Instead, I'll give you additional yardage as well."

Any ref can recite and penalize a false start or offside, but when a situation arises that a penalty results in an unfamiliar but advantageous administration, you have now presented yourself as someone who knows what's going on. The shocked looks on their faces or the softly spoken thank-you are small gestures signaling their acceptance of my presence on the field.

The demeanor in which you handle a chaotic situation also gains trustworthiness with players and coaches. In the final minute of a tight game, when a clock that should have stopped keeps running, a perfectly sane person can lose his or her mind. "Shannon," the coach will shout, "the clock is running. The clock is running!" He comes unglued, screaming and jumping up and down on the sideline.

In this situation, I can just calmly say, "Coach, the clock can run down to zero. It's okay. I've got this. There are 24.4 seconds left. I'll have them reset it." As officials, it's our responsibility to look at the game clock after every play.

It takes many different skill sets to be a referee of a crew, and not everyone can do it. From the start, I felt at home in that position. It takes leadership qualities and strong communication skills. Being a leader isn't about being the star of the show, it's about bringing everyone up to their highest level of work. In addition, communicating effectively is essential, like when you need to flip on your mic to announce a penalty. It's all tied together. Before I became a ref, the only practice I had speaking in public (not counting Bible Quiz) was in a junior college class on public speaking. I've never been afraid of the microphone and have never shied from the chance to turn it on and speak in front of a crowd, no matter the size. Talking clearly and authoritatively in front of fans without stumbling or hesitating allows me to demonstrate confidence and again gain credibility. And when I need to talk one-on-one with coaches, being able to give quick, strong reasons as to why a rule applied (or why it didn't) has helped my reputation as a ref.

As an official, you want to establish rapport not just with the coaches but with the players, too. Red Cashion was known for his camaraderie with his crew and the coaches and the players, and he's always been a good ref to emulate. Communication helps in this respect, too. Who doesn't like hearing, *Good job, good job*? And when the quarterback throws the ball, you call out, *Ball's gone, ball's gone* so the defenders know to slow up to avoid hitting the quarterback.

The key is to build rapport from the start. You never know when you might need to draw on it, as I would eventually need to with Coach Hill-Eley.

❧

The 2009 homecoming game I refereed was between Florida A&M and Norfolk State. The fans came just as hyped for the quality of the bands as they did for the quality of the football. The excitement was justifiable because Florida A&M has one of the greatest bands among the teams in the MEAC.

The members of the crew who'd worked this game in the past had given a heads-up as to how large the crowd would be, but I didn't fully understand or comprehend it until I stepped on the field. People had come out in droves for the homecoming game and the halftime show. The stands were packed, and the crowd had spilled out around the perimeter of the field. Outside the gates, many more milled around. I'd never seen a game so packed. The whole stadium buzzed with energy and excitement. What a truly awesome environment to work in.

With homecoming and with the popularity of the bands, halftime was extended to allow them plenty of time on the field. This halftime show went well beyond the allotted time. Norfolk's coach grew agitated over the delay of the start of the second half.

He came to me to complain. His frustration was clear, and he intended to let me know all about it. Around the same time, I was notified about a phone call for me coming from the press box.

It was Dan Evans, supervisor of officials for the MEAC.

"Drop a flag for delay," he said, "but don't penalize them with any loss of yardage."

I was glad for his expertise in such a rare situation. But even with the flag, the band played on in their tall hats and swinging orange capes. The Marching 100 had a fantastic show, and they had more of it, even playing a little Earth, Wind, and Fire. The crowd ate it up. And the band wasn't marching off the field yet.

The phone rang again. This time Dan had a different set of instructions. "Mark the yardage off against the home team."

The administrative delay of game came with a ten-yard loss to be enforced on the kickoff, and so that's what we did.

The game was delayed, but that performance was worth it to me and to many others. Watching that band counts as one of my fondest memories.

❧

I admit I have had my moments on the field when I haven't maintained my cool. For me, this happened when the problem on the field didn't lie with a player or a coach or even a band but with an official on my crew. Somehow, when an issue like this cropped up, we often seemed to be working one of Morgan State's games.

I'd already been refereeing one full season for the MEAC when Morgan State hosted South Carolina State in a nationally televised game. The Bulldogs quarterback handed the ball off to his running back, who was hit and then fumbled. Morgan State recovered the fumble—but during the play, while the ball was still loose, the head linesman blew the play dead.

When the information came to me from the calling official, the camera caught me mouthing, "You gotta be f—ing kidding me." The words were out of my mouth before I realized the camera was panning back its focus on me. Not one of my finer moments.

I took a deep breath and turned on my mic. "There was an inadvertent whistle while the ball was loose," I announced. "And the down will be replayed."

You can imagine how an inadvertent whistle like this can kill a team's momentum. With good reason, errors like this in officiating can draw instant ire from a coach whose team should have benefited from the play. But when I explained to Coach Hill-Eley that, although they recovered the fumble, I had to give the ball back to South Carolina State, he handled it much better than some coaches would have. He was rightly disgusted, but he accepted what I said and moved on.

Overall, Dan Evans must have considered my work solid since he placed me on one of two crews for playoff consideration should our conference receive the call to work. He told me the great news the week before my last regular-season game. I was flying high about being selected until I received a call back from him a few days later. He had to tell me that he didn't know why, but the two referees he'd recommended had been pulled off the playoff list by the commissioner. Dan never received an explanation.

The supervisor of officials is responsible for making these decisions without interference from the commissioner of the league. The supervisor is the one best suited to know which officials to assign to which games, including the playoffs—not the commissioner, who doesn't even know the officials. Instead, his duties are rooted in administration.

Dan continued to be supportive of me, but I didn't get a call the next year at playoff time. I figured I hadn't been selected. Years later, I found out he'd turned my name in again, and again it had been pulled. He said he didn't want to tell me because he didn't want me to get my hopes up just to have them taken away as they had been before. He was one of the guys I could count on to look out for me. As with everything else I'd worked hard for, that support helped—but I still needed to find other ways to show I could do the work if I wanted to keep progressing in my officiating.

∼

Even after refereeing for the MEAC for a few years, I still attended clinics in order to be seen. I hoped to move up to a higher D1 conference someday. In March 2011, I signed up for the prestigious Tom Beard Clinic. The classroom sessions were held at Morgan State. The main scrimmages would be held at colleges in the surrounding area. The best one you could be assigned to was the one at Rutgers University, which at the time was a member of the Big East. (It would join the Big Ten a few years later.) I kept my fingers crossed to get a chance to work the Scarlet Knights' scrimmage since that's where the legendary Jerry Markbreit would be observing.

We started with classroom sessions before working any scrimmages. After lunch, while I was mingling with some other officials, the Morgan State coach came up to me.

I prepared myself for what he'd say. I couldn't help thinking about what that camera had captured me saying after that inadvertent whistle.

"You know, you do a good job, Shannon," Coach Hill-Eley said kindly. "I've never had a problem with *you*, but some of the officials on your crew are making you look bad." He went on to say that he'd told the MEAC office I was a good referee and that they needed to surround me with better officials.

As luck would have it, Carl Johnson, the supervisor of officials for the NFL at the time, was standing a couple feet away from us. I said, "Hey, if that's the way you feel, Mr. Johnson is standing right over there. Could you tell him you like my work?" We were joking around then, but I wasn't completely kidding. I didn't know yet that by the next year, Carl would be looking for me at a finish line. I didn't know what I'd have to go through to get there.

For now, all I could see was my next step—getting the ref assignment I'd hoped for while at the Tom Beard Camp. And I got it! I drove to Rutgers, elated to be headed to where retired NFL referee Jerry Markbreit would be evaluating officials. He'd refereed for the NFL for twenty-three years. You may know him as the ref who made the famous Holy Roller call in a game between the Oakland Raiders and the San Diego Chargers in 1978, or you might have read his sports columns in the *Chicago Tribune*, which ran during football season until 2008. Along with Red Cashion, Jerry Markbreit has served as the face of refereeing for the NFL for years— his likeness has been used as the ref depicted in NFL video games.

At the clinic on that March afternoon, I rotated every ten plays with another chosen referee. We worked for more than three hours, which seemed much longer because this was one of the coldest days I could remember. My blood had thinned after living in Arizona so many years. I tell you, though, I would have worked another three hours in even colder weather to get as much advice as I could from such a football powerhouse as Mr. Markbreit. (Yes, I called him "Mr. Markbreit." It seemed only right.)

When the scrimmage ended, he met with the crew in the officials' locker room to discuss what he had seen. We got to spend about twenty additional minutes with the legend. After finishing his thorough evaluation with the group, he asked if he could talk with me alone.

He waited for the other officials to leave. "I want to tell you something," Mr. Markbreit said, after everyone else left. "And I am not sure how to say it."

I could tell he wanted to make sure that what he said came out the right way, and I waited until he was ready.

Finally, he continued. "When I watched you work," he said, "I didn't see a female out there. I just saw a good official."

This man, whom I had looked up to for so many years, had paid me one of the greatest compliments I could ever have dreamed to receive. That was exactly how I'd hoped to be seen out there on the field.

Mr. Markbreit had more to say. He answered some questions I had. Our time together flew by. I couldn't believe he spent a whole hour with me. At the end, he said if there was anything he could do for me, to please let him know. He said it again in his letter of recommendation.

At that moment, all my struggles and all my battles seemed a little further away.

18

UNSPORTSMANLIKE CONDUCT

Not everyone I worked with that fall would have given me such glowing reviews. While working down at North Carolina A&T, my three deep officials missed throwing a flag on the opposing team for twelve players on the defense late in the fourth quarter. Ultimately, this did not decide the game, but A&T's coach was upset by what happened. A short time passed before Coach Broadway called me over to his sideline to talk about a different play. After our exchange, I started to walk back to my position when he grabbed my arm.

I didn't flinch. I looked him right in the eye and called him out on it. "Don't touch me!" I said, using my sternest voice.

My tone mattered. I wanted to make sure my reaction conveyed that he was not intimidating me and that I would not allow him to do that ever again. I could have flagged him, which is typical when a player or coach touches an official, but at that point, my words were more important than throwing the flag. He'd been dismissive of me since our initial pregame meeting. He needed to know my authority came not from a flag but from within me.

Two weeks later, my crew was down in Tallahassee, where Florida A&M University (FAMU) was hosting North Carolina A&T. Facing the pregame routine with A&T's coach felt like facing a trip to the dentist's office. The way I saw it, it was my job to walk through the routine, and regardless of his noticeable lack of respect and professionalism, I was going to do my best to uphold the standards of a true professional. I'd approach him and introduce myself, and from there, I'd ask the standard questions and end it.

But the FAMU–A&T pregame conference with Broadway was worse than the last one. Normally, the meeting with the head coach takes place on the field. My umpire and I scanned the field, looking for Broadway. He was nowhere to be found. After a few minutes, we spotted him off the field on a bench behind the sideline and near the stands. When we approached and while we were with him, he gave us no eye contact, no handshake, and no respect. He didn't even stand up.

So we had the briefest pregame conference possible.

"Everyone legally and properly equipped?" I asked. Certain questions a ref needs to ask. "Any questions?"

We did what we could from our end.

"Alright," I said, "good luck. Have a great game."

The game started without any problems. Things began to head south at 5:58 in the second quarter, when A&T received the kickoff and ran the ball to the forty-five-yard line and out of bounds. Two flags were thrown during the play. One was for an illegal block in the back by A&T at the eighteen-yard line and the other a late hit by FAMU at the end of the run. This is a classic case of live-ball/dead-ball fouls, which are enforced in that order. We marked the first penalty off half the distance back (nine yards) to the nine-yard line. After that enforcement, we added fifteen yards for the late hit, bringing the ball back up to the twenty-four.[1]

Over on the sideline, Coach Broadway started yelling—loudly. He slammed his play sheet and headset to the ground.[2] He called a time-out, demanding an explanation as to how they could run the ball to the forty-five but now had to start on the twenty-four. I summarized the fouls called and the enforcement of each. I could tell by his reaction that my clarification of events fell on deaf ears.

"You don't know what you're doing," he said.

I headed back to the middle of the field to continue the game because there was no convincing him that what we had done and how we did it were, without a doubt, correct.

As the half was coming to an end, I was looking forward to heading to the locker room to regroup. But with forty-two seconds remaining in the second quarter, A&T punted the ball, and the field judge threw a flag for kick-catching interference (KCI). When the play ended, he blew a funny whistle—a series of short tweets—to alert me of the penalty. The back judge came in to confer with him, offering information as to what he observed during the play, as is common. With seven officials on the field, we are bound to have more than one set of eyes seeing any particular play. Sometimes a secondary official has the better view and sees something different than the primary official.

Once their brief discussion was over, they provided me the information on what they decided, which was KCI, so I made the announcement. Coach Broadway was visibly and vocally unhappy about it and even more so a couple of plays later when FAMU kicked a field goal and tied the game.

We went to halftime and started to make our way off the field toward the locker room. A crew member who had been a little behind the rest of us noticed Broadway making a rapid beeline toward me, which prompted the crew member to pick up the pace to catch up to me.

As Broadway got closer, he again questioned the KCI call. "How could you allow that to happen?"

I tried to respond, but before I could, he got up to my face, as close as he could without touching. "You're f—ing terrible," he said, his voice rising, the heat of his breath on me. "You don't have a f—ing clue!"[3]

All I wanted to do was get to the locker room. Nothing I did or said seemed to convince him of anything. I hadn't been the calling official on these plays—I'd just relayed information brought to me—but I was the referee. Whatever the crew did, right or wrong, fell on me.

The crew member with me tried to help me get away from him.

The coach was still going, still dropping the f-bomb, still saying— shouting—how horrible I was.

We somehow made our way to the area close to the officials' locker room. At this point, the entire A&T team and coaching staff were blocking the entrance to the locker room door. That's thirty-five men crowded around, most suited up in pads and full gear, many of them yelling and cursing, repeating what the coach had been saying.

So we tried moving farther and farther away as much as we could. A policeman pushed through to try to calm things down. A security guard from FAMU came over and escorted us down the hallway to our locker room via a far side door in the back.

As we crossed the threshold into our room, one last perfectly timed, ear-splitting curse sailed out of the coach's mouth.

For the rest of halftime, the police officer stayed by our door. "If you need anything, just let me know," he said. He gave me his contact information in case I needed his testimony as to what had happened.

After halftime, I assessed a fifteen-yard unsportsmanlike penalty on the head coach for his actions at halftime. That seemed like such a minimal punishment for something that required bringing in not only an officer of the law but also FAMU security.

I knew I'd handled things correctly, as was confirmed in the (standard) report e-mailed by the neutral observer at the end of a game. He complimented how I handled the situation. Once we had made it safely out of the stadium, I immediately called Rosie Amato, who'd replaced Dan Evans as supervisor of officials. I told him what had happened and followed up with an e-mail outlining the events. All the guys on my crew did the same. Rosie copied me when he forwarded my summary of events to Raynoid Dedeaux, who was the second in command behind the commissioner of the MEAC. Rosie added his take, too. "Unbelievable" was what he called the coach's conduct. "No one should have to put up with this kind of conduct," he wrote, pointing out that when I "tried to explain the rule enforcement to [the coach] he got more abusive." Rosie made clear what consequences should follow: "This coach should be fined and not be able to be on the sideline with his team for the rest of the season." Rosie acknowledged how emotions can sometime get the best of us "during the heat of the game, but that does not justify this kind of conduct." There had to be a limit. "If one of my officials addressed a coach in this manner he would be suspended for life."[4]

I could almost picture Rosie's thick eyebrows knitting together as he wrote this. It was nice to know he had my back.

The following Monday, Dedeaux pulled me in on a conference call with him, Rosie, and the commissioner, Dr. Thomas. Again, I started recounting the details of what took place. In my phone call, in the e-mail exchange, and in our discussion, the validity of my call never came into question. But the commissioner wanted to know why I had not tossed Coach Broadway out of the game.

"I couldn't—"

"What?" Dr. Thomas interjected. "What do you mean you couldn't?"

"NCAA rules don't support the ejection," I said.

"That's correct," Rosie said. "We would not eject him."

Even still, Dr. Thomas dug in on his point that he was disappointed in my decision not to eject the coach.

I was floored. I had abided by the rules, yet now I was being reprimanded for doing so. If I had tossed him, I could see the headline now: *Female Referee Can't Handle Irate Coach—Goes Outside NCAA Rule, Kicks Him Out of Game.*

Instead, I stayed true to myself—and to the rules—and did what I have always done. I remained calm and professional and did my job as if none of the hostile actions had taken place. I'd even waited until after halftime to throw the flag on the coach for his unsportsmanlike behavior.

At the time, the MEAC neutral observer, who by definition was there to observe everything, had complimented me on the job I'd done. Now the office wanted to scold me for it. I was damned if I did and damned if I didn't.

Ironically, the behavior that the conference office deemed ejection-worthy (and in my opinion suspension-worthy) in the end was found punishable by little more than a slap on the wrist. Dr. Thomas issued a public reprimand of the coach, stating that "the conference expects all student-athletes, coaches and athletic staff to demonstrate good sportsmanship before, during and after all athletic events." In addition, for the next game—and for only the next game—Coach Broadway was removed from the sideline and placed in the press box to coach.[5] I'm sure that stung.

When that game ended in a loss, though, Coach Broadway had some words to share—"not that he suggested his presence on the field would have made a difference," as the *Herald-Sun* put it.[6] "'We're just not good enough to win,' Broadway moaned. 'We're just not good enough right now.'"[7] But Broadway knew how to bring the Aggies along after that first year, and he would, winning five national championships by the time he retired.

Who knew what lay ahead for either of us then? As for me, by the end of the season, I found myself losing heart. Every weekend, I was traveling, usually from coast to coast. The money I spent on airline tickets and lodging was more than what I was paid in game fees. For three years, the weekly losses had been worth it, given how much I loved officiating. Yet with this latest season, I found it difficult to motivate myself to keep looking for another way forward. I continued applying to other conferences, and I applied everywhere. Many of them showed interest, but my efforts kept coming up short. I was beginning to think that my longtime dream of someday working in the NFL was nothing more than that—a dream.

Which meant that it might be time finally for me to quit. And that meant I could start thinking about getting a dog.

19

MY LUCKY CHARM

Heading into the summer of 2012, I was sure my time officiating was over. I'd become stuck in the MEAC, unable to advance—even though my list of references included both Red Cashion and Jerry Markbreit. Mr. Markbreit had sent me a copy of his recommendation letter, so I got to see that he'd written about being "very impressed with [my] mechanics and field presence" and with how "very dedicated" I was.[1]

Yet my heart wasn't in it anymore. I'd bumped into so many walls trying to get hired by another conference. I'd told myself I wouldn't get a dog until I was done once and for all with officiating. At this point, getting a dog was sounding better than officiating.

I set my heart on getting a puppy, a little Shih Tzu. I called a bunch of breeders and drove all around Arizona to see their setup. Out in Apache Junction, Puppy Love Shih Tzu had just had a litter of puppies. A male was still available.

"Can I come now?" I couldn't hop in my MINI Cooper fast enough.

Just thinking about a puppy filled me with excitement. It'd been too long since I'd felt like this. The whole way from Tempe, I had to resist the urge to speed.

Four puppies falling over each other are as cute as you imagine. Two were already spoken for by others, the breeder said. The runt she planned to keep. The one with a spot on his head in the shape of a horseshoe she said could be mine. She called that one Lucky, and he sure was cute, but I kept stealing glances over at Squirt, the runt who had to be bottle-fed.

I stayed an hour enjoying all the pups, trying to fall in love with little Lucky. As excited as I'd been, my heart wasn't with him. I left, promising to think about Lucky.

A couple of days later, I went back to try once again to connect with that little guy, but the one I wanted was Squirt. Once the breeder realized how much I loved Squirt, she broke down. "He's yours," she said. All the extra time I'd spent there talking with her, she'd learned what a good home I could provide him.

I couldn't believe it. He immediately became my best bud. I didn't want to do anything without him by my side. I smothered him with hugs and kisses constantly, probably more than he wanted, and my new favorite hobby became taking pictures of him. For months, I slept on the couch since it folded out into a bed much lower to the ground than the one in my bedroom. I didn't want to risk his falling out or trying to jump down until he was a bit bigger. He wasn't Squirt anymore. He was my little Cooper.

Not long after I got him, I had to go to San Diego for a few days to supervise officials I'd assigned to work at a youth football tournament. Mentally, I'd been preparing myself to reach out to Rosie to let him know I wouldn't be returning to the MEAC. I'd call once I got back home, I told myself. It was time. It felt right. Besides, I had my new best friend waiting for me.

News of what was happening with the NFL officials started floating around. The contract had expired the year before, but negotiations were under way to increase pay, improve retirement benefits, and bring on three more crews as part of their proposed transition to making some officiating roles full-time positions. But negotiations over a new collective bargaining agreement had apparently broken down. The NFL had officially locked out their officials. On June 4, the organization began hiring replacement officials.

In San Diego, I got an e-mail from Rom Gilbert. He'd been the neutral observer during the North Carolina A&T game. He also happened to be an NFL scout. He had an important question for me: Would I be interested in working for the NFL during the lockout?

Absolutely!

I went for a run down the beach, the waves lapping on a shore, not far from where a coach's son once rescued me under a pier and where a youth pastor had proposed as the sun sunk into a watery horizon. I ran past these memories and into my future. I ran as far as I could go.

Just a few weeks before, I'd been energized at the prospect of getting a puppy. Now I had a shot at being an NFL official after all. Turned out Cooper was my lucky charm.

I still had to clear a few last hurdles. I prayed nothing would stand in my way. Back at home, I had an appointment for a background check with Ben Nix, a former FBI special agent who had joined the NFL Security Department. When meeting someone new in officiating, I never knew what to expect. Sometimes they balked simply because I'm a woman, even before they get to know me. So I wasn't sure which way our meeting might go. But from our first handshake at a Starbucks, Ben seemed open and willing to find out more about me. He asked a lot of questions regarding my character and history. I was forthcoming and truthful and hid nothing—not even that I had played in a couple of events at the WSOP. I left the meeting believing he'd be supportive in his write-up, and I found out later that he was.

The background check was merely the first step. Next, I'd need to attend one of two clinics offered in which the NFL would evaluate applicants to decide who should be hired. Off I went to Texas.

As soon as I got to Dallas, I checked into the hotel and got to work. First, we got in line for weigh-in, and then we were shuttled off to a track at a local high school so evaluators could gauge our physical fitness. We were put into groups of fifteen to twenty officials. Billy "White Shoes" Johnson was our leader.

I knew who he was, of course. As a kid, I watched him do the Funky Chicken whenever he scored a touchdown. He was the one who started the tradition of dancing in the end zone when he was a kick returner with the Houston Oilers. He wasn't that tall of a guy, but he sure was fast. Three times he made first-team all-pro.

And now Billy "White Shoes" Johnson was standing there, dressed in his workout clothes, shorts, and a T-shirt, ready to lead us. We found out the nickname wasn't from any end zone celebration but from high school, when he dyed his shoes as part of a dare.

My group of about fifteen hopefuls waited for our turn on the field. One of the guys in my group had just moved to Arizona. He'd been working as a Division III official in Texas and hoped to go to up to the pros now, too.

Together, we all watched the groups ahead of us run through drills. At the start of each new skill, Billy said, "We won't be doing that." I thought that meant he'd cut us some slack on some of the drills, but that wasn't at all what he meant. The physical testing requirements started with "stretching and agility." When I say stretching, I mean everything but stretching took place. We ran forty-yard sprints and did lunges. We alternated shuffling, backpedaling, and running from cones placed twenty yards apart. We did so much more. As he ran us through these paces, he cheered us on, motivating us to greatness. After all this, we had to do a timed half-mile run.

On the last lap, I was exhausted—several of us were. One guy didn't even finish, and it was just a half a mile. But there at the finish line stood Carl Johnson, whom I'd met the year before at the Tom Beard Clinic. Seeing the supervisor of officials for the NFL waiting at the end for us gave me the surge of energy I needed. I sprinted the rest of the way.

With physical testing complete, the next stop was a classroom to review and discuss rules. There are numerous differences in officiating between college football rules and the ones in the NFL, particularly with regard to penalty administration. I pored over the rule book. I wanted to be fully prepared should I make the cut.

In those interminably long days waiting for the call, my pup was a great distraction. I had a camera on the little guy at all times. I was like a new parent documenting baby's every milestone with how constantly I was videotaping or taking pictures of my new puppy. Everything he did seemed like the greatest thing in the world.

Besides, by taking pictures, I kept my phone in hand. A call or an e-mail would reverberate enough to feel it. I had no idea just how much it would.

20

MAKING *HERSTORY*

My heart jumped up into my throat when I got the e-mail from a friend who'd been working as a replay official for the NFL. The subject line of his e-mail blared at me: *The Scab List.*

This wasn't the actual list of replacement officials, was it? I scanned the names listed. I checked it again. My name wasn't on it.

But I caught myself. Surely the NFL wouldn't send out an e-mail with a subject line of *The Scab List.* The logic of that finally clicked into place after I read what my friend wrote at the bottom under all the names: *I wanted you to have this so you would be prepared in case you weren't hired. I didn't want you to be disappointed.*

The problem was, I was disappointed. Though it was a fake list, it still bugged me that I wasn't on it and that the guy who hadn't even finished the last required run was.

I called Ben Nix from the NFL Security Department and told him about the e-mail. Within twenty-hours of our conversation, the NFL office was calling, asking how I got the list. I didn't want to tell. I pleaded with the gentleman not to make me. I didn't want to throw my colleague under the bus. Besides, he'd meant well. He'd meant to prepare me for the worst.

The next day, on June 4, the NFL sent the real roster to the officials—and I was on it! I was elated! I'd been assigned as a line judge, but I'd be a referee in training as well. I was given both a black and a white hat.

Being hired by the NFL, in and of itself, was a huge step for such a male-dominated institution. For them to put a woman in the referee position would have been more of a leap. Maybe too much of one. Instead, the NFL put me on a crew with referee Donovan Briggans, who was entering his second season as a referee in a Division II conference. I remembered working a basketball game with him before—back at New Mexico State, I think—so I was happy to be working with him again and grateful for the opportunity in the NFL.

A lot of officials work two different sports, but not many work D1 (or higher) for both. In the past, both Donovan and I had worked D1 basketball, and now we were both named as replacement officials.

After getting the official e-mail from the NFL, one of the first phone calls I made was to Rosie Amato, my supervisor for the MEAC. Late that spring, I had resolved to tell him I was going to hang up my hat that season. I had to tell him I wouldn't be available for a different reason now.

"What are you doing?" he asked after I'd already told him. He was so upset with me. "You could make it to the NFL without this!"

But I hadn't.

Many Division I guys hadn't applied because they didn't want to lose their college jobs when the lockout ended. For me, the timing felt right. My passion for the MEAC was gone. I was going to be done with it anyway, so this was my last and only chance for the NFL. It didn't matter what happened afterward. I had to go for it.

The labor dispute between the NFL and its referees' association had continued heating up that summer. In July, the association filed a complaint with the National Labor Relations Board, accusing the league of unfair labor practices and claiming the NFL had planned on locking them out all along. Hiring only a few officials from Division I and the rest from Division II schools and below put both officials and players at risk, they said, since officials from those levels wouldn't be prepared for a game that moved at pro speed. They were presenting their case to hold the media's attention and gain public sympathy, or else they'd lose their jobs for good.

I found out just how much the labor dispute had heated up when I returned to Dallas after the NFL hired me to attend a clinic to review rules and such. Down in Dallas, I ran into Chuck Stewart, who of course had always been in my corner. He was there as a replay official now, and that group wasn't among those striking. In the past, we'd always end up sharing a laugh about something whenever we talked. I was so glad to see his familiar face. I was smiling as I reached out for our usual hug hello.

But it didn't go as usual. "I'll hug you this last time," he said. "Then that's it. We're done."

My stomach sank. I couldn't believe it.

I knew my decision was not going to be popular with everyone, but I thought he would be one who'd understand. He'd been with me every step of the way and saw my hard work and how much I struggled to get a fair shake at times.

It was clear that was over now. From then on, I was cautious how I approached the guys who'd been there for me before.

My phone started ringing off the hook, and e-mails flooded my inbox. The media attention going into the first preseason game in San Diego was beyond anything I'd ever experienced.

In general, the NFL discouraged press interviews. They'd instructed us to decline them all and encouraged us not to be involved with social media. My rarely used Facebook account had begun blowing up with messages, so I ended up deactivating it.

But one particular aspect of the lockout the NFL seemed to want to bring before the public was that they'd hired their first woman official, so the NFL's vice president of communications coordinated a single conference call with all those requesting an interview with me. The call took place about a week before my first preseason game. About twenty news organizations were on the line, including reporters from CBS National News, CNN, and Good Morning America as well as those from outlets like *The Christian Science Monitor* and *Forbes*. Even a Dutch magazine was on the line.

The press pool took note that I had sixteen years of officiating experience. One of the first questions they asked was who'd been an instrumental influence for me during those years. I'd been thinking about this. Violet Palmer came to mind, considering what her breakthrough in officiating has meant for women. I had a few other names, too. At the top of my list, of course, was Red Cashion.

"I talked to Red recently," said one of the women reporters on the phone. "He said, 'That lady ref will be the best one on the field!'"

That put a big grin on my face. The whole call went well, in fact, with the tone of it being cordial and celebratory. Hearing about Red's faith in me had to count as my favorite part.

When it was over, more requests to speak to me continued to flow in. I was astounded by the number of people reaching out to congratulate me or to wish me luck—some people I knew, some I hadn't talked to in years, and many I didn't even know.

I was going in with "eyes wide open," as I told the AP. "She'll also come in with millions of eyes on her," they warned.[1]

And it felt like it, though my eyes—my focus—had to remain on the game and its rules. I spent countless hours poring over the *NFL Rulebook*. I kept it within constant reach. In it were the details that mattered.

People kept asking how I felt or how I was doing with everything. The two words I used to answer this question tended to include the words *a lot*! I had a lot to do in my time leading up to those first steps onto an NFL field—a lot to take in, a lot to absorb, a lot to wrap my mind around.

I should have expected it when Tom said he wanted to come to my first game. Frankly, though, I did not want him there. Our relationship wasn't in the best place then, but that's not the reason for my decision. I didn't want *anyone* to come, not even my mom. I didn't want to have to entertain anyone in any way. I did not want any additional distractions.

"If you come, you're not staying with me," I had to tell him. "I won't be able to see you at all. I want to focus only on what I'm there to do."

After all, this was going to be history in the making. I did not take that fact lightly, and I knew that it was important not only for me but for all women. Based on my performance, people would make decisions about what women could—or could not—do. I wanted to be focused on that and on that alone. I would see him when I returned home.

The day before the game, I flew to San Diego to meet Donovan and the rest of the crew for dinner and then a pregame conference. It seemed so familiar and so different to have the San Diego Chargers and the Green Bay Packers be the teams for which the crew discussed rules, mechanics, and game situations. We all wanted to do our best. We felt ready.

Once we finished, I headed to my room for my regular routine: a long bath with my rule book in hand. After that, rule book still in hand, I got ready for bed. I studied until I would (I hoped) fall asleep. Marriott hotel beds were my favorite, but I never slept well the night before a game.

When I woke up the next morning, it hit me. The time had come. What was about to happen was really happening—I was going to work on the greatest stage in professional sports. For years I'd worked so hard and had given my all to attain this goal. This was it. My dreams were coming true!

Then my phone rang. It was Carl Johnson, letting me know some of the union guys felt I shouldn't be allowed to officiate because of my poker playing.

ProFootballTalk.com had looked to a former NFL vice president of officiating for his thoughts. Mike Pereira was working as a football rules analyst for Fox. Even more pertinently, he'd played "a key role" in the last NFL lockout eleven years before. "In the normal background check process," Pereira claimed, I "would not have been hired."[2] Yet I'd disclosed everything about my poker playing to the former FBI special agent, and I'd stayed away from the tables since I started with the MEAC.

Other news outlets were picking up the story throughout the day. Some in the media didn't want the replacement officials to be working at all to strengthen the union's position.

I told Carl I appreciated him wanting to let me know what was being said. But I didn't see why that should stop me now. I couldn't let the media scrutiny get to me.

What could I do about it anyway? None of the reporters on the press call had asked about it. Later, when my time with the NFL was done, I'd see another NFL official at a poker table at Talking Stick. I pretended not to see him.

That morning before my first game, I didn't know what all was going to happen. All I knew was that I needed to maintain focus for the day. So I did what I do: continued my routine, took another hot bath—rule book still in hand—and prayed that I'd retain all I studied and that God would be with me every step of the way. In those days, I found myself returning to a constant state of prayer, and that helped me stay focused. I carried my prayer onto the field.

I wanted to do well. I wanted to prove the NFL commissioner right. In an interview not long after I was hired, he told reporters I was *well prepared*. "I think she'll do terrific," Roger Goodell said then. "So we're excited about that."[3]

The butterflies in my gut were in furious flight as I climbed aboard the shuttle to the stadium. I took a seat by myself and nestled by one of the wide windows. Not because I didn't want to interact or socialize with the other officials, but because I don't like small talk before a game, no matter if the conversation is silly or serious. There is a time and a place for that, and for me, it had to be after we finished working, not before.

I've always been this way, even as a kid. I remember my diving coach calling for silence when I climbed up onto the springboard. And when I was in judo, everyone knew to stay away from me while I sat in the stands, waiting to compete. I did not want to talk to anyone while mentally preparing for what I was about to do. Those who tried quickly realized that it was like talking to a brick wall, and they were happy to leave me alone.

I remained focused on the way to San Diego's field. When the bus pulled into Qualcomm Stadium, a broad-shouldered man from NFL security was waiting outside. He escorted us through a heavy steel door and down a long hallway to our locker rooms. My roller suitcase trailed behind me as our footsteps fell in sync and echoed.

The security guard came to a stop. "Guys, this is yours." He motioned to one of two doors. "Shannon, you'll be in the locker room over here." He gestured to the left.

I thanked him, my voice sounding calmer than I felt.

"And congratulations," he said, flashing a white smile. I couldn't help grinning back.

Then I stepped into my separate locker room, and the door closed behind me. Inside stood a gleaming row of metal lockers and a long wooden bench. Something about the place filled me with peace. I felt at home. That I belonged.

I rolled my black bag to an empty locker and unzipped the suitcase. Inside, my uniform lay neatly folded. I quickly changed into black pants and a striped shirt with the number twenty-seven on its back. As I draped the whistle around my neck, Mom's voice sounded in my head: *You'll do great!* Everyone I knew would be gathered in their living rooms all over the country tonight, cheering me on. I vowed not to let them down.

On my way out, I stopped before the mirror to tuck my ponytail under my cap with that NFL logo. I offered up a prayer of gratitude and asked God to abide in me every step of the way.

Outside the locker room, I met with the game clock operator to go over some instructions. (At the time, line judges had primary responsibility in case of a problem with the main clock.) In the distance, music blared across the field. Fans began to fill the seats. I was moments away from making NFL history. It felt exciting and also seemed right. I felt like I could finally breathe as I walked the field, waiting for the kickoff. The cameras were following me everywhere. I just kept on the move and stayed focused on what I was about to do.

The owners of the Chargers came down to meet me and asked if they could get a picture. I was naive and didn't want to do anything wrong. I'd been instructed to stay away from being photographed with fans or signing autographs. My goal was to represent the NFL in the most professional manner possible.

"Let me ask my supervisor if it's okay," I told the owners of the Chargers.

Then I walked over to Carl Johnson to run it by him.

Carl laughed. "Anything the owners want, you do."

Coach Norv Turner also wanted a picture with me. "This is history," he said, "and it will go on my wall."

I have that picture on my wall, too.

When you're in an NFL stadium and a pro game is about to start, everything feels bigger, more magnified. These field conditions were top notch, and there I stood on the home sideline. Ready. And then my first NFL preseason game was under way.

Not long into the first quarter, a defensive lineman came across the line fast, and the offensive lineman, who was clearly beaten, grabbed the defender's jersey and took him to the ground.

We officials have a saying in a situation like this: "When you're beat, you cheat."

I threw a flag for offensive holding. It was good knowing I'd clearly nailed the call. Later, I threw another flag for holding, and later still, I threw one for a defensive pass interference. All three were no-brainers.

Things weren't so clear cut for the flag that a fellow crew member had to throw. On this infraction, the penalty enforcement wasn't simple given the many differences between college and the NFL, especially with the rules all being so new to us at this point. As the yardage was being walked off, an assistant complained we were messing it up. He was right. I knew he was. I stepped in, and we tried to fix it. The assistant was appreciative of our efforts.

We got the enforcement closer to what it should have been. But we were still wrong. At a minimum, the ball should have been placed back at the line of scrimmage. This play still bugs me.

For the second half, it was business as usual while I was on the Packers' side of the field. I don't remember anything out of the ordinary taking place, though the AP reported that's when I heard boos from the hometown crowd when I called pass interference.

Note also that the AP judged that I "appeared to get [the call] right."[4] (Not that the AP is the final judge, but I do appreciate their unbiased reporting.) For what it's worth, I do remember Packers coach Mike McCarthy making a point of seeking me out as the clock wound down at the end of the game to shake my hand and let me know I'd done a great job.

Although I have worked countless football games and am confident in my abilities and though I felt this first game went well overall, it helped to get a nod of approval and recognition from both coaches, especially since Coach McCarthy is one of those all-time-great head coaches. Ray Anderson, NFL executive vice president of football operations at the time, was there and complimented us after the game, too. He was appreciative of how we'd helped the cause. Frankly, I think they wanted us to be successful so they didn't have to give in to the demands they were facing.

What capped off the experience for me was when Vanessa Streater, program director for Women Officiating Now, asked, "Would you be okay giving up your hat and whistle so that these items could be taken to the Pro Football Hall of Fame in Canton, Ohio?"

"Okay?" I asked. "I'd be honored!"

Even now, years later, it's hard to believe such a storied institution includes something of mine in a collection that encompasses the greatest football players, coaches, officials, and owners in NFL history.

Not everyone appreciated the work the crews did that day. A *Sports Illustrated* article complained that

> not a single current Football Bowl Subdivision official could be found among the 136 replacements. Instead, the league staffed up by drawing from the high school ranks and lower divisions, including some officials who had retired or been dismissed. (At least the situation has offered one breakthrough: Line judge Shannon Eastin, of the Mid-Eastern Athletic Conference, became the first female NFL official to work a game.)[5]

A friend had sent me the magazine. I didn't even know I was in it until I opened the envelope and flipped through the pages to find what he was talking about. I was surprised to find that the article inside about replacement refs began with a two-page spread of a photo of me, shot from behind, together with a Chargers tackle who was about a foot taller. The cutline reads in part that I'd "avoided the glaring mistakes of other replacements."[6] Considering how stingy *Sports Illustrated* had been with compliments that day, I'll take that one.

A few days after the game, Jen's brother invited me to a gathering at his house. He had taped the broadcast and wanted me to check out his favorite part of the game. What he queued up was a scuffle on the field between two players. The camera captured me breaking up a fight as ESPN commentator Jon Gruden said, "Way to go, Shannon; way to get in there!"

Breaking up a fight was no big deal because, as an official, that's what you do in a situation like that. However, it was extremely cool to hear him comment on it.[7]

It felt good to get the first game in the books. And I was glad it went as well as it did.

For week two, I'd already been assigned as an alternate to work in St. Louis, where the Rams hosted the Kansas City Chiefs. The NFL had to get the schedule out for the second week before week one games were finished. At first, I was disappointed but figured that the move was a fail-safe in case the female fell flat in the first game.

So, while in St. Louis, I stood on the sidelines as alternate. The line judge working my position was struggling, and I could see it. In his defense, he was not a wing official. He normally worked in the middle as an umpire. I couldn't just stand by.

I approached the NFL observer to ask if I could help the line judge during the game. "Yes, please do so," the observer said.

For the duration of the game, I backed up the line judge, aiding and helping him with mechanics. He was a great team player and was receptive to what I had to offer. Seeing as it was a preseason game, he came away from it relatively unscathed.

Now, with two preseason games in the books, the NFL would decide who would work on a crew and who would be alternates for the season.

At home, I pulled Cooper onto my lap and anxiously awaited seeing where the schedule would take me next.

21

LIVING THE DREAM

The NFL pulled together the crew from my first preseason game and sent us on to Dallas. At the risk of sounding overly confident, it did not come as a surprise that the NFL assigned me to the crew. I truly believe that, had the season gone the full distance, I would have proven myself as one of the strongest officials they had overall.

But at that point, we were still in preseason. The St. Louis Rams would play at Cowboys Stadium, as it was then known.[1] What an awesome venue—one of the best in the league. They do say everything is bigger and better in Texas. With training camp as well as two games behind me, I was more comfortable handing out tickets to people I knew. My mom could come, and Jen even planned to bring her son. She'd long been a Dallas Cowboys fan. But then Jen took seriously ill right before the game, so she and her son couldn't attend after all. That was heartbreaking.

But I had to stay focused. During the game, I was the covering official on a play as the clock was winding down to two minutes in the first half. As soon as the play ended, I looked at the clock and saw it stopped.

But an assistant coach starting challenging me that extra time had run. Since I didn't see that, I went to the deep official on my side to see if he had any additional information. He did not. No one of the crew had anything different to say indicating the clock was incorrect. I found myself finally having to say, "Coach, if what you're saying is what happened, then you're correct, and we missed it."

As an official, you don't want to be in a situation where you've missed something. But if you didn't see it, you can't make something up. If no one else on the crew has any additional information, then you have to move on. I did all I could, yet the assistant would not let it go.

Finally, Cowboys coach Jason Garrett jumped in. "That's enough," he said. "She gave you an answer!"

For the second half, as is custom for every game, I worked the other side of the field on Rams coach Jeff Fisher's sideline. I felt he was genuinely supportive of me and the other officials. We were, after all, learning (and applying) a complex set of different rules at an accelerated pace.

Not only are the rules different at every level; the rules and mechanics are also constantly being fine-tuned, addressing a range of concerns—from improving player safety to making sure the umpire is out of harm's way. These changes tweak important rules like those dealing with any illegal contact that targets defenseless players, and they tweak detail-oriented rules like those reconsidering which official should have primary clock responsibility (though all officials have some form of that responsibility).

As officials, it's our business to know all the rules and all the latest changes. And we've got to enforce them all correctly. It was important to follow the rules outside the game as well and represent myself as a professional. As part of that, I strove to follow NFL protocols, which stressed that we were there to do our job, not do interviews or take pictures. (Which was why I thought I needed permission for that pic with the owners of the Chargers.) Applying this rule seemed pretty black and white, but for me, sometimes it was difficult to decline requests to sign autographs or pose for a photo. Once a soldier in uniform approached me before a game and asked for a picture. How could I say no to a man who fights for our country? I couldn't. So I allowed a quick picture with him.

And there was the time before the game on Fan Appreciation Day when I heard someone calling my name. I glanced back toward the end of a long line of fans to see who it was. A woman waved at me. "My daughter loves you," she was saying. "Can she please get a picture with you?"

The answer was supposed to be no, but in turning back to the field, I caught a glimpse of the cutest girl with pigtails staring at me. A huge smile spread across her face. I could not resist this request. I strode over and told the woman to take it as fast as possible. I didn't want to get "caught" doing something I wasn't supposed to do.

For the next game I worked (the last of the preseason), the Houston Texans took on the Minnesota Vikings. At what was then Reliant Stadium, they put signs on both locker room doors for the officials. One just said *NFL Officials* and the other said *NFL Official Shannon Eastin*. It was so cool to have my name on mine. I thought it was a good sign. The locker room attendant must have thought so, too—he handed it to me on the way out the door. What a gift for someone who'd long been a fan of football memorabilia.

Of all the games our crew worked, the Texans–Vikings one turned out to be the most challenging. I felt our crew was among the strongest of the replacements, but this game proved to be one of our worst. We just weren't clicking. Routine mechanics, fouls, and keys were subpar in some cases. Maybe we'd let ourselves get too comfortable and we got sloppy. We all knew we had adjustments to make after this game and were committed to doing that. Luckily, so far, we seemed to be flying under the radar for the most part. Next up was regular season, where things would start to count. We had to be better.

We had ten days. I couldn't wait to get back on the field then and be stronger than ever to prove this had just been a hiccup.

Yet the thing about officiating is that it is impossible to work a perfect game. Even when you've worked your hardest and even when you've done your best, there will always be something that you can do better or learn from. As a perfectionist, I find this the most challenging part about being an official. At times, I have to remind myself no one has had a perfect game. Even Red Cashion ran to the wrong end of the field during a Super Bowl.[2]

∽

For the regular season, we opened in Detroit. I'll long remember Ford Field, how packed and loud it was. The call I remember making while there happened in the tunnel before the game. As I went through, the guy hanging over the tunnel kept begging me to sign a ticket for his son.

I knew what it was like to get an autograph after standing in line for hours. I knew how much it meant when I got it. So, as important as it was for me to follow all NFL guidelines, the one about denying autographs for little kids turned out to be a little too hard to stick to sometimes. Even for someone who works so hard to be a rules follower.

∽

For the second regular-season game, I returned to where I'd started in the NFL the month before. The first weekend in August, I'd worked Seattle's training camp, and there I'd been thrilled to have the chance to connect with Coach Pete Carroll. With his decades of experience and a national college championship under his belt, he was a rock star. His Seahawks would win the Super Bowl at the end of this season, and you could see that possibility with the way the team was playing from the start. I remember the inspirational quote on the poster outside his office and the simplicity and the complexity of his philosophy: "Always compete." If I ever played professional football, he'd be the coach I would want to play for. The week I worked on his field and with his team at the training camp, he'd been a bundle of intensely positive energy and an absolute joy to be around, so I looked forward to returning to Seattle for game two of the season.

Out on the gridiron, game time can pass so quickly. And so here I was at CenturyLink Field, with time running down in the half. Third down for Seattle, and the Seahawks needed just a few more yards to get within field goal range again.[3] They'd started strong in the first quarter but let the Cowboys get within striking range in the second.

With Seattle so close to securing their lead, the "twelfth man" showed up in force. The stadium was rocking. Among the Seattle fans were some members of the Frazier family. Tom's favorite team, and he couldn't come, but they could. It was good to know they were out there, supporting me, even as I tuned out the crowd noise, straddled the line of scrimmage, and focused on what would be one of the last plays of the quarter. Seattle's rookie quarterback Russell Wilson lined up under center and barked such a hard count that a linebacker jumped.

Coach Carroll yelled as I ran past. "Come on, Shannon," he said. "No flag?"

I knew he was disappointed I didn't make the call he wanted. The five-yard penalty would have given them a first down, keeping their drive alive, and they might have kicked a field goal before time ran out. But Seattle failed to convert on third down and punted the ball over to Dallas. And after Dallas ran a play, time expired.

I headed to the locker room. I had just enough time to quickly chart a couple penalties and stop by the restroom before getting back to work. For this game, I was one of the officials responsible for informing Seattle of the time remaining in the half and for escorting them back to the field. Halftime is the fastest twelve minutes of football.

While I was waiting outside their locker room door, one of the assistant coaches approached. "Shannon!" he said. "Why didn't you throw a flag when the defense jumped?"

The same issue Pete Carroll had, only the assistant wasn't letting it go. "Let me tell you what I saw," I said. "The defender wasn't crowding the zone. He was a couple yards off the line. Yes, he jumped," I acknowledged, "but when the ball was snapped, I could clearly see the ball, which indicated to me he wasn't in the neutral zone." If he wasn't in the zone, his movement wasn't a foul.

With that, the assistant coach straightened. "Well," he said, "you obviously know what you're doing."

Every game you have to show you know what you're doing. It wasn't enough for me to have sixteen years of experience; I had to show I could use it. The proof isn't just in recognizing a foul—it's in knowing the advantages and disadvantages of a play and in understanding the philosophies governing when to put a flag on the ground and when not to. Like that Kenny Rogers song (sort of) goes, you need to know when to hold 'em and know when to throw 'em. As an official, you also need to communicate what you've seen. At every level, you need to communicate effectively—ideally in a way the person you're speaking with will listen. So, had I responded with, "Coach, you're wrong. He wasn't offside," his reply would have probably been completely different. This exchange I'd seen not as a challenge but as a great opportunity to gain credibility through my response. To get to this point, I've had to take time to help others understand what I know, to see what I can do, and to trust me—and women like me—to do this work.

Later in that same game, the Cowboys had a close pass play on Seattle's sideline. I came up selling it, making it clear to all that this was a catch.

Seahawks cornerback Richard Sherman and a few other players descended toward me, all of them signaling that the catch had been incomplete.

Above us, on the big screen, the play I'd observed unfolded again, clearly showing the toe tap inside the side line. The catch was complete. I'd made the right call.

A hand touched between my shoulder blades. It was one of the Seahawks players.

"Good call," he said. "Good call."

❧

For the Indianapolis Colts–Jacksonville Jaguars game in September, my crew put ourselves where we needed to be, working our respective positions at Lucas Oil Stadium, where Super Bowl XLVI had been played earlier that year. Every NFL field has its share of history. They'd put my name in the books for being the first female officiating a preseason game and the first female officiating in the regular season, but I was working hard to be more than that. I hoped my work would be good enough to be considered simply good officiating. I wasn't alone in that. Our crew wanted to do a good job.

When things click for a crew and slide into place, there's not a lot to stick in your memory. At this point, our work was clicking together. So, as memorable as that fall was for me, I don't remember much about this game—though sports commentators talked a lot about the last minute of play.

For much of the game, the Colts led, though they let Jacksonville do all the scoring in the third quarter. The Jaguars took the lead at the beginning of the fourth. Then, with fifty-six seconds left, the home team scored a thirty-seven-yard field goal.

Home-team fans thought they had the game back in hand—until Jacksonville's second-year quarterback threw an eighty-yard pass to his wide receiver, who sprinted to the goal line and took a dive to avoid a tackle and score the touchdown. The ball crossed the goal line before his knee hit the ground, and we confirmed that by review in replay.

An NFL stadium can get incredibly loud, but when the home crowd falls silent, the quiet can feel incredibly close and so intense. The intensity of that moment came from the plays, not from the calls, as it should be.

I mention this game not because of that touchdown call but because of a different aspect of the final minute of play. In the weeks that followed, I got to thinking about the Colts coach Chuck Pagano and what he said about his players following the game. "This one's going to sit in the pit of their stomachs for quite some time," he said for an ESPN interview. "Obviously, we're going to have to get over it and move on and get better from here."[4]

I wondered later which final play he really meant. Just before the game, he'd met with team doctors about some bruises showing up on his arms. A few days later, we'd all learn that the blood tests they then directed him to take revealed he had leukemia. At the game, Coach Pagano had been so calm, respectful, and easy to talk to. A diagnosis like that can make you think. A moment like that can be such a life changer for so many.

❧

Next up, we were slated to work in Arizona. I got excited thinking about who all would be there for me. My friends. My dad. All the officials I knew who would come. The people who worked for me. I could hardly wait.

As soon as I got home from Indy, I started making plans for the following Sunday, collecting as many tickets as I could for everyone who'd want to attend. On the news, sportscasters were talking about how some crews were struggling. *SportsCenter* was pointing out every mistake the replacements were making. One ref announced a penalty on a team not even on the field. And the crew for the Baltimore Ravens–New England Patriots game had an especially difficult night. That was the crew my new friend Esteban Garza was on. Esteban was the D3 official who recently had moved to Arizona from Texas—the one in my try-out group in front of Billy Johnson. Another guy on Esteban's crew apparently got Patriots coach Bill Belichick so frustrated the coach ran and grabbed the official at the end of the game. "That's a few bucks," commentator Al Michaels said at the time. Fifty thousand dollars, the NFL later determined.[5] Having been in a similar situation, I imagined the ref would have his own account of what happened, though Belichick *said* he'd only wanted a clarification on the final call.

I only wanted the chance to keep living this dream. In the mail, I'd just received a new black NFL hat, one with pink piping for breast cancer awareness, to be worn the month of October. It even came with accessories—a pink wristband, a pink lanyard, and a pink whistle, too. I loved the pink, and I was super excited to represent breast cancer awareness. Since I've known some people who've battled the disease, the cause has been important to me.

Later that night, I gave Johnny Grier a call, and we were talking about the games, about everything. Belichick apparently wasn't alone in his frustration. Brandon Spikes and other players were tweeting complaints of their own.[6] It looked like the Denver Broncos coach and defensive coordinator would be fined for berating officials the week before.[7] Word had it that the Washington Redskins offensive coordinator had chased an official down a tunnel, swearing away at him because of their loss.[8]

"So how much longer before you throw the chick in at referee?" I finally asked.

"Another week like this, and it won't be long," Johnny said.

It was shorter than that. And with a more painful ending.

The next day, I cuddled up with my little man, Cooper, to watch Seattle host Green Bay on *Monday Night Football*. On the final play, Russell Wilson threw a Hail Mary pass into the end zone intended for wide receiver Golden Tate.

Before Tate caught it, he shoved Packers cornerback Sam Shields aside with both hands.

Foul, I called out to the TV, but no flag was thrown. Tate and Packers defender M. D. Jennings were in the air, their hands on the ball, both attempting to gain possession.

The two officials near the play initially gave separate signals—one touchdown, the other touchback. They conferred, then ruled the players had simultaneous possession, and that resulted in a Seahawks game-winning touchdown.

The game's announcers wanted to know why the penalty for pass interference wasn't called. Me, too. That would have negated the touchdown. You probably remember how the calls the officials made—and didn't make—in this particular game ended up being so heavily criticized in the media and even by NFL players. The NFL subsequently released a statement defending the touchdown ruling.

People couldn't stop talking about the end of that game. They asked, Was it a touchdown? Was it an interception? A *Fail Mary*, the play came to be called.

Two days after that fateful night, the replacements were no longer needed.

Roger Goodell, commissioner of the NFL, announced on television that the regular officials would be returning. The NFL instantly blocked our access to the officials' website. The next day, we had a conference call with Ray Anderson.

"Thank you for what you did," he told us. "And to our girl, Shannon, thank you."

I was a bit floored to be named personally in his thanks. That at least felt good to hear.

The only thing that would have been better would have been if I'd had the chance to work a game in New England, for my dad to see me on the field in Gillette Stadium. Of course, I would have also enjoyed working as referee. Had our season continued, I had every reason to believe the NFL would have moved me to that position. I still have the white hat. More important, I believe I was qualified to be the first woman ref, and other longtime NFL officials expressed that they believed this as well.

In the years since, no woman has been named as an NFL referee. At least not yet. It took three more years before the league hired any other woman as an official. It wasn't me. Since then, Sarah Thomas has even been able to work many playoff games, including the Super Bowl. I'm glad for her and glad to have paved the way for her and others, but back in 2012, I had to absorb the sting of sadness when my time as an official for the NFL came to an end. The rest of the season, I was essentially blackballed from officiating any college games.

It helped to hear from Red Cashion when all was said and done. He sent a kind e-mail, saying, "You will never know how many times I said when asked about the lady ref, 'She is the best official on the field.'"[9] Which made me think of at least one reporter who'd remembered he'd said that.

Count me among those who believe everything happens for a reason, even though it's not always easy to accept. God has a plan that's not always revealed in our desired timing, but his timing is always perfect—especially when it comes to our life-changing moments. I prayed there was still somehow more time officiating pro football for me. In the end, God gave me exactly that—time.

22

GAME CHANGERS

That spring, I kept busy with my usual work, with training and scheduling and rescheduling officials and fielding all the calls that go with that. Sometime around then, I heard from a parent who wanted to vent about a rule enforcement at her kid's youth game the day before. I listened first. "I hear you," I said. I tried walking her through the reasoning to give a sense of the philosophy behind the rule.

She cut me off. "You have no idea what you're talking about," she said and hung up.

Getting calls like that might not be my favorite part of my job, but I can tell you what is—floating from field to field, checking in on the guys officiating youth football for me.

One Saturday when I was out doing this, I saw that a longtime official I knew was working. I stopped to talk. Terry had always been one of those hard workers who truly cares about the game and the kids playing. I was glad to see him. He was having a hard time keeping it together.

It seemed he had something on his mind.

"Something going on?" I asked gently.

"Things aren't going well," Terry said, "for my grandson." The cancer had come back, he said.

I hadn't known what his family was going through.

The family had to plan a birthday party for Aiden pretty quick, he said. They weren't sure he was going to make it to his fourth birthday. Terry broke down telling me this.

The birthday was just a few weeks away.

"We thought he'd beat it," he said.

The little boy had been diagnosed not quite a year ago, at his third birthday, after some bad headaches. Turned out the tumor in his brain had been the size of a golf ball. The doctors took him into surgery the next day. After chemo, he'd lost his hair and his hearing, but it was worth it. The tests they ran showed the cancer was gone. Aiden was back to going to the barn and the park and all his favorite places.

Then he started limping on Easter Monday. After a day or two, the limp didn't go away. They found the cancer was back with a vengeance and had spread to his spine.

Terry showed me one more picture of his grandson. In this one, the little guy had a perfectly bald head. "My little stud," Terry called him. You couldn't see the tiny hearing aids. Through it all, Terry said, through all the pain and suffering this child endured, Aiden always smiled, and he never complained.

Terry bore the pain of his grandson's suffering as his own. I could see it in his face, his eyes.

"You want to go home?" I asked. "You should go home."

"No," he said. He shook his head. "No, working is a good distraction. It helps."

I gave him a hug before I left.

I couldn't get Aiden out of my mind. Terry had showed me pictures of the little toddler with blue eyes and blond hair and a smile that lit up his face. "He could light up a room," Terry had said. He'd talked about how little Aiden bounced and ran through parks, waving at strangers. How he made friends with everyone.

The story hit me hard. On my way to the next game, I thought about how I'd dealt with a few unsavory situations, and I quickly realized how insignificant some of my irritations were. We can all be upset and angry dealing with the stresses of our job or life in general, when things don't go as planned. Having to sit out most of a football season after officiating seventeen years looked like a different sort of problem after seeing how a three-year-old boy smiled his way through a cancer-riddled prognosis.

So, instead of driving to the next field, I went home and pulled off my shelf a Mickey Mouse dressed up like a referee. I also grabbed the only NFL game ball I had from my time officiating the previous fall. I carried both back over to Terry.

"I want Aiden to have these," I said, holding out the mouse and the ball.

Terry teared up at the gesture. He shook his head. "Not the ball," he said. "Not that, it means too much to you."

But I pressed the game ball back into the cradle of his arms. I wanted him to have it.

A few days later, Terry let me know that the little boy in the big hospital bed had told his grandpa he couldn't do the treatments anymore. Terry talked him through it, and little Aiden made clear he understood what that meant. The patient told his mom the same thing the next day, and she'd told the doctor.

Terry called Aiden his little hero. The three-year-old had just been discharged, and now he'd be home at grandma's house, until the end.

I'd been close to Terry to some degree before I found out about Aiden, but seeing how his incredibly gentle, loving soul loved Aiden with all his heart made me care for Terry all the more. I don't get attached to things like that NFL ball—or even my NFL jersey. It means more to me to share them with the right person for the right reason. Aiden was definitely the right reason.

Aiden died a few days later, on April 18. He didn't make it to his fourth birthday. Through the end, he was surrounded by those who loved him.

I wanted to do something more to support Terry and his family through their grief. I remembered how Terry said that Aiden was his hero. So after he passed away, I ordered 250 personalized rubber wristbands that read *Grandpa's Hero* and included the day he was born. Terry slipped the tie-dyed blue and white band onto his wrist his first game back. Every football official I employed wore the wristband to every youth game that entire season.

The anatomy of a life-changing event varies in size, intensity, time, and form. Whether intricate or simple, the details ultimately prove to be consequential. The event can give way to the decision to become a football official, then morph into a dream of making it to the NFL, a dream that takes many, many years to realize. Or such an event can take a matter of minutes in the form of a chance meeting with a stranger.

That's the thing about life changers. You never know when or how it's going to happen or if it's going to happen at all. The NFL and a little angel in heaven were life changing for me.

I never got to meet Aiden, yet his life changed mine. Through the stories, memories, and videos his grandfather shared with me, I felt I knew him. I knew I wanted to do even more. I wanted to use my voice to make a difference. I wanted to do something to celebrate Aiden's life as well as help children like him. I wanted to help spread a little joy the way Aiden had when he was here.

When I was as little as Aiden, I'd loved my Cubby Comfortable Jr. I remembered how stuffed animals helped when I wasn't feeling well.

Holding one comforted me. That gave me an idea, but I needed to enlist the help of a few close friends.

I sent an e-mail blast to all officials working for me, detailing a plan of donating teddy bears to Phoenix Children's Hospital. Would they be willing to donate a game fee back to help pay for the bears? The response was overwhelming. Some would donate one game, others would donate a whole day of game fees. One official let me know he had a contact with Gund bears, an extremely high-quality teddy bear manufacturer. He facilitated that connection. With the generous donation of all those game fees and with the connection made at Gund, we raised more than $9,000 and could order a thousand bears.

Once I received them all, I had the tedious task of removing the sewn-on shirts and redressing the bears with personalized shirts I'd ordered to let the kids know who was thinking of them. Each bear got a top featuring a picture of Cooper in a black and white striped referee shirt. Over each bear's heart, their new shirt read *Arizona Officials . . . a Family Who Cares*.

Finally, then, I stuffed my car with bears ready to be hugged by the children staying at Phoenix Children's Hospital. (And I'd thought my car was full bringing stuffed animals back from Circus Circus.) That first time, I couldn't go room to room. Instead, I met my contact person outside the hospital. I unloaded the big bags of bears from my car, and we loaded up her carts. I could only imagine the look on the faces of those little patients when she brought a bear in for them. That alone was enough for me to realize I couldn't let this be a one-time project.

Little did I know I was about to take another journey of the heart that summer.

∽

An NFL connection came calling, and I answered. That summer after my first season with the NFL, I flew out to American Samoa to help prep and train their high school football officials prior to the upcoming season. Troy Polamalu, a strong safety for the Pittsburgh Steelers, had made the camp possible through a foundation set up with his wife to give back to the community and islands of their heritage. The woman from his foundation who was organizing the event had searched the internet for football refs and found a story online about me from the previous fall. She thought it'd be great to have a female official included in the bunch.

At first, I'd hesitated to go. I didn't want to leave Cooper behind. But I'm glad I went out to the remote South Pacific island on the western edge of the International Date Line. My flight had an overnight layover in Hawaii, so I got some shopping in and enjoyed my old stomping grounds. A lot had been updated since I last ran past these palm trees with Cliff.

I'd lost touch with him along the way, though I'd heard he got a silver at the Pan American Games and went on to the 1996 Olympics, where he came in thirteenth. My judo days seemed so far behind me now, but they'd started me on my right path. Judo helped me understand the importance of finding the right training and preparation to achieve your goals and helped me learn how to focus during a match. I felt God's guiding hand through it all, and what a blessing he now gave me to have this chance to go to Pago Pago.

When we landed, it truly seemed as if everyone on the island had shown up to greet us—Troy is a hero to the island. And it turned out that there were many players and coaches on my flight. I can't say we realized it until we stepped off the plane and into the cheering crowd.

For the week's festivities, Troy brought in NFL players and college coaches from across the country. The high school players took part in football drills, scrimmages, and Manu Siva Tau war dance challenges. My work involved meeting with officials each day for a few hours to go over rules and football philosophies. I had my work cut out for me: Only two out of the group had a true grasp of officiating. I poured myself into the teaching.

While there, program coordinators asked what I knew about officiating basketball. They wondered if I could teach a class on that as well. A few years had passed since I'd worked the Division I level, but I had more than ten years of officiating basketball under my belt. I quickly pulled together a couple of classroom sessions. Fortunately, the basketball officials seemed a bit further along in their knowledge and skills.

For either sport, a week isn't nearly enough time to bring the level of officiating up to where it needs to be. But I was glad to do what I could to share what I know. Even more, I was glad to share my love of officiating with officials who were so eager to learn. Every minute there, on the field, on the court, and in the classroom, I loved.

While there, I had time to think about an e-mail that had just come through for me. The NFL wanted to let me know of an opportunity for me in the MEAC for the 2013 football season. This was both good and bad news. It meant my good on-field work had not gone unnoticed. Honestly, though, the last thing I felt up for was returning to the MEAC. But to be hired back by the NFL, I had to be working college football again. For the NFL, it was tempting.

The welcome my little pup gave me on my return home brought tears to my eyes. I couldn't stop hugging and kissing him. He did fine with my neighbors—maybe better than I did while we were apart—but right then, I knew I probably couldn't leave him for any length of time like that again. I also began to realize that maybe Cooper needed a buddy. Maybe I needed another dog. Maybe I'd do what I could to get back into the NFL again first.

Just a couple of weeks after my return from American Samoa, I had to leave Cooper once again. This time, my plane was headed east, to Norfolk, Virginia, for a preseason clinic for the MEAC. I wasn't sure how I'd be received. What had happened at the NFL clinic down in Dallas had stayed with me. Though I'd been to so many of these clinics and had always been the friendly professional who approached and talked to everyone there, I found myself sitting back this time, waiting for others to make the first move. I didn't want to put anyone else in a position that forced them to have to respond with rudeness or hurt me with their words. What Chuck Stewart had said to me the year before at the Dallas clinic had—I hate to admit— crushed me. I am a strong person, but I had valued his friendship greatly.

I looked for signs that others were giving. I didn't want to get hurt again. I struggled with what to do. Should I approach Rosie Amato, super-visor of officials, and thank him for bringing me back? But what if the NFL had pressured him to bring me in? Did I simply respect his feelings and stay away from him? I decided it was best not to approach him. We did not speak at all.

After the clinic ended, Rosie sent me an e-mail saying he was disap-pointed that I did not reach out to him. Maybe the choice I made wasn't the right one, but I can honestly say I made it with his feelings in mind as well as my own. All my life, I'd been lucky to have friends I could count on to help push when I was swimming against the current. The lockout changed some of that. I found myself far from shore and wasn't sure who'd be on board to help me back. I didn't want to isolate Rosie out there with me. I didn't want to put him in a position where he'd have to talk to me if he didn't want to.

I didn't want my supervisor not happy to see me anymore.

Technically, Rosie hired me back for the season. "Hired back" seems the wrong term for something that ended up being one assignment in Atlanta, not as an on-field official but as a red hat. The red hat is the one communicating with the media broadcast truck/data center about the length and number of TV time-outs per game. No other spot on or off the field with a hat could have less to do with officiating. I got the point.

Then I saw how much I'd be paid. Coming from Arizona and not somewhere on the East Coast, I never made much as a referee; I was paid a flat fee and was not reimbursed for the cost of travel or hotel stays. As a red hat, the game fee offered at the time was only $150. Accepting this assignment meant losing money, much more so than when I'd refereed. I reached out to Johnny Grier in the NFL office and asked for guidance. Johnny said to take the assignment. The NFL would reimburse my expenses. So I did as he said and worked the game.

The last time I'd worked a game in Atlanta, it was as referee for the Atlanta Classic. Instead of wearing a white hat for the annual (and much anticipated) football game between HBCUs, here I was, showing up in a red hat.

It was hard showing up for someone when I didn't feel wanted.

And then the security guard assigned to our locker room recognized me from a few years earlier. "Where's your white hat?" he asked.

"Story for another time," I said.

The story I wanted to hear was whether the NFL would let me back in the next season. They did, but they wanted me to play a different role at this point. By e-mail, they asked if I'd be interested in a job as a game day assistant. Because I lived in Arizona, the work wouldn't be for my beloved Patriots but for the Arizona Cardinals home games. Game day assistants were game clock operators, play clock operators, instant replay field communicators, coach-to-player cutoff operators, and many others. My friend Esteban Garza had also been contacted to work as my backup.

Since many game day assistants were or had been high school or college football officials, I knew the guys who filled the other positions. Paul Verna had been working as game clock operator for a few years by then. He had a long face and a wide smile. Mack Gilcrest was older, in his seventies, and had worked almost thirty years as a field judge for what was now the Pac-12. Since his retirement ten years before, he'd been training and mentoring officials as well as working as the coach-to-player cutoff operator for the NFL. Each quarterback had a speaker in his helmet that allowed him to hear the coach calling plays, and those communications had to be cut when fifteen seconds were left on the play clock. Johnny Price was the instant replay communicator. Instant replay officials in the booth would inform Johnny to stop the game if a play needed further review. Johnny then notified the short wing on his side of the field, and that official then alerted the referee to stop the game. All these roles, among others, helped games run smoothly and seamlessly.

As play clock operator, I'd be responsible to set the play clock after each play. Typically, I had to set it to forty or to twenty-five seconds, but special scenarios call for different timings on a reset. An hour and forty-five minutes before the first kickoff, Paul, Mack, and I headed down to the officials' locker room to meet with certain members of the NFL crew to confirm procedures. I'd once been among the crew meeting the game day assistants. Now I was the one waiting in the hall, holding a laminated card listing timing rules, resets, and guidelines for special situations.

Paul headed into the locker room to let the officials know we'd arrived. I waited outside in case crew members were still changing into their uniforms.

I was only one year removed from my work for the NFL and wasn't sure how I would be received, especially for these one-on-one meetings with the back judges. There were still mixed feelings from some officials toward those of us who had worked during the lockout. For the most part, the guys I encountered remained professional while working with me. They might not have liked what I did, but they weren't disrespectful.

Except for a couple of guys in particular, that is. A back judge who'd been with the NFL just a few years at that point delayed his conference with me for nearly fifteen minutes. I stood there outside the locker room wondering if he was going to come out at all. This was unusual because of the strict schedule we had to follow.

When he finally showed, he barely gave me the time of day, as the saying goes. "You have the card," was all he said. "You read it?" With that, he turned on his heel and punched back through the door into the locker room. He made it clear he didn't want to deal with me at all.

I would have rather met with him under different circumstances, too. I would have rather been an on-field official. Working the play clock wasn't a difficult job, but I took it seriously. I wanted to be so good that even if an NFL official didn't want to have anything to do with me, he'd still enjoy working in Arizona. I wanted to be perfect so they could focus on the game and not be distracted by the clock. I wanted to be a professional.

That wasn't always easy, like the time an (almost) fifteen-year veteran official emerged into the hallway for a routine pregame meeting holding his copy of the laminated card. The longtime back judge kept his gaze fixated on the card.

I automatically extended a hand and introduced myself.

"I know who you are," he said disinterestedly. He read through the to-do list robotically, then turned and disappeared back into the locker room.

From that point on, I hoped not to see either of their names listed as the back judge working a game. I did not look forward to my next pregame meeting with them but knew it was something I'd have to do. I was determined to represent myself and the NFL with the highest level of professionalism even if those two men would not. That was worth my time and effort, even if I didn't think I could change their minds.

That year what was happening at my condo was becoming more important than what was happening on the field. Back at home, I'd installed a security system with a camera so I could check in on Cooper when I wasn't there. Often, he rode along wherever I went, but sometimes it didn't work for me to take him, and hiring a babysitter at $10 an hour didn't always work for me, either. Yes, I hired a sitter sometimes. I knew he had separation anxiety but didn't know how bad it was until I peeked at the security video to see what he was doing.

When I was gone and he was home alone, he never stopped moving. He would not sleep, eat, or do anything other than pace or look at the door, waiting for me to return. That was hard enough to see, but then one day while peeking in on him with the camera, I saw him pacing up on the kitchen table.

I didn't know he could jump high enough to get onto a chair, much less climb onto the table from there, but somehow he'd managed. He was plainly distressed. That broke my heart.

I called Katie, his breeder, who had since become a friend. She knew I'd been struggling with whether to get him a buddy. So far, every time I came close to looking for another dog, I kept coming back to the problem of how getting around town and even just to the bank would be so much more challenging with two dogs.

Katie suggested we stop by for a visit since Cooper's sister had just had her first litter. "Bring him on over to see," she said. I didn't have to decide yet if I wanted another pup.

I chatted with Katie and her husband as Cooper tried to tell us what a good big brother he'd be, with how kind and gentle he acted around all the new puppies. I loved watching them climb over each other and snuggle all together. Katie let us keep playing with the puppies on a rug in the living room when she had to step away for a minute.

Of course, that's when one of the little guys squatted to pee on the rug. Katie's husband reached with his foot to nudge the puppy to stop.

"What are you doing?" I asked as the little pup's toenail caught on the rug. He tumbled and began to cry. I snatched him up. "You don't kick a puppy," I said.

Her husband felt terrible. He sat up in his chair. He hadn't meant to hurt the dog.

Katie came back out to find me holding a puppy and her husband and I not talking. She knew something had happened but didn't know what. She and I talked a while longer. I still hadn't put that little guy down. I didn't for the rest of the night.

Finally, I said, "Katie, I'm taking him home."

"Okay," she said and walked me to my car.

Once outside by my MINI Cooper, I told her what had happened. All I can say is, at the moment that little guy felt any pain, I knew I had to take him home. I found I have two loves of my life, and bringing the ones you love around town hasn't turned out to be as difficult as I thought it'd be.

My boys are never too far from me. When I have a free night, we settle on the couch and watch reality shows like *American Idol* or *The Voice*. Reality TV was something that I never understood or enjoyed before. I used to think it was silly. Somehow, the NFL changed this for me. It's hard to explain, but now I see shows like that as a way to watch people who are doing all they can to make their dreams come true.

These shows that I'd never tuned into before have since become something I can't get enough of. And that's true of almost any kind of reality TV. I get so caught up finding out about the struggles of all the contestants and hearing what sources of support and inspiration they've found. I can't get through an episode without lots of tears. And that Golden Buzzer on *America's Got Talent*? That sends me over the edge of emotion.

Each week, I watch these contestants getting closer and closer to reaching their goal. I see them all working toward their version of the NFL. So I find myself rooting not just for one but for all of them. Big dreams are something we all need.

And I was not done with mine.

23

REPLAY THE DOWN

The following spring, the supervisor of officials for a Division I conference asked me to participate in a scrimmage. I'd known the previous supervisor but didn't have high hopes the new supervisor would actually want me in the league. But to hold open any shot of working in the NFL again, I had to try moving forward with whatever opportunities this D1 conference offered.

The new supervisor said he'd be at the scrimmage, along with Johnny Grier and the NFL's director of officiating, David Coleman. I was hesitant about the situation but was still willing to do what was needed. David asked me to be patient and continue to work while the NFL got me through the interview process, which was one step that was necessary should I be hired back.

My friend Esteban Garza would also be working the scrimmage. You may remember he'd been a replacement official, too, but on another crew. Since we'd met at the first Dallas clinic for the NFL, I'd come to have a lot of respect for Esteban both on and off the field. He is a good Christian man, a man of integrity, as well as a CrossFit guru.

None of that seemed to matter to the new supervisor. Instead, he aimed a constant verbal barrage of degrading and sarcastic comments at me and at Esteban, so much that we felt we were marked. The supervisor hovered behind me to observe my work. He asked questions about what I saw during each play, though he never let me fully answer.

When he commented about the tackle on my side of the field, he added, "You probably don't know who the tackle is, anyway."

"For most of the scrimmage," I said, holding my voice even, "the tackle on my side was number 78."

He left me alone after that and turned his attention instead to Esteban. The new supervisor walked up to him, berating him for screwing up a play. Only it wasn't Esteban who'd made the mistakes the supervisor complained of. Esteban tried to set the record straight, but that seemed to infuriate the supervisor even more. He stopped the scrimmage and called for everyone to come over to where he was standing.

We gathered around him, and that's when he began ripping into Esteban. Esteban tried telling the supervisor he had the wrong guy, but Esteban only got into more trouble for pointing out the mistake. As the supervisor launched into how bad Esteban was, a smile formed on Esteban's face, the grin dissipating the misdirected criticism much like a car bumper dissipates the impact of a small collision. It was classic.

Then the new supervisor ran through his résumé for us again, as if his evaluations of us were spot on simply because he was an NFL official. All right.

After that scrimmage, he decided to hire me not as ref but as a head linesman and not on a regular crew but only as a supplemental official. That season, I received one game a plane ride away. In that game, early in the first quarter, I turned, taking off to follow a play, and my leg gave out.

I couldn't put any weight on it. The pain was excruciating, worse than any migraine and worse than that time I was hospitalized for judo. (The spinal tap itself was probably worse, though.) I had to be helped to the sideline.

The trainers took a look at what was wrong with my calf muscle.

"Can you give me a shot or something," I asked, "so I can get back in the game?"

"Let's ice it for a while and see how it feels," one of them said. After twenty minutes of ice, I tried to get off the table and walk. I could not.

"You're done," the trainer said.

Always before, I'd been able to fight pain regardless of the cost, but this time, I could not. My calf muscle was torn, and for the first time in almost twenty years of officiating, I couldn't finish a game.

I felt terrible. Thoughts of how this must look—a female who couldn't finish a game—weighed heavily on my mind.

Luckily, Esteban had worked this game, too, and was traveling back to Phoenix with me. It was hard enough getting around the hotel room by myself prior to heading home. I don't know how I could have made it through the airport without him. We found a wheelchair, and he pushed me. This one was super hard to maneuver, and he had to keep stopping.

We couldn't understand his struggles until we got to the gate. By then, he was drenched with sweat. We finally realized the wheels had been locked the whole time.

As soon as I got home, I immediately started treatments and rehabbing. I wanted to get back on the field as soon as possible to continue my pursuit of proving my worth to the NFL.

While going through rehab, I joined in with a crew on their weekly conference calls. The main topic of conversation was how difficult it was to determine what the new supervisor wanted from his officials. He would contradict himself from one week to the next. One game, he'd criticize a guy for throwing a flag in a certain situation, and the following week, when the exact same situation came up, he would rip into a guy for *not* throwing a flag. I watched the same game films and struggled to find consistency in what the supervisor had said.

I worked hard to rehab back and was ready to go when I received one more assignment to end the season. When the grades for the game came out, I didn't even look. He was ripping everyone regardless of what they did.

Later, Esteban called me and said that he and I graded out perfectly. This was unheard of coming from the new guy. There had to be a mistake, but I confirmed it. Talk about a shock.

However, in true form, the perfect grade was shortly followed by a letter saying I would not be asked back to work in the conference.

With how he approached training and how he treated his officials, I wasn't heartbroken, even though I hadn't yet found another path back to the NFL. It didn't look like another way would open up, either, since the guys on the inside helping and coaching me to get back into the league were now heading out in different directions.

Carl Johnson had supported me since we'd first met at the Tom Beard Clinic. He was the NFL official waiting at the end of the finish line at the NFL tryouts and the one who'd approached me at the end of my first NFL game to say I'd work many games in this league. That year, he left the NFL office to take a position back on the field.

Another supporter of mine was Ray Anderson, the executive vice president of NFL operations. He was a smart guy who'd gone to Stanford and Harvard Law. He'd been vice president for the Atlanta Falcons before joining the NFL's executive offices. When I ran into him in the press box while working play clock, he told me, "We need to get you back on the NFL field." In 2014, he joined his love of the game with a university setting when he became the athletic director at ASU.

David Coleman was still in the NFL office and still supportive of me. He said he wanted to get the Southwestern Athletic Conference to give me a look. As much as I appreciated Coleman looking for another way for me to possibly get back onto an NFL field, I had to pass.

～

That season at least, I was still working as play clock operator for the NFL. We had a change in protocol, and now we also had to meet after the game to address any outstanding issues. Because I had to wait outside the locker room, I made a point of asking the back judge during our pregame meeting if he wanted to meet right after the game or after he showered. No matter the role, communicating expectations matters in your work.

I like to think my professionalism made a difference in how the fifteen-year NFL veteran responded to me this second season. I was pleasantly surprised his abruptness from the year before had dissipated, and he talked to me as if I were no longer the enemy. I'm not entirely sure what caused the change in his behavior, but I was glad he seemed to put his issue with me in the past.

I can't say the same was true with the other NFL back judge. A pregame meeting in the fall of 2014 seemed a repeat of the year before, starting with the angry look he shot at me right out of the locker room. "Got the card," he said. "Can you read?" And he spun around to head back in.

"Excuse me, sir." We hadn't yet confirmed what I was there to confirm. I had to stop him. "With the new procedure," I said, keeping my voice even, "do you want me to meet you outside the locker room after the game?"

He was already pushing through the door. "Yes," he snapped over his shoulder.

The locker room attendant sitting out in the hall knit his brows together. "What's his problem?"

On our way back to the press box, Mack Gilcrest said he was going to send an e-mail to the NFL. "You've taken his bull long enough," he said.

It was as if he'd read my mind. In those days, it meant a lot to have someone standing with me.

Two years had passed since the lockout, and I still didn't know where I stood with everyone. After one game, NFL referee Walt Anderson called me down to the officials' locker room. Since my communication was generally always with the back judge, I was a little nervous about what he'd have to say. He'd reffed for about ten years after retiring as a dentist and had already officiated two Super Bowls.

He was waiting at the locker room door. He was so pleasant. Turned out all he wanted to do was say what a good job I'd done being on top of things and picking up his signal when he wanted the play clock reset. I was floored not because of the words he was saying but by the fact that he took the time to talk to me and make me feel appreciated at a time when there wasn't much appreciation coming my way.

During the next few years, I came to realize my love of football had taken a hit. If someone asks now about the Patriots and what I thought of Deflategate, the answer is I don't have much energy around it. In my work, I continued to officiate local games when needed. I did it to fill an open spot, to make sure the players got the best officiating possible.

Once in a while, I'd run into a coach who looked as if he'd never seen a woman walk onto the field before. It's rare, but it happens, and it's never gotten any easier when a coach like that directs his answers only to the umpire during a pregame meeting. In some ways, it feels worse.

Walking back after one such pregame conference, my ump turned to me. "Well, *that* was uncomfortable," he said. "Doesn't he know who you are? Doesn't he know where you've been?"

Yet what matters most still, I know, is the work I do in that moment, for that game. That's always been the case, and it always will be.

One night at about 9:30, I got a phone call from an official, checking in at the end of an all-day assignment I'd given him and his crew. They'd been out in Prescott Valley, a three-hour round trip. It'd been a fabulous day, he said.

He wasn't calling this late to tell me his day was completely fabulous. So I listened as he told me about how perfect the weather had been and how the players, coaches, and parents were so complimentary about the job we were doing. "Until the last play of the last game," he said.

"What happened then?"

There were only three seconds left, and the game was tied. The offense threw a pass that was intercepted and returned for a touchdown. "The problem was," he said, "there was an inadvertent whistle on the play."

"Well, that stinks." An inadvertent whistle is such a terrible mistake to make; it can weigh on you to think of how you affected the game—and it can happen at any level. Even on nationally televised games. There's never a good answer, though, when something like that happens.

What I told him, what I tell all my officials, is this: You're human. Mistakes will happen; they happen at every level. Learn from each one and next time make a different one. Officiating isn't just about learning from experience—it's also about growing from it. As you continue, over time you'll develop into the kind of official you aspire to be.

On the phone, the official was saying that when his crew conferred, they decided the whistle blew before the ball was intercepted. That meant the offense would get the ball back. Even with no time on the clock, the offense got one untimed down, meaning they had one more play. So the offense lined up and kicked a field goal to win the game.

"I'm sick to my stomach about what happened," he said.

"I'm glad you are sick about it, actually," I said. "That means you care."

It had been years, but I hadn't forgotten the time I'd felt the same way after a game. The problem popped up late in the fourth quarter after the team that had been losing scored a touchdown. On the kickoff return, they recovered the other team's fumble on the nineteen-yard line, putting a win within reach—except, while the ball was loose, the side judge had inadvertently blown his whistle. Unfortunately, that meant the ball had to be given back to the team last in possession of the ball. This time, the team that had fumbled retained possession and ran out the clock.

The thought that the crew I was on might have changed the outcome of a game literally nauseated me. But in the officials' locker room afterward, the referee went around shaking everyone's hand. *Good job, good job*, the crew said to each other. When they got to me, I had to ask, "Seriously, you think we did a good job?"

If the losing team had won this game and one more, they would have qualified to play for a national title. I still think about how we might have cost a team that chance.

"Caring about the officiating you do matters," I said over the phone. "When it doesn't bug you to make such a mistake, it's time to decide whether you should still be working."

Back when my crew had the potentially game-changing inadvertent whistle, I remember how the referee had answered me, saying they'd had plenty of opportunities to win. But what I wanted to know was, "When do we decide how many opportunities they should have to win?"

I'm glad this official had called looking for what he could have done better in this situation, that he values my insights. I can speak from experience, having been stuck in a similar place myself. I love being an ear to listen and serving as a voice to offer support and advice as others had done for me. Maybe it's even a better role for me now instead of being out on a field.

After I hung up, my little dog Riley tiptoed over and looked up at me. That little face. What he was trying to tell me was right. I'd talked too late and too long.

"Is it time to smell the rose?" I asked. That's what I say when he gives me his daily reminder of what's important. I scooped him up to give hugs and kisses. And Riley did what he does best, nestling his head on my shoulder, giving me comfort.

ᐲ

That next January, the Super Bowl came to Glendale. Not only was Super Bowl XLIX going to be in Arizona, but my New England Patriots were going to play the Seattle Seahawks there. Even better: I was asked to work the play clock and had an opportunity to work the NFL Experience before the big game. Out of everything, the NFL Experience was my favorite part.

That football-based extravaganza is full of interactive activities for fans. They get the chance to kick footballs through field goalposts or run like a running back with resistance bands tied around their waists.[1] Fans could also get an autograph from one of many current and former players there.

I got to work in an interactive attraction, *You Make the Call*. We escorted people into an NFL replay booth and showed a video of a controversial play. Participants, in turn, had to make the call as if they were the official on the field. *A Salute to Service* was similar, giving military veterans the chance to take a shot in the replay booth and ask us questions about officiating. Then they got to join us on a small section of turf resembling a football field to go over mechanics, positioning, fundamentals, and basic techniques of officiating. Veterans left with gift bags filled with *Salute to Service* NFL T-shirts, footballs, and other fun memorabilia.

Besides those attractions, I also worked the children's area, where kids learned about football officials—from the equipment we used to the jobs we had to the uniforms we wore. Kids made penalty flags and decorated them with NFL stickers. They used markers to color in the outline of a referee on a T-shirt. The many volunteers who worked alongside me there kept telling anyone coming through our section that I was the first female official to work in the NFL, and they'd point up at the huge wall right by us that displayed pictures of prominent football officials in their respective decades. Red Cashion was the picture of the 1990s, and I was the picture of the 2000s. You should have seen their faces when they connected me to the person in that picture blowing the whistle.

But it blew my mind, too, to see my picture right next to Red's, who is universally known as one of the greatest referees of all time. He was such an American football icon. He was my hero, my mentor, and, most important, my friend.

Several times, I was reminded that this area was meant only for the children, then word spread that I was there, and many adults without kids came to see me as well. They set up a place for me to sign autographs and take pictures. I signed literally thousands of autographs. The whole experience felt so surreal—as surreal as the cheering I'd heard every time I came out of an NFL tunnel, with all those fans calling out my name, cheering me for being the first woman officiating on an NFL field.

And that's what brought them into the line here, why the line to get my signature or picture taken grew so long. I took my time with each person. I wanted to make sure each child or adult got their questions answered, pictures taken, and autographs signed. I signed everything from the flags we made to T-shirts to footballs. When one girl asked me to sign right on her arm, I almost said no, but her mom came over to say it was okay, so I did.

Everyone kept thanking me for my time, but I was the one thankful for them. I felt so blessed for the chance to meet all those people, answer their questions, and hear their stories. Like the one woman who stepped forward with two children and three yellow flags for me to sign. I signed the ones her kids were holding, and then she raised the flag she held in her hand.

"Can you sign this one," she said, "to my angel in heaven?"

Her baby had only recently passed away, and somehow she found the strength to bring her living children here.

I couldn't help how my eyes brimmed with tears. I talked with her for a while. And after signing, I asked if I could give her a hug. I'll never forget her—or her angel.

It was hard moving on after that, but there were so many others in line. I gathered myself and continued.

Those days of the NFL Experience were meant to build up excitement for the big game at the end of the week, and by Super Bowl Sunday, I was as excited as I'd been as a teen ready to watch the Patriots play the big game with my dad. This time, I was on the inside.

We met the crew at their hotel to ride a bus to the stadium because of security and parking concerns. I remembered how I'd needed to focus before a game when I worked as an official and how some officials had socialized on the bus ride to the stadium. This bus ride felt different. A few officials clearly weren't happy to see me, so I kept to myself at first on the bus. I ended up talking only to the game day assistants, not any of the officials.

Up in the press box, we dove into our work. Just the week before, I'd worked the clock for the Pro Bowl—but this was the Super Bowl, with my favorite team playing. And when New England caught the interception on the goal line, sealing the deal for them to win, I almost jumped up out of my seat. But I caught myself. It was as if someone pressed down on my shoulders reminding me of the job I was doing. That weight I was willing to bear.

⌒⌣

In 2016, I got a call about an opportunity from the person who'd sent me the "scab list"—the one whose identity I'd protected when the NFL pressed hard for it. He'd just taken a position in the NFL office, and one of the areas for which he was responsible was the game day assistants.

"I have good news and bad news," he told me.

The bad news was he wanted to move me from the play clock operator position. The good news was he wanted to move me to the coach-to-player cutoff operator job. Physically, I would be moving one chair over in the press box. He commended my performance, saying that I was one of the best play clock operators they had and that in no way was this a demotion.

In the four years working this position, I'd worked two playoff games, a Pro Bowl, and the 2015 Super Bowl. I was a member of the Arizona game day crew that trained a new set of Los Angeles game day assistants at the Los Angeles Memorial Coliseum. I was also part of a select group of play clock operators asked to provide insight and suggestions about ways to improve the work we do on game days.

When this guy said I was one of the best, I believed him. In all my work, that's what I strive to deliver. However, he felt another official deserved an opportunity in the booth and wanted to move him into my position. He felt I had a better long-standing future working the coach-to-player spot.

This proposal left me confused. If I was indeed one of the best, then why move me? Why not just move the new guy into the coach-to-player position instead of a double move? I was also told it wasn't a demotion.

But after seeing the new contracts, as I suspected, the new position I was being offered paid significantly less. I knew how to read the hand I'd been dealt. So by e-mail, I replied that in the business world, less money seemed a demotion, though he'd specifically said it was not.

In his reply, he said he had never mentioned anything about a promotion or demotion.

I know what I heard.

I had a lot of respect for this person and truly felt he was one of the good guys. But the way he handled this with me was hurtful and disappointing.

First and foremost, the move wasn't about the money. The problem was that he wanted to move me into the position Mack was working. Mack had stood up for me when I was treated poorly. And what was the right thing to do for someone who'd always had my back?

I called Mack and told him what had been presented to me. He said he'd been told he was being moved out so younger up-and-comers could get a chance to work. He didn't have a problem with me being his replacement but also knew I wasn't an up-and-comer. He, too, felt the proposal was misleading and, worse, dishonest.

I told Mack I didn't want to be the one who pushed him out. "Friends and family are more important than the officiating world," I said.

He honestly did not have a problem if I decided to take it. He knew if I didn't, someone else would. Then he said something he didn't have to, something that meant a lot to me. "You are by far the most professional one we've ever had in the press box."

I thanked him and told him how truly appreciative I was for everything he'd done for me. It took little time for me to know what I needed to do. Mack had stuck his neck out for me when I needed help. Instead of turning a blind eye to the unjust treatment of a coworker and friend, he had exposed it. I could not be the one responsible for pushing him out of a job.

There are things in life far more important than stepping on someone to get what you want. I had already lived my dream. I'd worked as an official for the NFL. For this role, it was time for me to step down. Time to move on.

24

THE FINAL WHISTLE

One connection still leads to another for me, it seems. Dana Smith, the umpire from the great varsity crew I'd worked on years ago, has become my right-hand man for my officiating business. Over the years, we've become good friends, and he knew I'd stopped working as play clock operator for the NFL. Not long after that, he called to say the guy coordinating individuals to work the clock for Major League Baseball needed more people to cover spring training, and he asked if I was interested.

I called the number Dana gave me and was lucky enough to be assigned a game at the Salt River Fields over at Talking Stick.

As the coordinator watched me work, he said, "You really seem to get this." He knew from Dana that I'd once worked the clock for football. "So what's the biggest game you ever worked?" he wanted to know.

He must have like my answer. I became one of the main clock operators for home games for the Arizona Diamondbacks. In my time with them, I fell in love with the game of baseball. It's a new love. It's refreshing: It's not football.

For two years, I worked their home games. With my business and my job being so intensely busy, I was seriously overwhelmed. Then my dad started having health complications. I needed to be there for him. That had to be my priority instead. I made an easy decision to let go of working for Major League Baseball.

I tell you this so you know how pro ball played out in my life, how it changed, how it no longer carries the weight it used to. Now I shoulder other, greater parts of life. Strange how it works, but faith, love, and charity seem a lighter load.

❧

In my car, you'll find a couple of bears sitting in my backseat. I keep them there just in case I run into someone in need of a smile. Aiden's bears keep on giving—and cheering up children not only at Phoenix Children's Hospital but also in group homes, at an orphanage in Haiti, and throughout the United States. The fund-raiser has become an annual event. One of the officials who worked for me has never needed my e-mail request. "Keep my fees," he'd say whenever I'd try to pay him. "The kids need it more than I do." Because of the generosity of all those I work with, we've raised more than $40,000 to purchase stuffed animals to distribute.

Bringing cheer to kids in the hospital has meant so much to me. At times, people have told me that with this and other charity work, it seems I want to save the world. If only I could. Often, I have left the hospital bearing some of the pains and burdens of those inside, though that's not mine to carry. I feel things deeply, maybe too deeply at times. But I know God will give me the strength I need. He has entrusted me with this voice and has surrounded me with a family of officials who rally behind the causes I bring to them—whether raising money for teddy bears, helping members of our officiating family who are in need, or coordinating holiday parties for group homes or veterans. Those eager to take on all the games they can have likewise turned out to be eager to volunteer for all they can, too. As a team, we're ready to do our part to make a difference in this world.

Throughout the years, many officials have asked if they could help pass out the bears at the hospital. I've wanted to as well. Because of policy and other guidelines, we weren't allowed to at first. We took comfort in knowing that nurses often used our bears in the surgery center to show children going into an operation what's going to happen where on their body. But after a few years, I was finally given the okay to bring another official with me. I knew who that had to be. I picked up the phone and dialed Terry. I knew this would probably not be easy for him, but I had to ask.

He didn't say yes. Not at first. He needed some time to think about it. "Thanks, though," he said, "for thinking of me."

The next day, he called back. His voice was tight. He'd been thinking, he said. "It would be good for me."

Was that a yes?

"I would love to do it," he said.

A week later, we met at the hospital. We were escorted to different wings. We weren't allowed in any of the patients' rooms, but every time we saw a child in a hallway or a common area, we could ask if he or she wanted a bear. I knew the hard part for Terry would be the cancer center.

That day, techs were doing hearing tests on that floor, so we stayed away from the test area. As we did on other floors, we looked for kids hanging out in waiting areas with parents and with others. I grabbed a bear from the canvas basket we'd filled and veered toward the patient closest to me. Terry headed toward a kid sticking close his mom. When I came back to the cart for another bear, Terry was still talking to the little boy, so I brought another bear over to the next kid.

I connected with Terry once again back at the cart. I could tell something had happened. His eyes were shining, and he looked a little stunned.

"Everything okay?" I asked.

He said I wouldn't believe what just happened. The patient he'd just handed a bear had been playing with a Buzz Lightyear toy. The little guy was probably three or maybe four years old. So much in common with Terry's grandson.

And I remembered how much Grandpa's Hero had loved *Toy Story*.

Terry said that after giving the boy a bear—and after checking with the mom—he'd shown them the Buzz Lightyear tattoo on his leg in memory of his grandson. But that wasn't all, he said. After they'd all talked a while, the mom leaned in and said, "Aiden, say good-bye so he can give bears to other kids, too."

Aiden was this little boy's name.

I pressed another bear into Terry's hands and gave him a hug. I was sure Aiden was with us in spirit and said so.

Terry felt his grandson's presence, too.

I picked up the next bear from the cart, and holding on tight, I carried the little bit of the love we had to share forward to the next patient.

As Easter approached, Tom texted to see if I'd want to join him for the upcoming evening services at church. It's a different congregation than the one I used to go to—bigger and yet still a tightknit, bighearted community. We talked about maybe grabbing a bite to eat afterward. I mentioned my mom might end up coming to the service, too.

I was a bit surprised to hear from him and glad our friendship had reached this point. We'd known each other twenty years now. Starting out—and then for too long—we'd both made decisions that weren't in our best interest. Our time together was difficult, to say the least, with the love we shared and with the roller coaster of emotions along the way. My heart broke many times, but I don't think Tom's did until our relationship had ended for good. The finality of that decision took him to a very low place in his life, one that led him to reexamine his faith. Though Tom had been raised Catholic, he once told me he'd never had a close, personal relationship with God. He hadn't until recently, anyway. The year before, he'd given his heart to the Lord. Now, here he was on fire for God. And I'd decided to once again start serving the Lord the way I knew to, not as I had been.

It's amazing to me to see how God can take a situation so completely not pleasing to him and turn it for good.

Life changes but sometimes not as much as we want it to. The good news that Easter was that Tom had come to know God as his Lord and Savior. The good news was that I'd renewed my personal relationship with God. Good news is good news.

∿

When I was a kid, I learned to focus on an opponent in a judo match. As an adult, I learned to focus on keys while officiating a game. Now my dogs are teaching me to focus on enjoying what's important in life. Every day, they get so excited for their walk. We follow a route around the condos where we live. I know Cooper loves his walks because he skips the whole way. At least he does until we reach the stretch right before the front door. That's when he goes into super-slow-motion mode—he doesn't want the walk to end. Whenever I can, I'll say, "Okay, you want to go again?" And he'll scoot past the front door as fast as he can, as if I might change my mind.

Riley likes walks, too, but he likes to play with his toys more. He's a Shih Tzu who loves to fetch, and if I hold onto his stuffed toy, he'll stalk it, getting slower and slower the closer he gets. At a step away, he stands there, staring—sometimes up to a minute—until he pounces. He cracks me up.

In moments like these, my dogs remind me to love every minute of life. I need that reminder sometimes as I balance working as director of officials for CAA and running my company, SE Sports Officiating. I spend so many hours a day glued to screens that sometimes I need to cut short some exchanges. With four hundred people now working for me, I have to remember that when calls veer into becoming a rundown of what's going on in everyone's life, sometimes keeping an agenda is not as important as slowing down to be an ear to listen.

It was one of those days—actually, one of those weeks—when it was all work all the time. I was on the phone for the umpteenth time when

Riley came pawing at my leg. I ignored him since I had to finish the call. So he decided to take matters in his own hands—or paws.

He climbed up on his favorite chair and lifted his leg and peed.

"Listen, I've got to go," I said and finished my call. I snatched him up. "No no no," I scolded.

And he just nestled his head against me. He knew he'd done wrong. But he'd only peed a little and only to send a message. I couldn't be mad. For too long, I hadn't given him enough of a daily walk or time to play and chat and cuddle. He'd been trying to tell me he needed my time, and I hadn't listened.

I would now. I held him at my desk and smothered him with kisses. The whole time, he never lifted his head off my chest.

Riley taught me something that day. He taught me that work is not always the most important thing, that I need to stop and take time to show people (and my dogs) through word and action how important they are to me. It took my precious peanut to help me understand the importance of taking the time to slow down, step outside, and smell the roses. He is my Rose.

The importance of taking time now with those you care for has been underscored even more for me as I watch friends pass away. Before the pandemic, I lost three in the span of only a few months. One had been an official I used to work with at the high school and junior college levels and who was now working Pop Warner and NYS football for me. I knew something was wrong when he hadn't replied to confirm his assignments for several days. It was so unlike him that I sent someone over who lived close to him to see how he was. She found him, and I was the one who fell apart. I'd known how he was hurting in his personal life, and we'd even talked about having lunch, but I'd been too busy. I kept thinking how I could have been a better friend before he passed, taking time to smell some roses along the way.

The other person who came over to help that day was the same junior college supervisor who'd once pegged me as last on a list. In the world of officiating, when it comes to what matters, we are all connected.

Not long afterward, Scarduzio and I were talking about the friends we'd just lost and what we were going to do differently now. I'd been working on writing my story. "If you die before you read this book," I told him, "that will kill me." If Scarduzio hadn't given me the chance to officiate at the junior college level, who knows what would have happened? "I want you to know how important you are to me and the impact you've had on my life." I wanted him to see it in black and white.

"I know," he said.

"I hope you do," I replied. I didn't want him to ever doubt how much he meant to me.

Less than two months later, I got a call from Hank Mancini, a fellow official who'd been Scarduzio's friend for years and mine, too. He was crying. "It's bad," Mancini said. "You better get to the hospital as soon as possible."

Grabbing everything I'd written so far of this book, I left immediately. I wanted him to know that he'd live on.

When I walked into his room, my friend called out my name. "I've missed you," he said.

I hugged him and began to cry.

"Why are you crying?" he asked. "Am I dying or something?"

They hadn't told him yet that he was. I couldn't read what I had for him—then he would know.

Tom Scarduzio died by four o'clock that next morning.

I'm not good at viewings or funerals. Who is? But I am particularly bad at it. I knew I needed to suck it up and be there for him. When I showed up, I saw all the pictures spread out all over of him with his family and friends. Many were of him with his referee buddies.

It once again hit me that I couldn't let work be an excuse not to be a better friend, a better listener, or a better person. What Scarduzio did for me I needed to do more for others. It's still my hope to make a difference in the lives of those I come in contact with and more—I want the light of the Lord to shine brightly through me in what I do every day.

Looking through the record of Scarduzio's life that was laid out before friends and family that day, it was plain to see the impact he had on others. For decades, he'd practiced as a civil and criminal lawyer and worked as a judge pro tem in retirement, but his passion for football shone through and rose above all the rest.[1] He did so much for so many and asked a lot of those officials who worked for him only because he knew what we could give. I'd come across so many people who shook their head no, but Scarduzio was one of the ones who said, *Yes, you can do it.*

I hadn't even looked through all of his photos yet when one of his daughters threaded her way toward me. I reached out to hug her.

"Did you see what's back there?" She pointed to more pictures.

"No," I said. "What?"

"It's the picture you had framed for him," she said. "He was so proud of you, and it was one of the first things anyone saw hanging on his wall when you walked into his house."

At this, I couldn't keep it together. I just cried.

I knew the picture she meant before I saw it there on the table. It was a news article about my officiating for the NFL. On the border around the article, I'd written to him, *Thanks for taking a chance on a girl!* I'd signed it with love.

I'm still learning how precious life is. As it turned out, I didn't get a chance to tell Red Cashion one last time just how important he was to me before he died. Words like these are the things we should give and hope to receive. Over the years, I've cleared out my awards and even gave away my referee shirt from the NFL for an auction. It was worth it to help out a fellow official who was battling amyotrophic lateral sclerosis (ALS, or Lou Gehrig's disease). Out of everything I ever earned, what I've held onto have been the words of support that carried me through and lifted me up on every step I took toward my dream. I count myself lucky to have met those who believed in me early on—from that first session, when Larry said sure, it'd be great if I officiated football and vouched for me on the spot, though he didn't yet know me at all. Starting out, I'd never imagined Red Cashion and Jerry Markbreit would be among those helping me along the way. Now it's my turn to be someone who lifts up another every chance I can.

In that spirit, maybe it will help to know that sometimes the hardest moments can bring a cherished memory. I still have the apology Coach G insisted on giving me, back in my junior college days. Inside the card, he'd included a second note that read, *When a thoroughbred feels the crack of the whip, he responds with all the courage and desire in his heart. When a jackass feels the crack of the whip, he balks.* He thanked me "for being a thoroughbred" while admitting he "was definitely the jackass." It meant so much that he'd made amends for being so difficult.

Through the years, these words inspired me to be the best official I could, to respond with courage no matter the pushback. More than this, through what Coach G did, he provided a good example to me of the importance of making amends when needed and of recognizing you can be wrong when convinced you're right.

And even when you are right, when breaking tradition, you can get some pushback, as I imagine Dan Evans and Tom Scarduzio faced when they opened their ranks to a woman for the first time. And Dan didn't just bring me up a level in officiating—he also entrusted me to lead a crew. Because of what those two did for me, I'm mindful to do all I can to help others aspiring to move up in the officiating ranks.

Looking back, what has meant the most to me has been those times that people have gone out of their way to be kind. Like the time Johnny offered to pick me up from the airport for my first game with the MEAC. His empathy for my situation meant so much, and that's just one of many essential connections so many have provided me in officiating. I try to do the same now.

Friendships have made all the difference for me. I knew Terry, but not well, not until he told me about Aiden. In offering up what I could for him during that time of terrible loss, we became good friends. Our friendship has revealed the thousandfold benefit received when you take the time to make fuller connections and look for ways to give something back to your community. I've learned my responsibility to help others isn't limited to what I alone can do but extends to how I can pull together as many officials as I know to offer up the greatest good for as many as we can.

Obviously, I've not always done right, but I've tried. I am a continual work in progress, striving to be the best version of myself every day. In the end, I've found it doesn't matter that I received perfect scores as an official on written tests or in grading out on the field; what matters is whether I'm obedient to God's spirit in every moment.

Of course, my time working on NFL fields will always be a part of me. People still connect with me over it. When my days as an NFL official ended, a film producer interested in my story contacted me. We met in Canton, Ohio, at the Pro Football Hall of Fame. Canton was where the American Professional Football Association had been founded. That organization later became known as the NFL. The other reason the Hall of Fame is there is that the great Jim Thorpe, the first big-name athlete to play pro football, had played his first pro game for the Canton Bulldogs.[2]

At some point, you may have seen the original circular building—the one with a dome in its center in the shape of the point of a football. Its original footprint has been expanded a few times. There's a beautiful swoop of an entrance on one side of the building now. An escort met us at the door and led us in.

All the things about football that I'd heard and cherished through the years were there in that building filled with so many treasures. That day, I got to immerse myself again in the legends I'd long admired. I got to see the bronze heads of John Hannah and Andre Tippett, both of whom had played for the Patriots when Dad and I watched games on the couch together. I recognized both of them right away. The Vince Lombardi Trophy—which is given to the Super Bowl winner—is showcased there, too. So are all the Super Bowl rings, which started out simple and through the years have added diamonds galore. Our tour through the exhibits took a few hours. There's so much there to take in. The building opened seven years before I was born, and with more than three hundred inductees now, the Hall of Fame has so many items in their catalog that they can't display everything at once. Sure, it would have been amazing to see my things on display, but I get it. Being its first female official represents only a small part of the whole history.

And for my part, officiating for the NFL was the honor of a lifetime.

Our final stop was the archives room. I remember waiting with the producer as our escort retrieved my items. While standing there by the door, it hit me. I became emotional. To think, my hat and whistle are *here*.

The door opened back up, and the escort came out, holding what I once kept up on my shelf. It was all so incredible. It still is. I have been so blessed. Never in a million years did I ever imagine that someday I'd be a part of the Pro Football Hall of Fame. What woman would?

"Here, let's get a picture," the producer said, gesturing where I should stand. He took a couple of snaps, then rolled the camera as I held on to the hat and whistle I wore the first time I stood on an NFL field and worked as an official.

The smile that could not be erased from my face came to me again, remembering what it felt like standing on that Seattle sideline. I will always remember what it was like, standing ready and making the right call.

NOTES

CHAPTER 1

1. "Shannon Eastin Breaks Barrier," ESPN, 9 August 2012, https://www.espn
.com/nfl/trainingcamp12/story/_/id/8253836/shannon-eastin-officially-becomes
-first-female-referee-nfl-game (14 December 2022).

CHAPTER 2

1. Nikos Malliaropoulos, Mike Callan, and Babette Pluim, "Judo, the Gentle
Way," *British Journal of Sports Medicine* 47 (2013): 1137, https://bjsm.bmj.com/
content/47/18/1137 (18 December 2022).

2. "Judo 101: Rules and Scoring," NBC, 15 March 2021, https://www.nbc
olympics.com/news/judo-101-rules-scoring (13 December 2022).

CHAPTER 3

1. Dick Obert, "12-Year-Old Flips Her Way to Olympic Training Center,"
Arizona Republic, 6 October 1982, 74.

CHAPTER 4

1. Joseph Beyda, "Women's Sports Dominance Began with 'Innovative' Approach in 70s," *Stanford Daily*, 2 April 2013, https://stanforddaily.com/2013/04/02/
womens-sports-dominance-began-with-innovative-approach-in-70s (16 December 2022).

CHAPTER 8

1. The age the child is as of July 31 determines the age category for the season. "Ages and Weights," About, Pop Warner Little Scholars, https://www.popwarner .com/Default.aspx?tabid=1476162 (15 December 2022).

CHAPTER 10

1. "First in the NFL," *Referee* 25, no. 1 (January 2000): 30.

2. "Not Just for the Boys: Shannon Eastin to Become First Woman to Be an NFL Referee," *Daily Mail*, 7 August 2012, https://www.dailymail.co.uk/news/ article-2184821/Not-just-boys-Shannon-Eastin-woman-NFL-referee.html (18 December 2022).

CHAPTER 11

1. Alan Eisenstock, "Ultra Violet," *Referee* 25, no. 1 (January 2000): 35. Note that Barkley did later apologize. Aaliyah Kellogg, "NBA Referee Violet Palmer Is Still Breaking Barriers," *Sports Illustrated Kids* (29 September 2015), https:// www.sikids.com/kid-reporter/violet-palmer-still-breaking-barriers (18 December 2022).

2. Lyndsey D'Arcangelo, "The NBA's First Female and Openly Lesbian Ref Recalls 19 Years of Close Calls," *Vice*, 11 October 2016, https://www.vice .com/en_us/article/bn3jva/the-nbas-first-female-and-lesbian-ref-recalls-19-years -of-close-calls (18 December 2022).

3. Vanessa Van Edwards and Todd A. Fonseca, "Mirroring Body Language: 4 Steps to Successfully Mirror Others," *Science of People*, https://www.scienceof people.com/mirroring (12 June 2019).

4. Van Edwards and Fonseca, "Mirroring Body Language."

5. Van Edwards and Fonseca, "Mirroring Body Language."

CHAPTER 12

1. To get a chance to know some of Red's stories, be sure to check out his memoir: Red Cashion, *First Dooowwwnnn and Life to Go!* (Wilmington, DE: Stratton Press, 2019), 13.

2. Charles Stewart, e-mail message forwarded to Eastin, April 17, 2001.

3. Note that the Pac-10 didn't become the Pac-12 until 2011, when the universities of Colorado and Utah were added to the conference. "History of the Pac-12

Conference," About the Pac-12, https://pac-12.com/about-pac-12#pac12history (18 December 2022).

4. Thomas A. Scarduzio Jr., to All ACCAC Officials, 21 August 2002.

CHAPTER 14

1. John Marshall, "AP Explains: Super Bowl Stadium Full of Unique Features," AP News, 29 January 2015, https://apnews.com/article/079d610c9e7d44ecad055 21d6c6f40ba (16 December 2022).

CHAPTER 15

1. Richard Sandomir, "Johnnie Grier, N.F.L.'s First Black Referee, Dies at 74," *New York Times*, 11 March 2022, https://www.nytimes.com/2022/03/11/sports/football/johnny-grier-dead.html (12 December 2022).

2. Quotes pulled directly from e-mail message sent to Eastin, 20 August 2008. Copy of e-mail can be provided on request.

3. Daniel Evans, e-mail message to Shannon Eastin, 8 August 2008.

4. E-mail forwarded to Eastin, 5 September 2008. Copy of e-mail can be provided on request.

5. Nat Newall, "Cancer Can't Stop Female Ref/Annice Canady, a Breast-Cancer Survivor Who Became a Football Official for the Exercise, Has Reached the College Level," *The State* (Columbia, SC), 6 September 2002, updated 25 January 2015, https://greensboro.com/cancer-cant-stop-female-ref-annice-canady-a-breast-cancer-survivor-who-became-a-football/article_b94c6b82-315d-5859-8968-46f219dba657.html (12 December 2022).

6. Daniel Evans, e-mail message to Eastin, 10 November 2008.

CHAPTER 18

1. "North Carolina A&T vs Florida A&M (Nov 05, 2011 at Tallahassee, Fla.)," Play-by-Play Summary, MEAC Sports, https://static.meacsports.com/custom pages/stats/football/2011/famu09.htm#GAME.PLY (19 December 2022).

2. E-mail message from crew member to Rosie Amato provided to Eastin, 7 November 2011. Copy of e-mail can be provided on request.

3. Quotes pulled directly from contemporaneous account of the game provided by Shannon Eastin, e-mail message to Rosie Amato, 6 November 2011. Copy of e-mail can be provided on request.

4. Rosie Amato, e-mail message forwarded to Eastin, 7 November 2011.

5. St. Clair Murraine, "MEAC Reprimands N.C. A&T Coach," *Tallahassee Democrat*, 10 November 2011, 16; Thomas Grant Jr., "N.C. A&T Coach Gets Reprimand, Will Face SCSU from Pressbox," *The Times and Democrat* (Orangeburg, SC), 9 November 2011, 3(B).

6. John McCann, "Eagles-Aggies Football Same Ol' Broadway Act," *Herald-Sun*, 16 November 2011, 3(B). This Durham, North Carolina–based sports reporter was not the only one reporting that Broadway "sounded like a frustrated head football coach." MEAC/SWAC Sports Main Street had blogged that Broadway seemed that way even before his reprimand. "N.C. A&T Coach Gets Reprimand, Will Face S.C. State from Pressbox," *MEAC/SWAC Sports Main Street*, 10 November 2011, https://meacswacsports.blogspot.com/search?updated-max=2011-11-10T07:10:00 -05:00&max-results=25&start=173&by-date=false (13 January 2023). The coach had left a winning football program at Grambling State to live closer to his son in Durham, according to McCann (himself a Durham-based reporter). Now, with the FAMU and South Carolina State losses, the Aggies would finish the season "under .500 for the eighth consecutive year." All the more difficult to swallow, the MEAC/SWAC blogger suggests, considering that, less than a month before, Broadway "had North Carolina A&T among the leaders" in the MEAC. "N.C. A&T Coach Gets Reprimand, Will Face S.C. State from Pressbox."

7. McCann, "Eagles-Aggies Football Same Ol' Broadway Act," 3(B).

CHAPTER 19

1. Jerry Markbreit, e-mail message forwarded to Eastin, 22 January 2012.

CHAPTER 20

1. Barry Wilner, "First NFL Female Official Not Intimidated," *Arizona Daily Sun*, 8 August 2012, 4(B).

2. Mike Florio, "Pereira Says Eastin 'Never Would Have Been Hired under Normal Procedures,'" ProFootballTalk, NBC, 9 August 2012, https://profootball talk.nbcsports.com/2012/08/09/pereira-says-eastin-never-would-have-been-hired -under-normal-procedures (18 December 2022); Tom Polzer, "Mike Pereira: Shannon Shouldn't Pass NFL Background Check," *Sports Illustrated*, 9 August 2012, https://www.si.com/si-wire/2012/08/09/nfl-officials-shannon-eastin-mike -pereira-lockout (18 December 2022); Justin Tasch, "NFL Says Replacement Referee Shannon Eastin's Participation in World Series of Poker Is OK," *New York Daily News*, 9 August 2012, https://www.nydailynews.com/sports/football/ nfl-replacement-referee-shannon-eastin-participation-world-series-poker-article -1.1132804 (18 December 2022).

3. "Roger Goodell: Female Refs in Line," ESPN, 8 August 2012, https://www
.espn.com/nfl/trainingcamp12/story/_/id/8248024/roger-goodell-says-additional
-female-referees-possible (23 March 2023).

4. "Female Official Shannon Eastin Breaks NFL Gender Barrier," NFL, 9 August 2012, https://www.nfl.com/news/female-official-shannon-eastin-breaks-nfl
-gender-barrier-0ap2000000048210 (14 December 2022).

5. Pablo S. Torre, "Black and White, and Green All Over," *Sports Illustrated* 117,
no. 8 (17 August 2012), 46.

6. Torre, "Black and White, and Green All Over," 42.

7. Gruden went on to coach for the Raiders but resigned in 2021 over reports
of racist and misogynistic e-mails he sent. Eastin never received any such communication from him. Asia Cymone Smith, "Jon Gruden Resigns as Las Vegas
Raiders Head Coach," NFL, WRUF, 12 October 2021, https://www.wruf
.com/headlines/2021/10/12/jon-gruden-resigns-as-las-vegas-raiders-head-coach
(17 December 2022).

CHAPTER 21

1. "Cowboys Stadium to Be Renamed AT&T Stadium," *USA Today*, 25 July
2013, https://www.usatoday.com/story/sports/nfl/cowboys/2013/07/25/cow
boys-stadium-at-t-stadium/2586977 (17 December 2022).

2. Red Cashion, *First Dooowwwnnn and Life to Go!* (Wilmington, DE: Stratton
Press, 2019), 80.

3. "Seahawks Use Stifling Defense to Roll Cowboys," *Gamecast*, ESPN, 6
September 2012, https://www.espn.com/nfl/game/_/gameId/320916026 (17
December 2022).

4. "Blaine Gabbert's 80-Yd Pass Lifts Jags to Win," ESPN, 23 September 2012,
https://www.espn.com/nfl/recap?gameId=320923011 (18 December 2022).

5. Cindy Boran, "Bill Belichick Grabs a Replacement Ref, Draws NFL's
Attention," *Washington Post*, 24 September 2012, https://www.washington-
post.com/blogs/early-lead/post/bill-belichick-grabs-a-replacement-ref-draws
-nfls-attention/2012/09/24/df21a7b2-063d-11e2-a10c-fa5a255a9258_blog
.html?tid=a_inl_manual (18 December 2022). Belichick's frustration had been
building up over the course of the game, during which he counted thirty penalties
called. Really, Belichick hoped to replay the final seconds, as he noted in his day
-after press conference, citing a time Johnny Grier allowed just that back in 2000,
when the ref determined a fumble was indeed an incomplete pass, as Belichick had
argued as they walked off the field. That decision meant players had to be called
back out of the locker room (and dress again) after the end of the game. See Shalize
Manza Young, "Belichick Addresses End-of-Game Situation," Extra Points: Patriots Updates and Insights, *Boston Globe*, 24 September 2012, http://archive.boston
.com/sports/football/patriots/extra_points/2012/09/belichick_addre_3.html (18

December 2022). Belichick might have thought it was the better decision, but Johnny will tell you he kicked the hell out of that one.

6. "Can someone please tell these f—— zebras foot locker called and they're needed Back at work !!!! #BreakingPoint," Spikes tweeted, as quoted by Chris Mortenson, "More Uproar about Officials," ESPN, 23 September 2012, https://www.espn.com/nfl/story/_/id/8418497/referees-mistakes-shaky-calls-week-3-themes (18 December 2022).

7. John Fox was fined $30,000, and Jack Del Rio was fined $25,000. Mortenson, "More Uproar about Officials."

8. Mortenson, "More Uproar about Officials."

9. Red Cashion, e-mail message to Eastin, 13 October 2012.

CHAPTER 23

1. For some great pictures of some of the activities, click through this: Harry How, "NFL Experience," NFL, https://www.nfl.com/photos/nfl-experience-09000d5d80ca629f#7cee6f59-9918-47b1-9618-e35237d5e276 (19 December 2022).

CHAPTER 24

1. "Thomas A. Scarduzio, Jr.," Obituaries, *Arizona Republic*, 27 November 2018, https://www.messingermortuary.com/obituary/Thomas-ScarduzioJr (18 December 2022).

2. "This Is Football Heaven," About Us, Pro Football Hall of Fame, https://www.profootballhof.com/about (19 December 2022).

BIBLIOGRAPHY

"Ages and Weights," Pop Warner Little Scholars, https://www.popwarner.com/Default.aspx?tabid=1476162 (15 December 2022).

Austro, Ben. "Despite Inadvertent Whistle Panthers TD Is Allowed to Stand, Incorrectly," Football Zebras, 5 November 2012, https://www.footballzebras.com/2012/11/despite-inadvertent-whistle-panthers-td-is-allowed-to-stand-incorrectly (18 December 2022).

Beyda, Joseph. "Women's Sports Dominance Began with 'Innovative' Approach in 70s," *Stanford Daily*, 2 April 2013, https://stanforddaily.com/2013/04/02/womens-sports-dominance-began-with-innovative-approach-in-70s (16 December 2022).

"Blaine Gabbert's 80-Yd Pass Lifts Jags to Win," ESPN, 23 September 2012, https://www.espn.com/nfl/recap?gameId=320923011 (18 December 2022).

Boran, Cindy. "Bill Belichick Grabs a Replacement Ref, Draws NFL's Attention," *Washington Post*, 24 September 2012, https://www.washingtonpost.com/blogs/early-lead/post/bill-belichick-grabs-a-replacement-ref-draws-nfls-attention/2012/09/24/df21a7b2-063d-11e2-a10c-fa5a255a9258_blog.html?tid=a_inl_manual (18 December 2022).

Cashion, Red. *First Dooowwwnnn and Life to Go!* (Wilmington, DE: Stratton Press, 2019).

"Cowboys Stadium to Be Renamed AT&T Stadium," *USA Today*, 25 July 2013, https://www.usatoday.com/story/sports/nfl/cowboys/2013/07/25/cowboys-stadium-at-t-stadium/2586977 (17 December 2022).

D'Arcangelo, Lyndsey. "The NBA's First Female and Openly Lesbian Ref Recalls 19 Years of Close Calls," *Vice*, 11 October 2016, https://www.vice.com/en_us/article/bn3jva/the-nbas-first-female-and-lesbian-ref-recalls-19-years-of-close-calls (18 December 2022).

Eisenstock, Alan. "Ultra Violet," *Referee* 25, no. 1 (January 2000): 35.

"Female Official Shannon Eastin Breaks NFL Gender Barrier," NFL, 9 August 2012, https://www.nfl.com/news/female-official-shannon-eastin-breaks-nfl-gender-barrier-0ap2000000048210 (14 December 2022).

"First in the NFL," *Referee* 25, no. 1 (January 2000): 30.

Florio, Mike. "Pereira Says Eastin 'Never Would Have Been Hired under Normal Procedures,'" ProFootballTalk, NBC, 9 August 2012, https://profootballtalk.nbcsports.com/2012/08/09/pereira-says-eastin-never-would-have-been-hired-under-normal-procedures (18 December 2022).

Garza, Esteban L. *The Impossible Catch: A Football Story of Passion Meeting Fate.* (Scotts Valley, CA: CreateSpace, 2017).

Grant, Thomas, Jr. "N.C. A&T Coach Gets Reprimand, Will Face SCSU from Pressbox," *The Times and Democrat* (Orangeburg, SC), 9 November 2011, 3(B).

"History of the Pac-12 Conference," About the Pac-12, https://pac-12.com/about-pac-12#pac12history (18 December 2022).

How, Harry. "NFL Experience," NFL, https://www.nfl.com/photos/nfl-experience-09000d5d80ca629f#7cee6f59-9918-47b1-9618-e35237d5e276 (19 December 2022).

"Judo 101: Rules and Scoring," Olympics, NBC, 15 March 2021, https://www.nbcolympics.com/news/judo-101-rules-scoring (13 December 2022).

Kellogg, Aaliyah. "NBA Referee Violet Palmer Is Still Breaking Barriers," Sports Illustrated Kids (29 September 2015), https://www.sikids.com/kid-reporter/violet-palmer-still-breaking-barriers (18 December 2022).

Malliaropoulos, Nikos, Mike Callan, and Babette Pluim. "Judo, the Gentle Way," *British Journal of Sports Medicine* 47 (2013): 1137, https://bjsm.bmj.com/content/47/18/1137 (18 December 2022).

Marshall, John. "AP Explains: Super Bowl Stadium Full of Unique Features," AP News, 29 January 2015, https://apnews.com/article/079d610c9e7d44ecad05521d6c6f40ba (16 December 2022).

McCann, John. "Eagles-Aggies Football Same Ol' Broadway Act," *Herald-Sun* (Durham, NC), 16 November 2011, 3(B).

Mortenson, Chris. "More Uproar about Officials," ESPN, 23 September 2012, https://www.espn.com/nfl/story/_/id/8418497/referees-mistakes-shaky-calls-week-3-themes (18 December 2022).

Murraine, St. Clair. "MEAC Reprimands N.C. A&T Coach," *Tallahassee Democrat*, 10 November 2011, 16.

"N.C. A&T Coach Gets Reprimand, Will Face S.C. State from Pressbox," *MEAC/SWAC Sports Main Street*, 10 November 2011, https://meacswacsports.blogspot.com/search?updated-max=2011-11-10T07:10:00-05:00&max-results=25&start=173&by-date=false (13 January 2023).

Newall, Nat. "Cancer Can't Stop Female Ref/Annice Canady, a Breast-Cancer Survivor Who Became a Football Official for the Exercise, Has Reached the College Level," *The State* (Columbia, SC), 6 September 2002, updated 25 January 2015, https://greensboro.com/cancer-cant-stop-female-ref-annice-canady

-a-breast-cancer-survivor-who-became-a-football/article_b94c6b82-315d-5859
-8968-46f219dba657.html (12 December 2022).

"North Carolina A&T vs Florida A&M (Nov 05, 2011)," Play-by-Play Summary, MEAC Sports, https://static.meacsports.com/custompages/stats/football/2011/famu09.htm#GAME.PLY (19 December 2022).

"Not Just for the Boys: Shannon Eastin to Become First Woman to Be an NFL Referee," *Daily Mail*, 7 August 2012, https://www.dailymail.co.uk/news/article-2184821/Not-just-boys-Shannon-Eastin-woman-NFL-referee.html (18 December 2022).

Obert, Dick. "12-Year-Old Flips Her Way to Olympic Training Center," *Arizona Republic*, 6 October 1982, 74.

Polzer, Tom. "Mike Pereira: Shannon Shouldn't Pass NFL Background Check," *Sports Illustrated*, 9 August 2012, https://www.si.com/si-wire/2012/08/09/nfl-officials-shannon-eastin-mike-pereira-lockout (18 December 2022).

"Roger Goodell: Female Refs in Line," ESPN, 8 August 2012, https://www.espn.com/nfl/trainingcamp12/story/_/id/8248024/roger-goodell-says-additional-female-referees-possible (23 March 2023).

Sandomir, Richard. "Johnnie Grier, N.F.L.'s First Black Referee, Dies at 74," *New York Times*, 11 March 2022, https://www.nytimes.com/2022/03/11/sports/football/johnny-grier-dead.html (12 December 2022).

"Seahawks Use Stifling Defense to Roll Cowboys," Gamecast, ESPN, 6 September 2012, https://www.espn.com/nfl/game/_/gameId/320916026 (17 December 2022).

"Shannon Eastin Breaks Barrier," ESPN, 9 August 2012, https://www.espn.com/nfl/trainingcamp12/story/_/id/8253836/shannon-eastin-officially-becomes-first-female-referee-nfl-game (14 December 2022).

Smith, Asia Cymone. "Jon Gruden Resigns as Las Vegas Raiders Head Coach," NFL, WRUF, 12 October 2021, https://www.wruf.com/headlines/2021/10/12/jon-gruden-resigns-as-las-vegas-raiders-head-coach (17 December 2022).

Tasch, Justin. "NFL Says Replacement Referee Shannon Eastin's Participation in World Series of Poker Is OK," *New York Daily News*, 9 August 2012, https://www.nydailynews.com/sports/football/nfl-replacement-referee-shannon-eastin-participation-world-series-poker-article-1.1132804 (18 December 2022).

"This Is Football Heaven," About Us, Pro Football Hall of Fame, https://www.profootballhof.com/about (19 December 2022).

"Thomas A. Scarduzio, Jr.," Obituaries, *Arizona Republic*, 27 November 2018, https://www.messingermortuary.com/obituary/Thomas-ScarduzioJr (18 December 2022).

Torre, Pablo S. "Black and White, and Green All Over," *Sports Illustrated* 117, no. 8 (27 August 2012): 46.

Van Edwards, Vanessa, and Todd A. Fonseca. "Mirroring Body Language: 4 Steps to Successfully Mirror Others," *Science of People*, https://www.scienceofpeople.com/mirroring (12 June 2019).

Wilner, Barry. "First NFL Female Official Not Intimidated," *Arizona Daily Sun*, 8 August 2012, 4(B).

Young, Shalize Manza. "Belichick Addresses End-of-Game Situation," Extra Points: Patriots Updates and Insights, *Boston Globe*, 24 September 2012, http://archive.boston.com/sports/football/patriots/extra_points/2012/09/belichick_addre_3.html (18 December 2022).

ACKNOWLEDGMENTS

Above all, I give thanks to God for loving me unconditionally, for never giving up on me, and for leading me to an amazing church family, CCV.

Thank you, Mom, for all your love and support throughout my journey. And to Dad—I wish I could have shared this book with you before you passed away so you could have seen in writing how much I appreciated you accepting me immediately as your child. I will miss you always!

To my boys, Cooper and Riley, I'm the luckiest mama in the world! And thank you for welcoming Rosco into our home.

Thank you, Kate, for bringing my story to life. I want to thank Dawn for bringing us together, and thanks to Rowman & Littlefield for bringing this story to publication.

I want to be sure to thank all others who made this book possible and who lifted me up along my way, and so I offer a special thanks here to Dan, Dana, Jen, Sean, Larry, Scott, Terry, Coach G, and all the Toms—Scarduzio, Frazier, and Donithan.

And for those who work for me and with me in my business and with the CAA, I am so grateful to have a team so passionate about the sports we love and so dedicated to giving back to charities we support, especially in bringing comfort to children undergoing hospital care. I have pages and pages of thanks for all those who have helped me over the years—I wish I could list everyone here.

To all the players, coaches, owners, and fans of the NFL: The welcome I received countless times as I stepped onto the field—and the love still expressed to me to this day—continues to blow me away. Thank you! And this book would not be complete without one more special shout out to Red Cashion and Jerry Markbreit and Johnny Grier—thank you for helping to make my dream come true!

Shannon Eastin

I want to express my deepest thanks to Shannon for the honor of joining her crew. I'm so grateful for this opportunity to bring her story out into the world. Count me among her fans. Through the pandemic, we talked daily. Her calls were a bright spot in a dark time. I'm so thankful, too, that Dawn Frederick thought of me when she and Shannon first connected in early April of that year. Thanks to Christen Karniski, Samantha Delwarte, Nicole Carty, and everyone at Rowman & Littlefield for their excellent work in bringing this project to the goal line.

Thanks to my kids, Ash and Jen, and thanks to Jen's husband Charles, too, for cheering me on in so many ways. Love you all. And, most importantly, I want to offer special thanks to my husband, Jim. The long walks we take with Callie always count as the highlight of my day. I could not have written this book without your love and support. How wonderfully amazing our love continues to deepen through the years. Love that. Love you. Thank you.

Kate St. Vincent Vogl

ABOUT THE AUTHORS

Shannon Eastin broke barriers in becoming the first female Division I referee and the first female NFL official. Eastin continues to inspire people through speaking engagements and through organizing and supporting charitable events. She is director of officials for the Canyon Athletic Association and, for over twenty years, has mentored, trained, and assigned officials through her company, SE Sports Officiating. She is a devoted member of Christ's Church of the Valley, known as CCV,  and enjoys the connections being made through CCV small groups. Visit her at www.shannoneastin.com.

Kate St. Vincent Vogl has also cowritten *Iron Horse Cowgirls: Louise Scherbyn and the Women Motorcyclists of the 1930s and 1940s*. Vogl is the author of *Lost & Found: A Memoir of Mothers*, which was named among the best of the year by the *Akron Beacon Journal*. Her essays appear in best-selling anthologies such as *Why We Ride* and *Listen to Your Mother*, and her fiction has received support from the Minnesota State Arts Board and from the Anderson  Center. She teaches at the Loft Literary Center in Minneapolis. Visit her at www.katevogl.com.